HOW TO SURVIVE– AND PROFIT FROM– THE COMING CURRENCY RECALL

JONATHAN RICE AND FRANCIS CIABATTONI

CONTEMPORARY
BOOKS, INC.
CHICAGO • NEW YORK

Library of Congress Cataloging-in-Publication Data

Rice, Jonathan.
  How to survive and profit from the coming currency recall.

  Includes index.
  1. Currency question—United States.   2. Money—
History. I. Ciabattoni, Francis. II. Title.
HG540.R53   1986   332.4'973   86-6215
ISBN 0-8092-4998-7

The opinions and ideas expressed in this book are solely those of the authors and do not in any way reflect the opinions of the companies with which they are affiliated.

Published by Contemporary Books, Inc.
180 North Michigan Avenue, Chicago, Illinois 60601
Manufactured in the United States of America
Library of Congress Catalog Card Number: 86-6215
International Standard Book Number: 0-8092-4998-7

Published simultaneously in Canada by Beaverbooks, Ltd.
195 Allstate Parkway, Valleywood Business Park
Markham, Ontario L3R 4T8 Canada

CONTENTS

AS WE GO TO PRESS

The U.S. Treasury has just made a formal announcement, the latest in a series it has been making over the past five years or so, that it plans to replace our present paper currency with a new money that is "counterfeit-proof." In different newspaper articles describing the event, the following points were made:

1. The new design will carry a polyester thread bearing the inscription "USA ONE" for $1 bills, "USA FIVE" for $5 bills, "USA TEN" for $10 bills, changing to USA with numerals for $20, $50, and $100 bills;
2. The thread will be located between the Federal Reserve seal and the portrait on the $1 bill and between the seal and the left border on all other denominations;
3. These threads will enable Americans to hold a suspected bill up to light for a demonstrative visual examination;
4. The legend "United States of America" will be printed around the border of the portraits in type so tiny, it will be

undiscernable unless viewed with a magnifying glass of 7×
power or better;
5. Printing will begin in 12 months with the first notes ready
for circulation in 15 to 18 months;
6. There will be a gradual replacement of bills that will take
two to three years.

While a number of news sources have previously reported
radical changes being planned in our currency—including a
possible currency recall, as well as the embedding of elements
in the new currency that will allow the government to track
and trace the movement of cash throughout the economy,
whether aboveground or underground—the U.S. government
has always downplayed these assertions. Thus, there is really
nothing new in the U.S. Treasury's most recent statements.
If anything, they are as misleading as all the previous
statements have been. This was evidenced by Treasury
spokesman Robert G. Stone, who when asked about the
previously proposed use of holograms, replied that the hologram may still get a chance since "we are still looking for
alternatives down the road." In other words, the newly announced changes are not definite and most likely will be
reconsidered. For example, government surveys have revealed the American public is very opposed to any type of
change that will require obvious overt display to determine
authenticity such as a security thread would necessitate. If
the government is as concerned about public opinion and
reaction as they claim, then in all likelihood the threads will be
dropped in favor of other changes. According to official
government statements, and as will be explained in the text,
these changes will be totally useless in the prevention of
counterfeiting. Their only intention is to prevent the casual
use of color copying machines for this purpose, a fear which
is so small and unimportant it becomes obvious, after an
examination of the facts, that all this talk must be an attempt
to cover the government's real intentions:

1. Attack and attempt to control the alarming growth of the
underground economy;

2. Install a new international currency of sorts;
3. Eliminate Federal Reserve branch bank reserve requirements;
4. Introduce a new process that can allow the currency to be tracked and traced electronically;
5. Install currency that can carry secret messages.

Even the most recently announced changes are inconsistent with the alleged goal of preventing the use of color copiers. For example, what good is tiny print which cannot be copied by the copying machines but must be viewed with a 7× magnifier? Does that mean all Americans must carry magnifying glasses? If a security thread is good enough, why bother with "invisible" painting? If the threads are not enough and must be backed up with invisible writing, then what good are both changes? And if the American public is adamant in its opposition to security threads, as revealed by expensive government research, what will be the fate of the proposed threads over the next twelve months?

In any event, all these changes will ultimately result in the continuing loss of freedom for all Americans, a process that has been gradually occurring for so long as to have gone on practically unobserved. All these points will be examined in great detail in the text.

ACKNOWLEDGMENTS

In appreciation of Ron De Cristoforo, Joe McCollough, Buzz Cromwell, Jeanie Derago, and Joshua Greene whose guidance and inspiration helped bring this work to fruition. And special thanks to Denise without whose strong moral support nothing could have been accomplished.

INTRODUCTION

Much has been written in the last few years on the subject of the coming currency conversion, but little of this information has surfaced in the popular press, and what has appeared usually has been found hidden in the back pages as secondary news. Most of this information has appeared in expensive newsletters and relatively obscure financial digests. Because of this news blackout of sorts, most people have no idea that a currency conversion is about to take place, and those who do merely have some vague concept of what a currency conversion is and what the consequences of this type of monetary manipulation will be. Indeed, if the currency conversion is actually to take place, it must be swift and secretive for it to succeed—unless, of course, we swallow the government's version, which is that the conversion is being made solely to deter counterfeiting. For several reasons, there has also been some confusion as to whether this conversion will actually take place.

Over the last years, rumors have spread that the government has plans to issue a new paper money to replace our present currency. It appears that the main feature of this new money will be to introduce colors not found on our current paper money. The notion the government has tried to promulgate is that new colors will somehow make our paper currency more counterfeit-proof in the presence of a new generation of photocopiers now emerging in the marketplace. Even astute members of the "underground economy" who feel (and rightly so) that one of the main reasons for a conversion is to flush out or contain the underground are not taking this move seriously. After all, there have been many attempts in the past in other countries to try to pull in the reins on the underground via currency call-ins, which at best have only created a temporary disruption in underground activity.

What is not generally known is that the new colors on the new money are a secondary if not altogether insignificant feature designed primarily to act as a smoke screen for other characteristics earmarked for this new paper currency. For the first time in history, elements will be embodied in the new paper that the government is hoping will make it possible to track and trace electronically the movements of cash throughout the economy, regardless of whether it is aboveground or underground, even to the point where customs officials will have the ability to ascertain secretly whether large caches of money are moving across borders. Given this ability, not only will the anonymous nature of cash be destroyed, but also the government will have a powerful, even overwhelming, new tool in its arsenal to further subjugate the people to its wishes. An exchange of this type not only jeopardizes individual wealth, but has far-reaching ramifications in terms of lost freedom and mobility as well. Because of these ramifications, every citizen, whether rich or poor, has something to lose. It therefore becomes incumbent upon all those who wish to protect themselves from such a predicament to gain as much knowledge about the exchange as possible.

This book represents an effort to assemble this knowledge and make it accessible to the common man and woman so that they may place their houses in order and not be caught unaware. We will discuss different angles and strategies designed to keep our financial affairs private; preserve wealth, freedom, and opportunity; and present opportunities for making quite a bit of money from this coming conversion.

It is said that to be forewarned is to be forearmed and that the future favors the prepared. If enough people become knowledgeable about the exchange, it might be possible to foil the plans of those who wish to foist this whole scenario on us, even though the apparent schedule for the conversion indicates that it is rather late in the game for this to happen. However, nothing is impossible. Therefore, this book will present both strategies for the individual and a monetary system that, if adopted nationally, would prevent governmental oppressors from ever having the ability to abridge the freedoms of the people or cheat them of their wealth through a worthless paper money system that plans to incorporate Orwellian *1984*-type features.

This books begins with a brief history of coins, gold, money, inflation, and other monetary matters, from ancient times to the present, so we can better understand the nature of currency, economics, and the ways by which the rulers and governing elite have sought to control us through the last few thousand years. This historical review will take the reader from Greek and Roman times up to the introduction of paper money in the Middle Ages and into the modern world of governmentally controlled money and economies. We will see how money manipulation and debauchery go hand in hand with the rise and fall of empires and societies and how parallels can be drawn between the past and current world events. Through this study, we can see how history is attempting to repeat itself. By understanding the past, we can develop a clearer understanding of what is going on today in this never-ending saga of oppressor and oppressed and, with this understanding, prevent ourselves from becoming victims.

1
THE ANCIENT MONEY MANIPULATORS

With common sense and a good understanding of history and current events, anyone can become a prudent financial analyst and forecaster in his own right, rather than having to depend on professionals or the government-sponsored economic news and media that tend simply to parrot official lines. History is always repeating itself, so astute observers armed with this knowledge can take heed and arrange their affairs so that they may not have to repeat the same errors themselves. As a foundation for this knowledge, this chapter presents a historical review of coin, currency, and economics.

Just as a steady normal temperature is a sign of good health in the human body, we can see that often wild fluctuations in interest and mortgage rates, inflation, gold and silver prices, stock and bond prices, deficits, balance of payments, and so on, are indicators of the social body's poor economic health. Because the leaders and money managers in government are responsible for this illness, we must conclude that either they are totally inept and, therefore, must desperately supply us with constant misinformation in order to cover their blunders, or they are purposely creating situations to confuse us that are intended to be used to slowly strip away our powers and freedoms in order to deposit them in the hands of a few men or internationalistic "one-worlder" groups hell-bent on dominating the world. The former may be true to a small degree: there may be a few sincere but misled government men who are trying to sort out this mess with their impotent economic theories, but history has shown that they are vastly overshadowed by the power mongers who want to seize it all for themselves. Historically, political and economic power tends to centralize itself. To paraphrase what Franklin Delano Roosevelt once said, nothing in government happens by chance; everything is carefully planned. We will see in this chapter and those that follow how this is actually taking place.

THE PATTERN OF DEVALUATION

Inflation and currency controls are not new. There have been many kings and emperors throughout history with the propensity to devalue coinage through clipping, filing, reducing, or debasing. Imperial Rome was particularly notorious for this maneuver. There also were many instances of frantic and desperate hoarding of coinage in the ancient world. The pattern that has emerged is as follows: (1) you spend good coin, but you receive in return a new debased coin of less intrinsic value; (2) you then spend that coin and receive a newer coin ever further devalued; (3) this goes on and on until you learn to hoard the old coin, which will buy in the future 10, 20, 50, or even 100 new coins. This has led to the observation by Sir Thomas Gresham (1519–1579) that is now known as Gresham's Law:

> When coins of equal value but different intrinsic value are put into circulation side by side, the coin with the higher intrinsic value will be hoarded and only the coin of lower intrinsic value will be permitted to remain in circulation. [It is sometimes put in the form of an aphorism: "Bad money drives out good

money."] Despite the incantations of the New Economics, the events of recent years have shown rather conclusively that Gresham's Law has not been repealed.*

Those present-day pundits who push fiat money and other cheap money doctrines delight in pointing to the money hoarders as proof that gold (or any sound currency that has intrinsic value) is impractical and dangerous. In a classic example of Orwellian doublethink, they charge the hoarder with the unpatriotic aim of trying to undermine the economic system, when we can see that the only thing the hoarder actually is guilty of is self-defense.

Since the 1930s U.S. gold grab, the government has tried to force negative public opinion of gold as a barbarous relic of the past as it continues to pave the way for its "funny money." The government has been trying to convince us since then, as have other governments in the past, that the value and type of money we use is actually a function and convenience of government and not what the people perceive to be valuable.

Strong, sound, independent money, whether it be wampum or gold, is indicative of a strong, independent, free-spirited people. This creates a dangerous situation for those who wish to control our lives. Because gold currency is a major obstacle in the powercrats' plans to centralize all power in their hands, they engage in constant and often arrogant schemes to coerce us into believing they know better than we what is best for us. A good example of this was the argument by the money managers and the U.S. Treasury in the '60s that, since the Treasury was paying $35 in paper for one ounce of gold, the dollar must be superior to gold. The hypocrisy and emptiness of this argument was rudely exposed in 1968, when the international price of gold soared above $35 an ounce in spite of all the maneuvers, manipulations, threats, and intrigues employed by the U.S. government to prevent it.

---

*Donald J. Hoppe, *How to Invest in Gold Coins*, (New York: Arco Publishing Co., 1970), 289.

GOLD: THE PERMANENT SOLUTION

This book supports a return to specie based on gold as a permanent solution to our economic problems. Why this solution can be effective can be seen in the physical attributes and historical significance of gold.

Actually, a return to the gold standard is only one part of the solution to our economic woes. Also necessary is the repeal of the Federal Reserve Act of 1913 and the 16th Amendment to the Constitution, which gave us income tax and the most oppressive bureaucracy ever created—the IRS. These may seem like radical ideas to some, but consider the facts: we can trace directly to these institutions the 95-percent-plus erosion of the dollar's purchasing power since 1913; the depressions, recessions, inflations, deficits, wars, and panics; the systematic transfer of wealth from one class of citizens, the producers, to another class of citizens, the nonproducers; and the establishment of worthless paper.

Depressions, recessions, inflation, deficits, and the like, are reactive forces to artificial or external manipulations of the economy. Since the Federal Reserve has total control over the issuance of money, it has become the heartbeat of the economy and the major force in causing depressions and other economic conditions. It's almost common knowledge that most wars are fought for economic purposes. A good case in point was the Vietnam War, which many veterans claimed could have been won in a very short time but was prolonged for economic reasons. Thus, even wars come under the influences of the Fed. The Fed also perpetuates the existence of fractional reserve banking, which has destroyed countless numbers of people through usurious lending practices. And it is these big banks that make huge sums lending to select parties, such as government, and make profits from long drawn-out wars. The Fed is also at the root of the establishment of worthless paper money, which is the ultimate in currency debauchery.

The IRS is responsible for the collection of taxes, which enables wealth to be transferred not only to nonproducers but to other government agencies, which expand their power and influence over people they are supposed to serve. These bureaus, especially the IRS, become increasingly arrogant and insensitive to the people and each year increase their harassment and attacks on them. The IRS is responsible for collection of money that is used for illegal government programs, military build-up, and the aforementioned wars. The IRS is also a favorite weapon of the government. By threatening them with jail and/or confiscation of their property and assets, the government forces into submission dissidents who battle illegal, unconstitutional, and oppressive government maneuvers. These points will be discussed further in coming chapters.

In the face of such evidence, we can see that the only radical idea is the continued support of these systems. And those who support these institutions, no matter how eloquently they state their case, are easily revealed as the enemies of economic freedom. To expound in detail on the effects of central banking and the tax system, as well as the issue of the coming currency conversion (although all these topics are closely related), is beyond the scope of this book. These issues will be dealt with briefly, however, throughout the text.

Gold has been the standard of money since ancient times, even though other metals, such as platinum, silver, copper, bronze, and even iron, also have been in use. Other objects of recognized common value have also been used at times, ranging from animals, slaves, and spices to ivory, gems, and jewels. Gold, though, has always reigned as the king of money because of its truly unique physical properties, which make it the ideal medium for coinage.

Because it is the most malleable and ductile of all metals, it is the best suited for the minting of coins. It can be pounded into sheets as thin as 1/360,000 of an inch, a measure 1,000 times thinner than paper, thin enough to read through. One ounce can be stretched into a single strand of wire 50 miles long without breaking. It is so dense that a cubic foot of gold weighs in at 1,204.8 pounds (at $325 per troy ounce, a cubic foot is worth $5,727,300). It is said that from 3000 B.C. to present day approximately 80,000,000 tons of gold have been taken from the earth, 85 percent of which still exists. (The remaining 15 percent has been lost.) If all this gold were to be amassed in one spot, it would create a cube of only 50 feet per side. It is obvious then that small but very valuable amounts can be stored, shipped, stashed, or smuggled rather easily.

Gold is practically indestructible. It is the most stable and chemically inactive of all the metals, and it is impervious to rust, tarnish, and corrosion. It is unaffected by time, weather, water, acids, or pollutants. Coins that have been buried in the earth or under the sea for over 20 centuries and then recovered have remained just as sharp and brilliant as the day they were minted.

Gold is divisible; that is, one ounce of gold, whether it is in dust, coin, or bullion, is worth $\frac{1}{10}$ of 10 ounces. You cannot split a painting or even a diamond such that its fractional parts are equal to the whole.

Gold also has consistent quality. Unlike antiques, artwork, gems, etc., gold does not need constant expert appraisals. There are no different grades of gold. You either have gold or you don't. Gold cannot be created out of thin air in the same manner that this is done with our printing press money. Gold, then, has all the physical prerequisites of a perfect value standard.

The only reason a government stamp should be on gold coin is to guarantee its purity and weight. However, the government labors under the illusion that it is not only the guarantor of money but also the actual creator of wealth. Historically, governments that have deluded themselves with this belief and severed their ties to gold money have done so with catastrophic results. To push a fiat currency on the populace requires coercion and ultimately brute force. When the state depends more and more on police powers to check its populace, it sounds its own death knell. Public confidence in government based on integrity, justice, honesty, and morality is the government's greatest asset. Its money is a direct reflection of these qualities. The integrity of its money is proportionate to that government's own virtues.

Typically, in the beginning, a government is based on sound moral and religious principles with a sound and popular currency, usually gold and sometimes silver. Then begins the work of the money manipulators and the power mongers, who slowly infiltrate the structure. As the populace becomes complacent and apathetic with the passing of time, these social parasites impose their plans on an unwary public in a gradual and covert manner. The gold currency is replaced with gold-backed paper money, fractional reserve central banking, and coinage of debased value. Gresham's Law goes into effect, and hoarding commences. With public confidence in the government and money declining quickly, the people seek other means by which to preserve their wealth, such as investing in antiques, jewels, precious metals, real estate, stamps and coins, etc. Speculation becomes a way of life. Government retaliates with gold and silver confiscation, wage and price controls, severe punishments for hoarders, interest rate and foreign exchange rate controls, travel restrictions, and a host of other measures designed to force the people into accepting their fiat money.

The results of these measures are always the opposite of what is intended; trade stagnates, prices rise even faster, black markets develop, gold and silver disappear entirely, speculation becomes frantic, evasions and dishonesties become commonplace and all remaining confidence in the government evaporates. The government itself becomes the victim of its own inflationary debasement. Tax revenues decline due to the erosion of legitimate trade, the diversion of goods to the black market, and the pouring of money into nonproductive speculation. The costs of government rise rapidly and the burdens on it increase as a result of economic instability. In the end the government is obligated to create still more fiat money or debase the currency still further in order to finance its own operation—and the spiral gets another vicious twist. With each turn of the cycle the descent becomes more rapid. There is no way out except to return to discipline of gold, and this requires that the debased purchasing media be officially devalued in terms of their gold equivalent or written off entirely as in a bankruptcy. In either case, the holders of the debased coin or fiat money are the losers.*

We now have a classic case for a currency exchange: debts that cannot be satisfied, soaring inflation, and a burgeoning underground economy. Governments are, of course, loath to admit that their true aim is to renege on debts, to favor debtors over creditors, and to assuage the public's fear of inflation. When rampant counterfeiting is presented as the reason for a currency exchange, the public must look beneath the surface for the real reasons.

A currency exchange also can further the political goals of the one-worlders; namely, a world take-over and new economic and political order based on their own egocentric desires. Their goals include the complete and final demonetization of gold, the destruction of the independent dollar, the implementation of a new international paper currency, and the eradication and replacement of nationalism (especially American) and independent statism with socialistic internationalism and interdependent statism. In short, we have an international "big brother" vying for supremacy. More on this theme later. For now, let us continue our review of history and examine coin and currency debasements and exchanges that have actually taken place.

A REVIEW OF DEBASEMENTS AND EXCHANGES

Ancient Greece

The introduction of coined money into the Greek world relieved the Greeks of the restrictions of barter and created a great economic boom. Mighty city-states emerged, trade flourished, banks were established, and a previously unknown entity appeared on the scene—the money changer. In this age,

---

*Donald J. Hoppe, *How to Invest in Gold Coins*, (New York: Arco Publishing Co., 1970), 53.

creditor and debtor classes emerged, with the moneylenders becoming very powerful. In loan transactions, these money-lenders not only accepted the usual forms of collateral, such as land and animals, but also allowed a man to pledge his wife, his children, and himself as a loan guarantee. On default, these human chattels were sold into slavery. The moneylend-ers were not reluctant to accept this human chattel; they reasoned that there could be no better form of security than one's own freedom and life. (For those who have a 30-year mortgage, this may ring a bell.)

After a century of prosperity and expansion, the Greek economy began to sour. A great depression ensued due to a burgeoning trade with developing Italian states that were able to undercut domestic prices for food and manufactured goods. In addition, the situation had been greatly aggravated for many decades by the moneylenders' cheap money credit inflation. How similar this is to America's current problems, in which she is finding herself losing industrial productivity to cheap foreign imports, listing increasing numbers of farm foreclosures and bank failures, and experiencing monetary instability due to inflation and other economic aberrations!

The Greek depression led to massive defaults on loans, with subsequent foreclosures on farms, bankruptcy for artisans, and the threat of slavery hanging over much of the popula-tion. With such severe suffering, armed uprising was immi-nent and extreme action was required in order to rectify these inequities, assuage the populace, and restabilize the economy.

A learned aristocrat named Solon, in about 600 B.C., was appointed minister and given the task of solving the crisis. Solon proved to be a skillful statesman, and he immediately issued a decree repudiating all debts and releasing all people in and under the threat of bondage. Farms and shops were released from foreclosures, but many bankers and other creditors were wiped out by this decree since now they also could not meet their own commitments to their creditors. To help relieve their plight somewhat and restimulate the econ-omy, Solon introduced a currency devaluation of 37 percent. Before this devaluation, 73 drachma were minted from 1 mina (Greek pound). Devaluation allowed the minting of 100 drachma from a mina.

Other social reforms Solon instituted were the prohibition of human chattel loans, the reformation of citizenship laws, the mediation of new trade treaties for fair pricing of goods, and the abolition of the oligarchy that was controlled by some of the most vulturous moneylenders of the period. Most amazing was that, for the remainder of classical Greek history, the people had learned their lesson well and the cheap money credit inflation policies were never allowed to be repeated. In the democracy that was subsequently established, every major official was required to swear by oath annually to maintain purity of coinage.

After the Solonian reform, a new and even greater economy developed based on the silver drachma (66 grains, 99 percent pure). Gold coins were also minted to a lesser degree, but silver was more widely available and remained the standard until the conquest by the Macedonian Empire, which introduced small gold staters, which afterward became the most prized money in the Near, Middle, and Far East long after the empire was gone. The Macedonians also left behind the Hellenic legacy of sound, pure money, which has survived even to this day in those parts of the world where there is a long-bred respect for gold and silver as the standard bearer of wealth.

The Roman Empire

To the west in Rome, a different story unfolded. In the western world, our legacy comes from ancient Rome, and we have benefited greatly from the systems of law and politics, the arts and literature that have been handed down to us. So it is interesting to note that we also seemed to have inherited the Romans' enigmatic ineptitudes when it comes to dealing with coin and currency.

The first Roman money was a bar of copper called the *as*, which weighed one pound and while in circulation was checked by weighing. Later, it was stamped with the official state seal and was circulated by sight only. Sometimes it was broken into smaller pieces but still passed, along with its official stamp, by visual inspection only. This system tempted both the authorities and the general population to debase the as by reducing its weight slightly, to the point that from constant filing and clipping it dropped in weight from one pound in the fourth century B.C. to four ounces by the middle of the third century B.C. This trend continued until, by 70 B.C., the as had been reduced to a mere half ounce.

Around 300 B.C., the Roman denarius of silver (66 grains, 99 percent pure) was introduced to compete with the Greek drachma. Two hundred years later, when Julius Caesar came to power, the weight of the denarius had dropped only slightly, to 60 grains, which reflected the basic integrity of the Roman republic. With the advent of the Roman Empire, however, the coinage fared differently. Julius Caesar and his successor Augustus, the first Roman emperor, who ruled from 27 B.C. to A.D. 14, established a new money system based on the gold aureus, 126 grains of fine gold minted at the rate of 40 to the libra (pound). The silver denariis was continued at 84 to the libra, and its value was 25 denarii to 1 aureus. This standard remained undisturbed for 75 years, until the ascension of the infamous Nero (ruler from A.D. 54 to A.D. 68), who devalued the aureus by reducing its weight from 40 to 45 to the libra and the denarius from 84 to 96 to the libra and who, with this act, we might say formally ushered in the moral decay and corruption that set the empire on its long downward spiral to its ultimate demise.

Following this, a series of devaluations occurred with each successive emperor, with Trajan (A.D. 98–117), becoming the first to reduce purity as well as weight, up to Severus (A.D. 193–211), who reduced the denarius to only 26 grains and 50 percent base metal. Caracalla (A.D. 211–217) reduced the aureus from 45 to 50 to the libra, but this was purely cosmetic since the imperial mint for some time had been secretly issuing the coin with a base content of 40 percent to 50 percent while the silver content of the denarius had degenerated to a point where it was little more than a copper penny.

A new silver coin weighing 84 grains, called the *antonius*, was struck to replace the denarius, but this coin suffered the same fate as its predecessor, so that by the reign of Gallienus (A.D. 253–268), the antonius was merely a base metal coin with a thin coating of silver. This gave Gallienus the dubious distinction of introducing us to the first clad coinage.

Disdainfully, the treasury still demanded that taxes be paid with good gold and silver coin while it paid out in debased coin, but this proved impossible to enforce. All good gold and silver that could be had escaped to lands outside the borders of the empire, and, despite a flurry of edicts that attempted to control prices and debt payments, the Roman monetary system was in a complete shambles.

As the monetary system fell apart, so did the empire. A civilization that had made great strides in many areas became stagnant, anarchistic, and bankrupt, and eventually succumbed to barbarism, the Huns, and the Vandals.

Byzantium

While the Roman Empire in the West fell into ruin, there was a rebirth of the old empire in the East through Byzantium, which was to endure for over 1,200 years with its capital city of Constantinople (Istanbul). Here in the eastern remains of the Roman Empire, a mixture of Roman and Hellenic culture and tradition blended to create a new order under the leadership of Constantine I (A.D. 306–337).

Constantine instituted a gold money standard and introduced a new gold coin called the *bezant*. The bezant was only slightly modified in succeeding years until it was finally fixed at a standard of 65 grains of fine gold. Drawing on its Greek heritage of maintaining a pure money standard, this coin was minted at this purity for an astounding 800 years, which is undoubtedly the greatest achievement in the annals of monetary history. That it was minted at this purity for that length of time makes it the most important coin in the history of Western man, and it was this coin that for 800 years dominated in all trade, commerce, and money matters all the way from the barbarian camps in northern Europe to the opulent courts of royalty in India.

The power of the bezant was legendary, and many monarchs throughout the world never even bothered to mint their own coin, but instead kept their accounts recorded in bezants. Based on the unshakeable bezant, the Byzantines built an empire that was held in awe and respect throughout the far reaches of the world. While Europe mired in the Dark Ages, Byzantine culture and wealth flourished. The Byzantines were able to maintain vast armies, launch great fleets, build magnificent palaces, and expand in religion, the arts, and the sciences.

The empire was able to maintain its borders and repel one assault after another, and for 900 years its capital city was never seriously threatened by enemy forces. It is interesting that the Byzantines did not enjoy the reputation of being the best fighters, and military incompetency ran high. But those enemies that could not be fought off were bought off. Even the most savage barbarian chieftains could not resist the spell cast by the mighty bezant.

Of course, Byzantium's sound money system was not the sole cause of such commercial and social advancement. A reflection of other governmental equities can be seen in Byzantine banking laws: all the bankers and money changers were required to swear by oath never to clip, file, or in any way devalue the coinage, never to issue any counterfeit coin, and never to give charge of their business to any servant during an absence. The punishment of this oath was severe: the offender's hand was cut off.

A most interesting lesson can be learned from the Byzantine money experience by all those who oppose gold as a money standard with the claim that there's not enough gold to go around. No restrictions were ever enacted barring the travel of bezants. Bezants were freely exported and reached all parts of the world, yet the empire never experienced any shortage of gold. During the 800 years of sound money practice, gold poured into the empire from mines and stockpiles from all parts of the earth to be sold and exchanged with the highly prized bezant. As for those bezants that reached corners of the globe far from the empire, most eventually found their way back to be spent again with Byzantine merchants. Note this contrast with latter-day Rome, when neither by law nor by force could a single gold or silver coin be extracted from the people, and the base metal tokens that passed for money in the empire were so universally loathed and rejected that its once thriving and extensive foreign commerce all but vanished.

As in the case of other dynasties and governments, the decline of Byzantium corresponds with the decline of its money. Eight centuries of pure money coinage, along with the integrity and economic wonders that accompanied it, were brought to an end by a very unpopular ruler named Alexius I Comnenus (1081–1118). In order to pay for his corrupt and lavish government, he debased the bezant and resorted to the old Roman tactic of paying debts with devalued coinage while mandating that all taxes be paid with good coin. For the remaining 250 years that the Byzantine Empire existed before its fall to Islam, it never was able to regain its former status and distinction. Steady decline brought further debasements, governmental cheating, scandals, and social and political turmoil until dishonesty and immorality permeated the society at all levels. In the end, the name Byzantium, which had once set the standard for honor and integrity, became synonymous with degradation and debauchery.

The European Monarchs

With the onslaught of the Islamic conquests, all vestiges of the old Hellenic world disappeared, and with it the stabilizing influence it had exerted on the money policies of the West. With this tradition destroyed, the West once again reverted to its Roman heritage and began a mad money rampage that lasted until Napoleon. Following this Latin example, the European monarchs added to it with their feeling that, as an important source of revenue for the crown, it was their divine right periodically to devalue and debase their currencies, regardless of the economic confusion and hardship they imposed upon their subjects and their commerce by doing so. They pursued this policy with vigor. When they conquered new territories that had sound currencies, they immediately set out to squeeze revenues from the newly acquired currency through devaluation.

An example of this is the Arabian dinar after it fell into Christian hands. The Arabs had been great admirers of classical Greek philosophy and the Byzantine money experience. Following in their footsteps, they had established their coin, the dinar, at 65 grains, .975 pure gold (patterned exactly after the bezant) and had maintained this standard throughout the entire Arabian world for over 400 years. Moslem Spain, under the control of the Moors, had kept its accounts in dinars. No sooner had the Christians conquered Spain in the 12th century than they began to rape the dinar. Its name was changed from the dinar to the maravedi, and it was immediately reduced in weight to 56 grains. Its debasement continued unabated until, by the rule of James I of Aragon (13th century), the maravedi had been reduced to a meager 14 grains. Under Alfonso the Wise, it had only 10 grains, and soon after it became too small to circulate.

The maravedi then had a short-lived rebirth as a silver coin of 26 grains, but it suffered the same fate as its gold predecessor until it became so debased that it could be used only as a theoretical unit of account.

There are many more examples of centuries of European coin debasement, but they are too numerous to mention here. In any case, all this was only a precursor to the incredible experiences that were to come with the introduction of the magic currency—paper money.

2
THE DEBUT OF PAPER
MAGIC MADNESS

Because of the colonization and exploitation of the newly discovered Americas, huge stores of gold, silver, and other wealth began to pour into Europe from these new lands. This created a new boom and prosperity on the Continent, but it seemed that, no matter how much wealth was exported to Europe, it was never enough to satisfy the greed of certain monarchs. The French experience beginning with Louis XIV (1643–1715) illustrates this propensity.

THE RISE AND FALL OF JOHN LAW

With his unending military exploits and his lavish and corrupt squanderings on palaces, gardens, and the like, Louis XIV managed to leave the country in debt to the tune of three billion livres (one livre equals one pound of silver) at the time of his death. With net government income of only three million livres, the nation found itself on the brink of collapse.

To raise revenues, the new regent tried the same old tactic of coin debasement, but this served only to aggravate the problem, with the usual results of economic despair, pauperism, and social strife and contention among the people. Everywhere, talk of revolution filled the air.

Into this scene strode a dashing Scottish-born gambler and adventurer, John Law, who had become familiar with the new regent in the gambling halls of Paris. As a youth, John Law had worked in his father's bank in Edinburgh but had fled Scotland after killing a man in a duel and had supported himself on the Continent since that time with his uncommon gambling abilities.

Law, an amateur economist, had written some pamphlets espousing a scheme for the issuance of bank notes based on the value of land or other wealth, rather than gold or silver reserves. Through his acquaintance with the regent, he was given permission to open a bank in Paris and allowed to test his theories.

Law proved to be a very ingenious banker. He immediately began to release bank notes that carried a unique guarantee, which was that his notes promised to pay on demand not only valid coin but coin in amounts current at the time of the note's issue. This made the notes appear depreciation-proof. To secure further public confidence in his notes, he boldly declared that any banker who issued notes for greater amounts than he could redeem should be immediately put to death. These strategies did the trick, and his notes were soon widely circulating at great premiums over all other coin and notes issued by the state.

With the amazing success of John Law's notes, the regent began to view paper currency not merely as a currency supplemental to metal, but as a means to eliminate all metallic currency completely, as well as the fiscal responsibilities and limitations that go with it. John Law's next proposal was therefore greeted with open arms and great enthusiasm. That familiar marriage of politician and banker had taken place.

France's vast Louisiana Territory in the New World presented great promise. It was a wild, unexplored land, perceived to be an immense untapped store of wealth containing huge lodes of gold, silver, minerals, and other natural resources. John Law's plan was to sell shares of stock in a new jointly held company that had exclusive rights to all trade and commerce in the Louisiana Territory as well as the Mississippi River. In no time, investors were caught up in a frenetic speculative fever as they all rushed to buy stock in this new venture.

The regent and his court were also swept away by this wave of enthusiasm, and with each passing week John Law was given newer privileges until finally he was granted a monopoly on the entire tobacco trade and the exclusive right to all gold and silver refining, and his bank was designated the Royal Bank of France.

Enamored by success, Law soon became overconfident and began to forget his own rules. When the regent approached him to issue a billion new livres in paper currency, Law indifferently agreed, brushing aside his earlier dictum that any banker who would issue paper currency beyond that which he could redeem was deserving of death. After all, now he was the Royal Bank. With this new wave of money pumped into the economy, a false sense of prosperity swept the nation, which was further fueled by the booming rise in price of Mississippi stock.

In 1719, the Mississippi Company was given exclusive rights to all trade in France's territories in the South Seas and Far East. With two more monopolies under his belt, Law created yet another wave of new currency and Mississippi stock issued on the strength of the soon to be discovered wealth these lands contained.

Law's influence was augmented by the economic ignorance of France's regent, who saw nothing wrong with the theory that more is better. A second billion livres of paper money was issued, and even more notes were issued against the rising value of the Mississippi stock.

By 1720, more sagacious investors deduced the end was coming and quietly began to cash in their stocks and notes for specie, which they quickly smuggled out of France and into hiding. This steady drain of the bank's gold reserve soon left it precariously posed on the brink of collapse. In a futile attempt to salvage the economy, coins were devalued to 10 percent below paper currency value, and strict limits were placed on both bank payout amounts and amounts individuals could hold.

Further edicts and displays of force ensued but did not succeed in stemming the flight of gold and silver from France. Mississippi stock prices dropped drastically and were dumped for whatever price could be gotten. Coin and bullion soared in value, despite all measures to prevent it. Another decree was issued, making it illegal to pay debt with any coin or metal. Debt could be paid with paper money only, and another 1.5 billion livres of paper money were issued.

But it was too late. By the end of 1720, this great paper money experiment had failed miserably. The bank had no reserves left and suspended payment in specie. The royal treasury was bankrupt, as all gold and silver had disappeared entirely from circulation. The Mississippi Company stock was worthless, and 2.7 billion livres in bank notes remained unredeemable. An angry populace publicly burned all paper currency and Mississippi stocks, and by decree all further business was once more to be conducted in gold and silver. Law's experiments had left France in worse shape than before, he was forced to flee with his family, and all his estates and holdings were confiscated. He died nine years later in Venice, an unknown pauper.

THE FRENCH REVOLUTION AND THE ASSIGNAT

The French monarchy never recovered from this experience and was ultimately to pay for its mistakes 70 years later when once again France found itself in the throes of a huge debt, in severe economic depression, and primed for revolution. Great debates raged in the National Assembly, and the cry went up to issue irredeemable paper money in order to stimulate the economy and pay the debt. Opponents argued that irredeemable-in-specie paper money, once issued, would be followed by more and more issues, with fiscal suicide inevitable. The memory of John Law's bank notes had been short-lived.

The advent of the Revolutionary Government, in 1790, provided the paper money advocates the opportunity they desired. It seized all lands owned by the church (which amounted to one-third of France) and proposed that a new paper be issued based on the value of these lands. These notes, in theory, would be able to be presented to the state for the purchase of land at fixed rates, and the notes themselves would carry an interest rate of 3 percent per year. In April of 1790, 400 million livres of these new paper notes were issued under the name of assignats ("mortgage notes"). Unlike John Law's notes, which were ultimately backed by illusory promises of wealth, these notes were backed by actual state-owned land and would grow in value if left to circulate.

The introduction of these notes seemed to solve the problem. Commerce was revived, and the government reduced debt and paid expenses until five months later, when the government, after having spent all the new assignats, once more found itself in financial straits. The call for a new issue was sounded again. The original opponents of this irredeemable currency had been correct when they had said, once started, there would be no end. Nonetheless, the Revolutionary Government declared the first issue of assignats a success and ordered a new issue of 800 million livres.

But with this new issue, Gresham's Law began to take hold, and all gold, silver, and copper coin disappeared from sight. Desperate to keep good coin in circulation, the government confiscated all gold jewelry, silverware, and even the king's housewares and carried them to the mint. The church was also required to submit all its gold and silver vessels, except for the bare minimum necessary for the saying of Mass. Even church bells were melted down for coin. Despite all these measures, Gresham's Law continued to operate.

The government responded in 1791 with the printing of 600 million livres more of assignats with even more printings after that. By 1793, the illusion that inflation is prosperity was realized. There were new riots, the monarchy was abolished, the king and his family were sent to the guillotine, and the Reign of Terror began.

Unbelievably, instead of enacting currency reform, the Revolutionary Tribunal idiotically imposed stricter price controls, outlawed all dealing in specie, imposed the death penalty for violators and hoarders, and then issued 1.2 billion livres of its own, followed by another 3 billion in 1794. By 1795, 35 billion livres (or francs, as they had come to be known) of assignats were in circulation. And as in all runaway inflations, business collapsed, shortages of food and other necessities prevailed, and rioting and lawlessness ran rampant.

During this period, the louis d'or grew from a value equivalent to 25 livres to 7,200 francs in early 1796. By December 1796, the louis d'or was worth 15,000 francs in paper money. That year, with starvation and death now gripping the land, blind to its own tragic absurdity, the government issued a new paper called the *mandat* to replace the worthless assignat. These mandats were also to be backed with the best government lands, but before they could be put into circulation they were devalued 40 percent and were worthless by the end of the year.

This madness finally came to an end in early 1797. Outstanding remained 40 billion francs in assignats and 2.6 billion in mandats. It was decreed that all paper money was void as legal tender (except for payment of debt to the state at the rate of 1 percent of face value). The printing presses and plates were destroyed publicly, and the hated assignats were burned in great bonfires throughout the land. This action, however, left France with no paper money and, since all coin laid in hiding, put France in the incomprehensible position of having no currency whatsoever.

At first, a bewildered public was uncertain as to what would happen, but coin gradually came out of hiding and circulated when needed. Nonetheless, in 1799, when Napoleon came to power, France still was economically crippled. Its treasury was empty, its debt astronomical, its armies, engaged in war, unpaid for months, and the collection of new taxes an impossibility. In the first meeting with the new Council of State, Napoleon was pressured to issue a new paper currency, to which he replied, "Never—I will pay cash or nothing."

Napoleon was true to his word, and never, throughout his entire career, did he buckle under to pressures put on him to issue paper money. It has been said that his refusal to issue irredeemable paper caused the Rothschilds (a prominent banking family) to withdraw financial support, one of many factors instrumental in bringing the ultimate destruction of his plans for a world empire.

Because of Napoleon's determination to place France on a sound, gold money system, in little time she had no trouble garnering whatever gold was necessary for the economy. Napoleon resumed payment in specie whenever possible and restored France to a full specie monetary system so strong that when France fell to the allied invasion after Waterloo and had heavy indemnities levied against her, she was able to rebound from the setback easily. Even 50 years later, when France was soundly defeated in the Franco-Prussian War and levied the largest indemnity ever to that time ($1 billion) by the occupying Germans, she astounded the world by paying the fine in less than three years.

THE AMERICAN EXPERIENCE

Across the Atlantic, the American colonies also were to experience a currency exchange. These colonies had declared their independence from Great Britain but had no resources or tax revenues with which to wage war. The Continental Congress convened and decided to solve the problem by issuing a paper money, the Continental dollar. Even though these notes bore the inscription "bearer entitled to a Spanish milled dollar, or Value thereof in Gold or Silver," with no assets to back up these notes, they were in reality irredeemable. In June 1775, the Continental Congress authorized the first issue of $2 million of this new money and continued to pump out increasing quantities of the Continentals throughout the next five years of war. In November 1779, a final issue of $10 million brought the total amount of Continentals in circulation to $241 million.

A trusting and naive public had at first accepted these notes, but with each issue their value fell more and more, until in 1780 they were worth 1 percent face value. The government had created the classic case for inflation; that is, it had expanded the money supply as it simultaneously ate up increasing amounts of manpower and goods, which resulted in decreasing amounts of services and products available to the public.

The inflation cycle took hold as prices of goods and services increased to keep par with the currency. Government then issued more paper to cover higher costs it also had to pay. Prices again rose, with more paper following. Enraged by these price hikes, the Continental Congress passed different resolutions and edicts designed to prevent the continuation of the cycle. Price controls were enacted. Those who refused to accept payment with notes at face value were denounced as traitors and legally lost their right to collect their debt. They also had to face fines, imprisonment, and corporal punishment. But no matter what sorts of coercion were attempted, they were useless in forcing the people to accept this fiat currency.

The politicians had encouraged this inflation as a source of indirect taxation to pay for the war. But there were other ramifications as well. In runaway inflations, debtors, including the government, are the big winners as they pay back present loans with future depreciated currency. Holders of the paper are robbed of their wealth even as it sits in their pockets. Many creditors who were forced to accept those future Continentals were wiped out.

Inflation, loss of savings, and price controls were not the only effects of the note issues. As is *always* the case during monetary inflation, all classes of society were caught up in a rage for speculation, while the fundamental virtues of thrift, honesty, and honor were swept away.

When this spate of paper had finally ended and with it all attempts to force its acceptance, the newly formed Congress of the United States was confronted with a new dilemma. With the war over, it faced an angry populace that demanded restitution for Continentals that promised repayment in specie. This Congress was no better off than the previous since it still had no substantial assets of its own. Congress considered leaving the notes in circulation with the promise to redeem them in specie at a lower rate than that for which they had been originally issued or to institute a currency call-in and exchange the old notes for new, at a lower rate. Both solutions were actually the same action in slightly different forms, and the public stood to lose either way. The government decided on the latter course, figuring it would have a psychological edge in its attempts to mollify the people. Finally, in 1789, there was a 100-for-1 exchange of old dollars for new ones. Out of the original issue of $241 million, only $168.3 million were redeemed, which means that it cost the Treasury only $1.683 million dollars to pay off its debt. The only one to profit was the government, a presage of what was to come in the modern world.

3
MODERN DAY
INFLATIONS AND
DESTROYED
DESTINIES

Since World War II, the world has been in what may be described as the "age of inflation." In South America, many countries fell victim to the printing press and had to undergo currency reform. Argentina, Bolivia, Chile, and Uruguay had exchanges. Brazil called in 1,000 old cruzeiros for 1 new one. In eight short years (1959–1967), the cruzeiro went from 18 to the dollar to 3,500 to the dollar.

One of the most tragic results of the modern-day inflations took place during the Nationalistic-Communist War of 1946–1949 in China. The postwar Chinese paper money, the yuan, had deteriorated to where it traded for up to 10,000 to 1 U.S. dollar. The cause of this was the asinine attempt by the U.S. and Nationalist Chinese governments to finance the entire war with printing press money. The Communists paid their troops with hard cash, while the Nationalists paid in paper. This despite the fact that the Nationalist government had a cache of silver and gold worth nearly $300 million that was never used. Defections by Nationalist troops were massive as they were bought off by a promised payment of four

27

Chinese silver dollars (equal to two U.S. dollars) per month by the opposing Communists.

The U.S. Treasury also had $24 billion in gold bullion and 2 billion ounces of silver in stockpiles. Had a fraction of this amount been coined and allowed to circulate in China, then in all likelihood China would have been spared from Communism.

In Europe, one generation of Germans were to see in their lifetime the deutsche mark wiped out not once but twice by hyperinflation. In seven years ending in 1923, the deutsche mark zoomed from 4.2 to 1 U.S. gold dollar to 4 trillion, 2 billion to 1 U.S. dollar with black market rates of 12 trillion to 1. Many have heard the story of the German householder who went to the store to buy a loaf of bread for his family with a wheelbarrow full of notes. When he arrived at the shop he found the wheelbarrow too big to pass through the doorway, so he left it outside and went in to get the shopkeeper. When he came back outside, to his surprise, the money was still there, but the wheelbarrow had been stolen!

In 1948, when once again the deutsche mark was totally destroyed by inflation, Germany underwent a complete monetary overhaul by instituting sound money practices, which forbade budget deficits and resisted the great pressures put on them by the Keynesian economists of the Allied governments attempting to impose their socialistic monetary policies on them. Since then, Germany has had one of the strongest currencies in the world.

In 1946, there were bank notes in Hungary as high as 100 sextillion pengö. In this case, it was the Communists who stabilized the money by recalling the old currency and issuing a new currency tied to gold. In Russia, after it fell to Communism, the Bolsheviks had tried to pay their way with the printing press. As usual, there was runaway inflation and economic collapse. Industrial output vanished, agricultural production fell disastrously, people in the cities were starving, and millions of Russians died or fled abroad.

In 1921, Lenin forced through his New Economic Policy over the protests of his own Marxist advisors, which replaced many of the socialist measures started in the beginning of his rule. Small businesses were permitted to resume limited operations, and retail trade was allowed again. Balanced budgets were mandated, a central bank was established, and the old paper sovznaki ruble was recalled and replaced with the new gold unit, the chervonetz, which equaled 119.5 grains of fine gold. In 1923, the Soviets also minted a 10-ruble gold chervonetz. All bank notes were backed by a minimum of 25 percent gold reserves. It is ironic that since then the Soviets have rigidly adhered to an economic system of strict banking and accounting practices in contrast to the credit-happy Keynesian high rollers in the West. (Present-day Soviets more than likely run budget deficits at home. Their ruble is worthless on the world market, so they must pay in gold and take only short-term loans from Western creditors. This is one reason the West has no qualms about doing, and even seeks, business with them, although they are "enemies" who have vowed to "bury us.")

In post–World War II France, economic trouble had been brewing. Two losing wars, one in Algeria and the other in Indochina, were draining the country. The government had made socialistic handouts to both the public and industry and attempted to stimulate the economy through spending. The government failed to raise any revenues or curb other spending to pay for these measures. The result was an inflation that took the already inflated war franc of 1944 from 50 to 1 U.S. dollar to 500 to 1 dollar in 1958. When de Gaulle came to power in 1958, he instituted massive reforms to curb inflation. The war in Algeria was concluded with a negotiated withdrawal. He brought government spending to reduced levels by different means and introduced a gradual currency call-in of 100 old francs for 1 new heavy franc.

There have been many other currency destructions and call-ins, involving the Austrian krone, Czech koruna, Korean won, Greek drachma, etc., but the story is basically the same everywhere. There is always economic chaos, social disturbance, dishonesty and immorality, death and starvation. Sometimes it takes years and sometimes decades or even centuries, but whether fast or slow, destruction, instability, hardship, and great loss of personal freedom always go with it. Why are these scenarios, with all their human misery, constantly repeated? Can no one take a lesson from history, one that has been continually restated?

Traditionally, the rise and fall of societies run parallel with the rise and fall of their money. It is not hard to see where America is presently situated in terms of this traditional rising and falling money. Why is it, in our society, with all its advancement in material wealth and knowledge, that we lack an even elementary understanding of money? Remember FDR's statement, that nothing in government happens by chance, everything is carefully planned. Why have we been denied information about these plans? Money is the lifeblood of the society, and whoever controls the money controls the direction in which the society flows. Who stands to benefit from this money manipulation, and what is the goal behind it? What extra-special problems do we face in this modern age of electronic wizardry? Are we actually heading for an Orwellian one-world society?

To answer these questions and more, let us specifically review, in the next chapter, American economic and monetary policy for the last 200 years. In Chapter 4, we will also see how the government has selectively "leaked" certain pieces of information in order to prepare us psychologically for the currency exchange that is being planned for us in the very near future.

4
THE ROOTS OF INTERNATIONAL BANKING AND FED POWER

Before 1800, in Europe as well as the United States, there were no real standards in the money systems. Gold, silver, bank notes, and government fiat paper all circulated together, and, although there were a few feeble attempts to attune this jumble, nothing substantial was accomplished. Because of this, gold was usually hoarded, in response to Gresham's Law, and silver became the standard exchange in many places. Without standard coins, foreign trade was often burdensome and vexing. In the early 1800s, Great Britain took the lead and made all its paper money, whether held at home or abroad, fully convertible to gold coin at a fixed rate and made all paper as "good as gold." The 100 percent gold-backed pound sterling became the world's most important currency and established London as the international banking center. The rest of the European nations followed suit and tied their currencies to gold.

In the American colonies, most commerce had been carried out through barter. In New England, wampum was used as well as beaver skins, and in Virginia, tobacco was the medium of exchange. These early settlers had little use for coined money until traders arriving from foreign lands demanded coinage in payment for goods. Any foreign coin was accepted, such as French louis, German talers, Dutch ducats, etc., and especially Spanish doubloons and Spanish milled dollars or pieces of eight. The milled dollar became the colonial standard and was used with official sanction up until 1857. England had consistently ignored the plight of the American colonies and made no effort to provide coinage for them. Consequently, private individuals as well as some states began to mint and circulate their own coin until there were dozens of different coins of gold, silver, and copper in circulation.

After national independence, the Articles of Confederation of March 1, 1781, provided that Congress had the sole right to regulate the content and value of coin struck under its own authority or that of the states. Each state had the right to coin its own money, with the Congress serving as the overseer. Many of the states did then officially strike their own coin.

Throughout the colonial years, Americans had grown used to the Spanish milled dollar, and whenever national coinage was discussed the Spanish dollar was mentioned. Many colonial states had made the Spanish coins legal tender, and the Continental paper issue of 1775 was based on the Spanish dollar.

Over the years, different value and unit systems for a national coinage were submitted, until on July 6, 1785, Congress formally approved the dollar and decimal coinage ratio for a national coinage. But more pressing matters delayed implementation of any resolutions. Only after the Constitutional Convention had placed the republic on solid ground and George Washington was elected president did the Congress once again return to the topic of coinage.

On April 2, 1792, the Coinage Act established an independent monetary system, with the dollar designated as its basic unit. The gold dollar was defined as 24¾ grains fine gold, and the silver dollar 416 grains standard, 892.4 fineness (equaled 371¼ grains pure silver). The act did not call for mintage of a gold dollar, though. Gold pieces in denominations of $10, $5, and $2.50 were authorized. Silver coins in $1, $.50, $.25, $.10, $.05 denominations, and a copper cent and half-cent completed coinage values specified by the act. A mint in Philadelphia was established and began its production of gold, silver, and copper coin. Free circulation of gold and silver coin was hindered, however, because of speculation. The new silver dollars were easily replaced with old, worn Spanish dollars (which contained a little less silver content because of wear), and the gold coins had been slightly undervalued, causing both coins to be snatched up and shipped to Europe, where they would bring higher prices as bullion. Both these conditions were ultimately corrected by acts in 1834 and 1837 that stabilized the weights and values of these coins.

Due to pressures from silver mining interests in the West, our system was actually a bimetal one until 1900, when the Gold Standard Act officially put us on a full gold standard. Silver continued to be used and enjoyed unlimited legal tender status, but it was actually a subsidiary coin, and its value was far below face value in terms of standard gold.

This golden age lasted for almost 33 years. Then, on March 5, 1933, FDR seized the country's gold through the proclamation of a national emergency, threatened all hoarders with imprisonment, stopped the minting of gold coin and any transactions in gold, and turned all our gold over to the quasipublic Federal Reserve System.

The "Fed" is a unique organization that has found a special niche. It is not a government, public, or private agency, even though some claim it is all of these.

Most people believe that the Federal Reserve is part of the government because the word *federal* appears in the title. Most people do not realize that the Federal Reserve is not a government institution but in reality a government-granted monopoly to private bankers. As evidence that it is not a government agency, it is not listed by the federal government as a government entity, it does not respond on a daily basis to the Congress, nor is it subject to congressional action. It is a top-secret organization functioning within full protection of the law. It operates its own off-budget programs without any jurisdiction by the Congress. It receives its money from buying Treasury securities, which the Treasury must pay back with interest, and then by using these billions in interest to run its own show. In other words, it is empowered to create money out of thin air, lend the thin-air money to the Treasury, and then use the interest paid back on the thin-air money as its own.

The Fed cannot be categorized as public or private either. Public and private corporations are required to have their books audited in order to fulfill the Securities and Exchange Commission (SEC) requirements. However, the Fed never gets audited and will not allow an audit. Yet this is not considered a violation of the law. It would seem that the Fed is, perhaps, the most powerful organization in the country. It has full control over our money, thus giving it power over every single one of us. It runs a tightly veiled operation answering to none of us, including our president or Congress, while enjoying the full protection of our laws.

It is essential, then, to examine how banking has evolved and developed into a power-stricken entity whose leaders would like nothing better than to enslave us to a new world order under their dominion.

THE HISTORY OF AMERICAN BANKING

There are two types of commercial banks in this country: state-chartered and federally chartered. Banking got its start in the United States through prosperous merchants who lent out their own money to creditworthy customers. The interest these merchants charged for loans often exceeded what they could make in their own businesses; hence, they evolved into full-time bankers.

In their early days, these bankers were cautious and utilized what was called the *real bills doctrine*. This meant they would make only short-term loans to commercial accounts, which would be paid back quickly through sales made by the borrowing company. These banks worked only with commerce and became known as *commercial banks*, the term by which they are still known today.

These early bankers found that, after they had established a good reputation, they could issue their personal IOUs or notes in lieu of gold or silver. The borrower would then use the bank note as he would money, to buy whatever he needed. The bankers would maintain reserves of gold and silver and would pay off the note whenever it was presented for redemption. Those bankers who had firmly established themselves in the community found that many times the notes would not come in for redemption right away but began to circulate instead as money. Out of this evolved one of the most insidious mechanisms ever devised to defraud—fractional reserve banking. Bankers would lend out and collect interest on their notes in greater amounts than they had in actual reserves. Assuming that many notes would circulate and not be redeemed quickly, they could collect interest on loans for money that they really did not possess. They ran the risk, though, that if they inflated their quantities of notes too much, and too many notes were presented at one time for redemption of reserves that they did not possess, they would be broken or bankrupt. Conservative bankers would therefore be careful to keep their issues low, while the less scrupulous bankers would run high issues, hoping to make a killing before being discovered.

From 1792 to 1834, when the country underwent a severe coin shortage due to the previously described actions of the speculators, a great assortment of state and private bank notes flooded the markets as the de facto currency. These notes were known by colorful names (which also implied their worth), such as *wildcat, red dog, stump tail,* and *shin plaster.* These notes were so overissued that they always traded for less then face value, and as today when someone checks the financial columns of a newspaper for stock prices, the people of that day would consult local newspapers and publications listing the discount prices of individual bank notes to find out their actual worth.

This situation was relieved when the bugs were worked out of the system in 1837. But there were still federal government issues to contend with, such as national bank notes, greenbacks, and Treasury notes. With the Gold Standard Act of 1900, all of this currency was tied to full parity with gold and was 100 percent convertible into gold coin or bullion. This golden age lasted until 1933, when our gold was stolen from us through nationalization.

In the early days, our nation had a primarily agriculture-based economy, and almost everyone was self-employed. Individuals who increased their wealth would invest in more land or livestock, and the merchants and manufacturers would increase inventories and raw materials, or they would merely store their wealth in gold or silver buried in the ground. The arrival of the Industrial Revolution caused a switch from an agrarian economy to an industrial economy. This resulted in more and more people working as employees.

At first, most banks avoided deposits from the general public. When they did accept them, they would charge the depositors a fee for storing and guarding their money. But with more people moving into urban and industrial areas as employees, whatever excess wealth they accumulated went begging for places to be invested. This gave birth to the savings bank and other investment vehicles, such as the securities and insurance markets, which all provided specialized opportunities for the wealth of the growing middle class. Bankers now found themselves with even greater stocks of money that could be exploited as reserves. Banking grew larger than ever.

In those early days of the U.S., both the states and the federal government were in need of money to operate. The power the politicians had for taxing purposes was very limited. When they wanted to finance a project, the usual method was to sell bonds and securities and pay back the buyers of these issues with revenue generated from the project. Still, to sell bonds was no easy task as most people had little faith in the integrity of politicians, whose undertakings were usually pork-barrel projects designed to enrich their financial supporters. A natural attraction then resulted between bankers who had extra money and the politicians who needed money.

At first, the state politicians did not go directly to the bankers, but attempted to get into the banking business themselves. They chartered state-owned and -operated banks that issued their own bonds to garner reserves. After acquiring the needed reserves, they issued notes, finally in such large quantities that the notes quickly depreciated and these banks collapsed one by one.

In the meantime, the private bankers had been doing a good business lending to Wall Street stock speculators. The problem was that, whenever stock prices fell or for whatever reason a minor recession occurred, the number of people rushing to withdraw their deposits from the banks increased. Many times a panic would result, with depositors lining up outside to withdraw their funds before the bank went under. Banks found that, if they did not keep approximately a 50 percent gold reserve, there was every chance of their failing during a crisis. Because the reserves had to be maintained at this 50 percent level, and the amount of gold in the system remained rather constant, the banks were limited in their ability to inflate to about twice their reserves.

Therefore, a great demand arose for some method to circumvent this reserve requirement. The bankers wanted a system that would reduce their required reserves and eliminate bank runs, the businesspeople wanted a source of low-cost loans, and the politicians, who did not have sufficient power to tax, wanted money to finance the ever expanding government. But they all already knew what that method was. It was to use reserve assets other than gold. Although the people had chosen and still wanted gold as their money, it was now up to the politicians and bankers to convince them that some other asset would be better and should be used instead.

One group, which represented the silver interests in the West, tried to have the huge quantities of silver being mined used as new reserve. At that time, silver had very little commercial use, and if it had been adopted as a banking reserve, the miners would have had a new market for their increasing production.

The bankers and politicians had another idea in mind for assets, though, and that asset was debt. The state politicians had failed at their own banking attempts, so they turned to the private bankers for assistance. By seizing on the public's natural distrust of banks, it was easy for them to enact legislation that professed to regulate the banking industry.

The states passed laws requiring the banks to obtain state charters. These charters stipulated that the banks were to maintain minimum reserves in relation to their note issue. It appeared that these charters would protect the public from the bankers by forcing them to keep reserves in certain proportions to their notes.

This was only a front. The banks were given the choice of maintaining their reserves in gold or in interest-bearing debt securities of the state. The bankers were no fools. Gold reserves would pay no interest, while state debt would. They became willing buyers of state IOUs. The politicians had found a source of easy money, and the bankers had found a way to increase profits while simultaneously gaining an air of respectability and stability from their status as state-chartered banks with so much in reserve.

In reality, the bankers had wanted to use the IOUs of their loan customers as reserves. After all, they reasoned, these short-term commercial IOUs were real assets of the bank that would eventually be paid off. They figured that during business expansions these IOUs would increase and during business slowdowns the IOUs would decrease. The note issues backed by these IOUs would also temporarily expand and then contract with the business cycle. They knew that, with government debt, the permanent expansion would result in inflation. But the depositors would not go for either idea. They wanted to be sure they could get out their funds in real money—gold, not hot-air IOUs.

What the bankers really wanted, though, was to set up a central bank that would have special powers to issue "legal tender" currency in exchange for IOUs at the bankers' request. Their idea was that, if a bank run started, that bank could go to the central bank with some of its IOUs and sell its IOUs to the central bank for some of its legal tender currency. In this way, the banks would have the necessary funds to meet any banking crisis.

A competition then ensued between federal and state officials over who would be able to control the issuance of money. Many attempts had been made throughout the early life of the U.S. to set up a national bank under federal jurisdiction. Both the First and Second National Bank of the United States did not survive due to the people's well-founded fears and prejudices against banks. The Second National Bank had actually failed, leaving over $23 million of its notes outstanding, which served only to strengthen these prejudices.

The National Bank Act of 1863

In 1863, during the Civil War, under the guise of reforming the abuses of the wildcat period, the National Bank Act was passed, taking away the rights of state banks to issue bank notes and giving this right only to banks that were chartered by the federal government. It was deemed a free act in the sense that any group or individual could easily obtain a federal charter, provided it met certain requirements found in the act.

The real motivation behind passage of this act is revealed by the requirement that banks keep amounts of U.S. federal government securities equal to the amount of notes issued by the bank. This move was made to bolster the government, not society.

In summary, it can be said that the state and federal dual system of banking evolved into a contest over who would be the beneficiary from the issuance of debt-backed currency. Although the politicians and bankers widely touted the benefits the public would derive from these measures, the root cause of these actions actually was to satisfy the selfish desires of both politician and banker.

State and federal banks continued to grow and thrive, but the bankers were still not satisfied. The big bankers in the East wanted to consolidate their powers and quash competition from the new banks that were developing. And because of the great public distrust of banks, all banks still faced the possibility of failure when even the slightest rumor of trouble started. The bankers continued to push for a central bank, and the politicians were very receptive to the idea, provided that the bank issue was backed with government debt rather than the bankers' commercial IOUs.

There were many opponents of all of these schemes, however, who could see them for what they really were. The American public remembered well the devastating effects of inflation during the Revolutionary and Civil Wars, caused solely by debt-backed currency. They could see these schemes as nothing more than a system to bilk the people of their wealth at the hands of special-interest groups, namely the bankers and politicians.

The Federal Reserve Act of 1913

The bankers and politicians were tenacious and not easily deterred. They continued to pound away at the voters, with much rhetoric centered around the public's fear of banking failures. Then came a Wall Street crash, causing the Bank Panic of 1907, in which many New York banks were wiped out and with them the savings of most of their depositors. Capitalizing on the public's tremendous anger about this event provided the additional sway needed to ram through the Federal Reserve Act of 1913. This act finally granted to the private bankers the monopoly they had so longingly sought.

The government claimed the act was a victory for the public because it provided formal supervision of the big bankers by a presidentially appointed board of governors. The bankers claimed a public victory in that the government was now inhibited in its power to inflate (government debt was not permitted to be used as reserves). In reality, this act placed the monetary power in private hands, with the real victors the bankers and politicians. As usual, the public lost.

The 1913 act created the Federal Reserve System, which consisted of a board of governors headquartered in Washington, DC, 12 regional banks, and a total of 25 branch banks. All nationally chartered banks were required to join, and as many state chartered banks that desired could also join the system.

The 12 regional banks would have the power to buy up debt securities from their member banks using the newly invented Federal Reserve Note (FRN). These FRNs became the new legal tender currency of the country, and all other banks were prohibited from issuing any private bank notes at all.

The Federal Reserve Bank became the "lender of last resort" whenever its members faced any difficulties. The Fed would simply create money out of thin air, purchase the troubled bank's IOUs, and pump them up with as much "money" as was needed. These private bankers had finally gotten the power to create currency at will, thus preventing any chance of a bank run. They claimed panics and depressions would become a thing of the past.

As mentioned above, the original act had put limits on the Fed's power to inflate. There were two major restrictions: The first was that it could inflate only to the point of having a 35 percent gold reserve backing for all FRNs issued. The second was that the IOUs it was able to purchase with these FRNs could be in commercial paper only, not in government debt securities. But now this would all change.

When the Great Depression hit, the Fed's power to inflate was greatly disturbed due to its commercial IOU reserve requirements and gold hoarding by the people. Another banking crisis developed, and a record 4,004 banks failed with deposits of $3.6 billion. At the behest of the bankers, FDR, in 1933 and 1934, through the Emergency Banking Act and the Gold Reserve Act, nationalized and demonetized gold and turned it over to the Federal Reserve. He also devalued the dollar from $20.67 to $35 per ounce of gold. This allowed for great expansion of the currency to pay for government programs. The Fed also turned from its previous policy of buying commercial IOUs to government debt IOUs. This allowed freedom from the benign restrictions that a commodity-based money system inherently imposes. The government and bankers now had the power to inflate without limit, and individuals could never again feel free to save money without fearing a great loss in its value.

The Monetary Control Act of 1980

Many other details about the evolution of the banking system are of interest, but they are not really pertinent here. What *is* relevant is the Depository Institutions Deregulation and Monetary Control Act of 1980 (commonly known as the Monetary Control Act). This act is probably the single most inflationary bill ever enacted outside of the original Federal Reserve Act of 1913.

The act began as a bill intended to deal with state usury laws and consumer loans. Along the way, in the congressional banking committees, it was merged with a monetary control bill, and one or two well-placed members of the committees slipped in some sleeper clauses. According to an interview with Daniel J. Piro, Chairman of the Committee to Establish the Gold Standard and a chief lobbyist against the act, only 3 of the 26 congressmen who voted for the act while in committee understood its potential impact. The others were told they were merely voting on the issue of "voluntary vs. mandatory" membership in the Federal Reserve System. It was called for a vote in the House only two days after it cleared conference, and nobody on the House floor even had time to read it. It wouldn't have mattered anyway, since it was a very complex bill with the obscure sleeper provisions written into 85 pages of technical legal jargon that would have taken days or weeks for a nonspecialist to decipher. It received no attention in the popular press or other media, and only a few lawmakers understood the implications of the bill. After it was quietly rushed through the Congress, President Carter signed it into law March 31.

The questionable circumstances under which this bill was slipped through Congress demonstrates how much of a stranglehold the bankers have on us. The title of the act itself is written in Orwellian doublespeak. It neither deregulates depository institutions nor controls money. In fact, it does the exact opposite in both cases. Let's examine how the Monetary Control Act came into being to clarify what it actually does.

First, the Fed is always seeking ways to concentrate more

power in its hands and to expand its control over the money system and all banks. The Fed controls member banks through its authority to set reserve requirements and its ability to demand reports from each bank. Moving reserve limits up or down dictates the lending powers of the banks, and the reports the Fed requires enable it to monitor the money supply and set policies. Membership in the Fed is mandatory for federally chartered banks but optional for state-chartered banks. The last few years before passage of the act saw member banks rebelling against these controls of the Fed by switching over to state charters and dropping out of the system altogether. Many state charters allow interest-bearing reserves or require no minimum reserves at all. This gives them a competitive edge over the member banks, which must maintain minimum reserves in non-interest-bearing accounts. The Fed's ability to control member banks through reserve standards was broken when banks changed to state charters. Also, state-chartered banks report only to their state agencies and do not have to supply any information to the Fed. This action was greatly eroding the powers of the Fed. The Monetary Control Act restored these powers by subordinating all "depository institutions" to the control of the Fed and reducing reserve requirements. All depository institutions, such as state banks, savings and loans, credit unions, mutual savings banks, etc., are now under the control of the Fed. The Fed also has the authority to set reserve requirements for all institutions with deposits exceeding $25 million. No longer can a bank avoid the Fed by simply reorganizing its structure. This was the "voluntary vs. mandatory" provision mentioned earlier. So much for the deregulation referred to in the act's misleading title. The Fed also opened up its discount window to all these institutions to provide emergency funds for any problem. This allows the Fed greater opportunity for and facility in expanding the money supply.

To pacify the bankers' dissatisfaction with having to maintain non-interest-bearing reserves, the Fed was empowered to lower its reserve requirement from 16½ percent to 12 percent, the amount banks must carry against demand deposits. The act also allows for the rate to be reduced to 8 percent if the Fed deems it necessary. Under renewable periods of 180 days, the Fed has special powers to set the reserve requirements at whatever level it pleases, even to reduce them to zero. At 16½ percent, the banks can create $6 of demand deposits for $1 held. Twelve percent reserve moves it to $8.50 for every $1 held, and at 8 percent it is $12 for every $1. This means that the lowering of the reserve requirements to 12 percent allows for a 28 percent increase in the money supply and at 8 percent up to a 76 percent increase in the money supply. And if some emergency necessitated a zero reserve, all hell would break loose with hyperinflation the result.

An obscure provision of the act also has helped allay the fears that have developed within large corporations in response to the gaining momentum of grass roots balanced-budget movements. Many corporate heads hold positions as district directors in the Fed. These corporations have a vested interest in seeing inflation continue. Most of the biggest corporations are unprofitable and are now living on cash flow and borrowed money. They know they can pay back present loans with constantly depreciating dollars.

The Monetary Control Act has changed the definition of collateral to mean any "asset" the Federal Reserve Banks buys or sells in the open market. This expands the types of securities the Fed can hold from U.S. Treasury securities to include obligations of corporate, state, and municipal entities. This means that, if any corporation, state, or city is in trouble, it can bypass the Congress and go directly to the Fed for help. It has been argued that careful reading of the original Federal Reserve Act will reveal that the Fed always had this power. Well, if there was ever any doubt, this new provision obviates the need for further debate.

However, there is one new authorization that no one debates. Not only can the Fed buy up corporate, state, or municipal debt, but it now has been given the authority to monetize bond issues of foreign governments in the exact same fashion it has been doing in monetizing U.S. Treasury debts. This power can be used to buy up the debt of any foreign nation that defaults on its loans with the international bankers. A massive default would cause the whole banking system to come tumbling down. The threat of this action is no longer as menacing since the Fed can now step in and act to prevent such an occurrence.

There are two more areas the act affects. One is the usury laws, which placed limits on the interest rates of different types of deposits. These laws were originally installed by the big banks to prevent competitors from advertising higher rates that would take business away from them. Even so, the entire industry profited from keeping these rates low at the expense of the saver. Inflation forced interest rates to rise so high that these usury ceilings began to work against the banks. Borrowers such as corporations and governments were not bound by these usury limits and were able to offer higher interest rates (through bonds, money market funds, etc.) than could the banks. This was causing a drain of funds from banks into these other areas. The 1980 act voided these ceiling rates. This is both good and bad. The saver and lender can get more of a return on their investment, but in areas such as home mortgages the borrower is strapped to exorbitant rates and pays three or four times the worth of the property.

The final area affected by the act involves the Federal Deposit Insurance Corporation (FDIC). The FDIC came into being through the Banking Act of 1933. The big bankers thought they had solved the problem of bank failures with the establishment of the Federal Reserve System in 1913. Their fallacious logic was exposed by the banking crisis that engulfed them that year (over 4,000 banks failed in 1933). They then hit upon the idea of creating a type of insurance fund to stem the fears of depositors potentially fleeing with their savings. Coverage was started at $2,500 and raised to $5,000 per account in mid-1934. It had been upped a number of times throughout the years until it stood at $40,000. The insured banks at first contributed $\frac{1}{12}$ of 1 percent of their total deposits as a premium. This had been lowered to $\frac{1}{3}$ of that in recent years. The act of 1980 increased FDIC protection to

$100,000 per account, which has reduced the fund's reserve even more. As of January 1, 1984, about $12.25 billion or only 1.25 percent of deposits are in reserve.

In summary, the Monetary Control Act is likely to have these consequences:

- The money value will be cut in half in the next few years.
- Interest rates will rise as high as 50 percent and will reach at least 15–30 percent over the next ten years.
- Interest rates on consumer loans will be 50–100 percent, with the largest corporations able to borrow at half these rates.
- Chrysler Corporation-type bailouts will become routine.
- Legalized governmental manipulations of stocks and bonds will be commonplace.
- Rallies in the securities of very weak companies will come when they are least expected.

The Fed will pick and choose opportunities as it plays the role of rescuer and steps in at the 11th hour to end a crisis or save the economy.

A CASE FOR THE DISSOLUTION OF THE FED

The power and functions of the Fed are coming under closer scrutiny now than ever before. The public is looking for answers to the problems of increasing taxes and inflation. Most Americans remain confused, especially with the endless stream of incomprehensible babble coming from the economists who grace our TV screens and newsprint, but the minority that looks to the abolishment of the Fed as one major solution to these problems is growing rapidly. Americans are beginning to realize that the Fed is controlled by the big international bankers who are out to destroy the American way of life while providing the means to maintain their own financial and political empires.

Lately, a group of Fed apologists have tried to dispel this attitude by claiming that the Fed is a government-controlled committee. They have tried to stifle the Fed "haters" by labeling them as right-wing kooks. The debate centers around who owns the Fed. Technically, the Fed is owned by its member banks, which are supervised primarily by a presidentially appointed board of governors and by secondary district directors comprised of bankers, industrialists, and private citizens.

The apologists admit that the creation of debt-backed money by the Fed is a technical action of the Fed, but they point to the fact that the Fed does not benefit from this money at all. After the Fed's expenses are paid, the remainder of this money is returned to the Treasury Department in the form of an excise tax. For example, in 1980, of the $12.8 billion it earned on government debt, $11.7 billion was paid back to the Treasury. Even so, though collecting $1.1 billion in interest on money created out of thin air to pay to perpetuate itself is not really a profit per se, this is not where the real power of the Fed rests. After all, what need is there to worry about profits when the Fed can create all the money it wants by simply "printing" it?

The Fed is a government-granted monopoly to the private banks and, like all government-imposed monopolies, works for the good of its established firms to the great detriment of the public. The Fed controls the American economic and political system and enables its member banks and shadowy insiders to maintain this power lock through the preservation of the fractional reserve system of banking. With this system, they can lend out at least 10 times more than their reserves of cash or government securities, all of which came to them at no cost and on which they collect interest that has to be created by the hard work of the borrower. An excellent illustration of this involves the home mortgage. The banks lend this "nonexistent" money, which the homeowner must pay back with interest in "real" money or face foreclosure.

But even more important is the power to create the money necessary to perpetuate this sham. This is achieved by the Federal Open Market Committee (FOMC). The FOMC is the authority that guides the Fed's security transactions. It is responsible for the purchase and sales of securities in the open market. This is the means by which the Fed contracts or expands the bank reserves and thus the money supply, which is the single most important determinant in the nation's economy. Through this activity, the Fed can control interest rates, inflation, recessions, or depressions.

As a fringe benefit, the insiders who have access to the activities of the FOMC receive advance information concerning the decisions that will be made. This small elite cabal, who avail themselves of this knowledge, can exploit the market-place for billions. Who among us would not mind being privy to this information just once, so that we might also be able to reap the benefits and maybe retire in style?

The committee is comprised of the seven members of the board of governors and the presidents of five of the regional Federal Reserve Banks. (The remaining seven sit in on all meetings but cannot vote.) The seven members of the Federal Reserve Board are nominated by the president of the U.S., and confirmed by the Senate. One full term is equal to 14 years, and a term begins every two years on February 1 of even-numbered years. A board member may not be reappointed to another term if that member has served a full term. If the member was completing an unexpired term, then reappointment to a full term is permitted. Terms end on their statutory date regardless of the date on which a member is sworn into office. The chairman and vice chairman are chosen by the president from the existing board members and serve a four-year term. These choices must also be confirmed by the Senate. Having the position of chairman or vice chairman does not affect that member's term on the board.

It can be said of this group that, with the life-and-death grip they have on the American people and their money, they are the single most important decision-making assembly in the nation. Who are these people, and what do they stand for? Let us examine their backgrounds.

Federal Reserve Board of Governors

Paul Volcker. Born September 5, 1927. Volcker is the present chairman of the board of governors and the FOMC. He is serving his second four-year term as chairman of the board and was initially appointed by President Jimmy Carter. He became a member of the board of governors on August 6, 1979, on which date he also began his four-year term as chairman of the board. His term as a member of the board expires on January 31, 1992.

Volcker earned his B.A. at Princeton University in 1949, received his M.A. from Harvard in 1951, and did postgraduate work at the London School of Economics in 1951–52, which, at that time, was well known for its "Fabian" socialistic leanings.

He began his career working for the New York Fed as a summer employee in 1949 and 1950. He returned to the New York Fed in 1952 as a full-time economist and remained there until 1957. He then went to work for the Chase Manhattan Bank as a financial economist until 1961. In 1962, he went to work at the U.S. Treasury as director of financial analysis until his promotion, in 1963, to the position of deputy under secretary of monetary affairs for the Treasury, which he held until 1965. From 1965 to 1969, Volcker returned to work for Chase Manhattan as vice president of the bank. In 1969 he went back to the Treasury, appointed to the position of under secretary of monetary affairs for the Treasury, where he remained until 1974. During this time Mr. Volcker was the principal United States negotiator in the development and installation of a new international monetary system departing from the fixed-exchange-rate system installed after World War II. He returned to the New York Fed in 1975, this time as president of the New York district bank, where he remained until his appointment to the board of governors in 1979.

Volcker spent a total of 14 years working at the Treasury and 13 years working for David Rockefeller at the Chase Manhattan Bank. Referred to as an "eastern money man, one of the New York banking crowd," and a high interest rate enthusiast, he established himself as a leading spokesman for the Fed and became the Establishment's logical choice to succeed Chairman G. William Miller upon the termination of Miller's tenure in 1979.

Preston Martin. Born December 5, 1923. Martin is the vice chairman of the board. He received his B.S. in finance from the University of Southern California in 1947 and an M.B.A. in 1948. He received a doctorate in monetary economics from Indiana University in 1952. He has served on the boards of a number of major corporations, including Sears, Roebuck and Co., and has been a professor at the University of Southern California. He amassed most of his work experience in the savings and loan industry, including a 10-year stint from 1956 to 1966 as director of Lincoln Savings & Loan of Los Angeles. He served three years, from 1969 to 1972, as chairman of the Federal Home Loan Bank Board (the savings and loan equivalent of the Federal Reserve Board) before coming to the Fed board of governors as vice chairman in 1982. His vice chairmanship will end on March 31, 1986, and his board membership ends on January 31, 1996.

Henry C. Wallich. Born June 10, 1914. Wallich was educated in Germany; at Oxford University in England, 1933–35; and at Harvard University, where he received his Ph.D. in economics in 1944. He worked at the Chemical Bank & Trust Co., 1935–36; at Hackney, Hopkinson & Sutphen (Securities), 1936–40; and on to the New York Fed for 10 years, 1941–51, as chief of the bank's foreign research division. He taught economics at Yale off and on from 1951 to 1974, was assistant Secretary of the Treasury, 1958–59, and was a member of the President's Council of Economic Advisors, 1959–61. He has also served on the research advisory board of the private Committee for Economic Development, an institution that has openly supported corporate agribusiness in favor of the American family farm system. Wallich was sworn in March 8, 1974, and his term will end on January 31, 1988.

Emmett J. Rice. Rice hails from South Carolina and earned his B.A. and M.B.A. at the City College of New York and a Ph.D. in economics from the University of California at Berkeley. Prior to his appointment to the board, he was senior vice president of the National Bank of Washington, DC, the city's second largest bank. Like most of his colleagues, he got his start at the New York Fed as an economist. He also worked in the Treasury Department as a deputy director and later as acting director of the Treasury's Office of Developing Nations. He was also the U.S. alternative executive director of the International Bank for Reconstruction and Development at the World Bank (a multinational lending institution that channels billions of American tax dollars into Third World regimes that use the money to repay debts to the international bankers). In addition, he has been a director in different big corporations such as Trans World Corporation and Trans World Airlines. He was appointed to the board in 1979 to fill an unexpired term and will be up for reappointment on January 31, 1990.

Martha Romayne Seger. Born February 17, 1932. Seger replaced Nancy Hayes Teeters in 1984 when she was appointed by Ronald Reagan, and her term ends on January 31, 1998. She was educated at the University of Michigan, where she received an undergraduate degree, an M.B.A. in finance, and a Ph.D. in finance and business economics. In 1981–82, she was the commissioner of financial institutions for the state of Michigan. She has been a professor of finance at different universities, including the University of Michigan, as well as the director of many banks and life insurance companies. Between 1964 and 1967, she was an economist for the board of governors, after which she joined a banking firm. She then worked for 10 years as chief economist for the Detroit Bank and Trust Company, following which she became vice president of the Bank of the Commonwealth in Detroit.

Wayne D. Angell. Resides in Ottawa, Kansas. He received his B.A. at Ottawa University in 1952 and his M.A. and Ph.D. at the University of Kansas, in 1953 and 1957 respectively. He has been a professor of economics at Ottawa University from 1956 to the present and dean of the college, 1969–72. He has been director of the Federal Reserve Bank of Kansas City from 1979 to the present. He was a state representative, Kansas House of Representatives, from 1961 to 1967; chairman, Kansas Third District Republic Convention, 1964; and Republican primary election candidate for the U.S. Senate in 1978.

Manuel H. Johnson, Jr. Born February 10, 1949. Johnson attended the University of Alabama, Tuscaloosa, 1967–68; got his B.S. in economics at Troy State University, 1973; received his M.S. in economics (1974) and Ph.D. in economics (1977) at Florida State University, Tallahassee. He was assistant professor of economics, 1977–80, and associate professor of economics, 1980–81, at George Mason University. He then went to the U.S. Treasury as a deputy assistant secretary for economic policy, 1981–82, and since 1982 has been an assistant secretary for economic policy there.

These board members have several things in common: (1) most went to major Establishment universities and have worked as economists for the Federal Reserve System; (2) they all have been affiliated with big banking; (3) they have all worked in different government bureaucracies. In short, they are that breed of professional bureaucrat proficient in playing the political games necessary to reach the top positions of influence. They get there by not making waves and by kissing the hands of those who put them there.

The position of Chairman Volcker is most interesting. Most of his career outside of the Fed was spent working for David Rockefeller's Chase Manhattan Bank and the Treasury Department. He switched back and forth, working for a few years at Chase, then for a few years at the Treasury Department, then back at the Chase, and then again at the Treasury. It has been said that this was part of his grooming for the position he now holds.

When the FOMC makes its decision to buy or sell government securities, it gives its orders directly to the manager of the New York Fed, which has the exclusive responsibility for the purchase and sale of these securities. Of the 5 voting members picked from the 12 district presidents to be on the FOMC, the president of the New York Fed is a permanent member. The other 11 members rotate as voting members.

Volcker was a key figure in the FOMC when he was president of the New York Fed. While he was president there, the chairman of the board of directors and most important member of that district was none other than Volcker's old boss at Chase Manhattan, David Rockefeller. It is not hard to deduce from the observation of this cozy arrangement the enormous amount of power David Rockefeller wields in this country (and the world).

Federal Reserve District Directors

There are 12 districts in the Federal Reserve System. There are 12 presidents, one for each district. There is also a board of 9 directors for each district, who choose the president for their district, subject to the approval of the board of governors. These presidents are the most influential members of their district but are of the same mold as all the rest of the career bureaucrats; that is, they don't buck the system, and they bow to the requests of their masters who have appointed them.

The nine directors from each district are broken down into three categories. There are three Class A, three Class B, and three Class C directors. Class A directors are bankers who are elected by the banks of that district. Class B are also banker-elected but must come from the industrial community. Class C directors are appointed by the board of governors and cannot be bankers or hold stock in banks. They must come from the public. This is intended to provide representation from banking, industry, and the public, thus serving the interests of the entire community. This is a joke. Class A and B directors are chosen by the bankers, and Class C are chosen by the board of governors, who will always choose ex-bankers, university presidents, or other individuals who know what will be expected from them.

These district directors do not set policy but are only advisors to the officers in their district bank. The bank president makes the decisions in the course of day-to-day business, with the board of governors having the last say-so. The directors are able to exert much pressure in the direction of policy, though. For example, if the industrial community is

being burdened with high rates of interest, the Class B directors will push for lower rates.

These directors represent the biggest and most powerful
bankers and corporations in the country. The following is a
list of the directors of each district and their positions.

New York District

Name	Primary Affiliation
Louis T. Preston	CEO, Morgan Guaranty Trust Co.
T. Joseph Semrod	Chairman, United Jersey Bank
Robert W. Moyer	President, Wilber National Bank
Richard L. Gelb	Chairman and CEO, Bristol-Meyers Co.
John R. Opel	Chairman and CEO, IBM Corp.
John F. Welch, Jr.	Chairman, General Electric Co.
John Brademas	President, New York University
Virginia A. Dwyer	Senior Vice President, AT & T
Clifton R. Wharton, Jr.	Chancellor, State University of New York

Boston District

Name	Primary Affiliation
Joseph A. Baute	Chairman and CEO, Markem Corp.
George N. Hatsopoulos	Chairman, Thermo Electron Corp.

William S. Edgerly	President and CEO, State Street Bank and Trust Co.
Harry R. Mitiguy	President, The Howard Bank, N.A.
Homer B. Ellis, Jr.	President, Factory Point National Bank
Richard M. Oster	President, Cookson America, Inc.
Matina Horner	President, Radcliffe College
Michael J. Harrington	CEO, Harrington Company
Ralph Z. Sorenson	Chairman and CEO, Barry Wright Corp.

Philadelphia District

Name	Primary Affiliation
John H. Walther	Chairman and CEO, New Jersey National Bank
Ronald H. Smith	President and CEO, CCNB Bank
Clarence D. McCormick	President, Farmers and Merchants National Bank
Carl A. Singley	Dean and Professor of Law, Temple University School of Law
Charles S. Seymour	Chairman and CEO, Jackson Cross Co.
Nicholas Riso	President and CEO, Giant Food Stores, Inc.
Nevius M. Curtis	Chairman and CEO, Delmarva Power & Light Co.

Robert M. Landis	Partner, Dechert, Price, & Rhoads
George E. Bartol III	Chairman, Hunt Manufacturing Co.

Richmond District

Name	Primary Affiliation
K. Donald Menefee	Chairman and CEO, Madison National Bank; Chairman and President, James Madison, Limited
Robert S. Chiles, Sr.	President and CEO, Greensboro National Bank
Robert F. Baronner	Chairman and CEO, One Valley Bancorp of W. Virginia, Inc. and Kanawha Valley Bank, N.A.
Edward H. Covell	President, The Covell Co.
Thomas B. Cookerly	President, Broadcast Division, Albritton Communications
Floyd D. Gottwald, Jr.	Chairman and CEO, Ethyl Corp.
Robert A. Georgine	President, Building and Construction Trades Dept. AFL-CIO
Leroy T. Canoles, Jr.	President, Kaufman and Canoles
Hanne Merriman	President, Garfinckel's

Atlanta District

Name	*Primary Affiliation*
E. B. Robinson, Jr.	Chairman and CEO, Deposit Guaranty National Bank
Virgil H. Moore, Jr.	Chairman and CEO, First Farmers and Merchants National Bank
Mary W. Walker	President, The National Bank of Walton
Bernard F. Sliger	President, Florida State University
Harold B. Blach, Jr.	President, Blach's Inc.
Horatio C. Thompson	President, Horatio Thompson Investments, Inc.
John H. Weitnauer, Jr.	Chairman and CEO, Richway
Bradley Currey, Jr.	President, Rock-Tenn Co.
Jane C. Cousins	President and CEO, Merrill Lynch Realty/ Cousins

Chicago District

Name	*Primary Affiliation*
John W. Gabbert	President, First National Bank and Trust Co.
O. J. Thomson	President, Citizen's National Bank of Charles City
Barry F. Sullivan	Chairman and CEO, First National Bank of Chicago

Max J. Naylor	Owner and Operator of a Grain and Livestock Farm
Leon T. Kendall	Chairman and CEO, Mortgage Guaranty Insurance Corp.
Edward D. Powers	President and CEO, Mueller Co.
Marcus Alexis	Dean of the College of Business Administration at the University of Illinois at Chicago
Robert J.Day	President and Chief Operating Officer, United States Gypsum Co.
Charles S. McNeer	Chairman and CEO, Wisconsin Electric Power Company

Cleveland District

Name	Primary Affiliation
William A. Stroud	Chairman and President, First-Knox National Bank
J. David Barnes	Chairman and CEO, Mellon Bank, N.A.
Raymond D. Campbell	Chairman, President, and CEO, Independent State Bank of Ohio
Daniel M. Galbreath	President, John W. Galbreath Co.
John R. Hall	Chairman and CEO, Ashland Oil, Inc.

Richard D. Hannan

Chairman and
President, Mercury
Instruments, Inc.

E. Mandell de Windt

Chairman, Eaton Corp.

John R. Miller

Former President and
Chief Operating Officer,
Standard Oil of Ohio

William H. Knoell

President and CEO,
Cyclops Corp.

St. Louis District

Name	Primary Affiliation
Paul K. Reynolds	President and CEO, First National Bank of Pittsfield
Clarence C. Barksdale	Chairman and President, Centerre Bank, N.A.
H.L. Hembree, III	Chairman and CEO, Arkansas Best Corp.
Robert J. Sweeney	President and CEO, Murphy Oil Corp.
Frank A. Jones, Jr.	President, Dietz Forge Co.
Jesse M. Shaver	Consultant, Allis-Chalmers Corp.
Robert Virgil, Jr.	Dean, School of Business, Washington University
W. L. Hadley Griffin	Chairman, Brown Group, Inc.
Mary P. Holt	President, Clothes Horse

Minneapolis District

Name	Primary Affiliation
Curtis W. Kuehn	President, The First National Bank in Sioux Falls
Burton P. Allen, Jr.	President, First National Bank
Duane Ring	Chairman and CEO, Norwest Bank
Richard Falconer	District Manager, Northwestern Bell
Harold F. Zigmund	Chairman, Blandin Paper Co.
William L. Mathers	President, Mathers Land Co., Inc.
Michael Wright	SuperValu Stores
John Rollwagen	Cray Research
John B. Davis, Jr.	Interim Executive Director, Children's Theater Company and School

Kansas City District

Name	Primary Affiliation
Robert L. Hollis	Chairman and CEO, First National Bank and Trust Co. of Okmulgee
Donald B. Hoffman	Chairman, Central Bank of Denver
Jerry D. Geist	Chairman and President, Public Service Co. of New Mexico

Richard D. Harrison	Chairman and CEO, Fleming Companies, Inc.
Duane Acker	President, Kansas State University
Irvine O. Hockaday, Jr.	President and CEO, Hallmark Cards, Inc.
Frederick W. Lyons, Jr.	President and CEO, Marion Laboratories, Inc.
Robert G. Lueder	Chairman, Lueder Construction Co.

Dallas District

Name	Primary Affiliation
Gene Edwards	Chairman, First Amarillo Bank Corp.
Miles D. Wilson	Chairman and CEO, The First National Bank of Bellville
Charles T. Doyle	Chairman and CEO, Gulf National Bank
Robert T. Enloe III	President, Lomas & Nettleton Financial Corp.
Kent Gilbreath	Associate Dean, Hankamer School of Business, Baylor University
Robert L. Pfluger	Rancher
Bobby Inman	President and CEO, MCC
Robert D. Rogers	President and CEO, Texas Industries, Inc.

| Hugh G. Robinson | President, Cityplace Development Corp. |

San Francisco District

Name	*Primary Affiliation*
Spencer Eccles	Chairman, President, and CEO, First Security Corp.
Rayburn S. Dezember	Chairman, Central Pacific Corp. and American National Bank
Donald J. Gehb	President and CEO, Alameda Bancorp and Alameda First National Bank
Togo W. Tanaka	Chairman, Gramercy Enterprises, Inc.
John C. Hampton	Chairman and President, Willamina Lumber Co.
George W. Weyerhaeuser	President and CEO, Weyerhaeuser Co.
Caroline S. Chambers	President and CEO, Chambers Cable Com., Inc.
Alan C. Furth	Vice Chairman, Santa Fe Southern Pacific Corp. and President, Southern Pacific Co.
Fred W. Andrew	Chairman, President, and CEO, Superior Farming Co.

A summary description of the board members, district directors, and district presidents follows:

They are individuals who are team players, accepting appointive jobs that they hold at the whim of others. They reach their positions by knowing how to play the political game and satisfy the needs of the people who put them in their jobs. They may have demonstrated efficiency at tasks given them, and may be excellent at delegating authority and managing people, but they lack the willingness to take the risks that accompany the free market. It is in this sense that their actions might be predicted. *They will follow the rules.* And the rules are clearly set down by seventy years of precedent. The job of the Federal Reserve is to preserve the status quo in the banking system and the economy, to prevent any disruptions that might come from deflation, and to do so in a way that forestalls any disruption from too much inflation.*

The Fed was created to facilitate the expansion of credit. It has encouraged reckless government spending and encouraged weak lending practices by diluting reserve requirements, removing the benign restrictions of gold currency, and acting as a "lender of last resort" to those that engage in irresponsible profligate lending. This has been done at the expense of the public, which has lost stable prices, purchasing power, and the ability to store wealth. With the final barriers removed, there are now no restrictions to bar the way to hyperinflation. The Fed will continue to monetize whatever amount of debt is necessary to keep the system solvent. The federal government will deficit-spend more in the next five years than it has in the entire history of the country. In our present economic system, with such massive budget deficits on the horizon, the worst inflation we have ever known is inevitable.

Thomas Jefferson prophesied: "If the American people ever allow the banks to control the issuance of their currency, first by inflation and then by deflation, the banks and corporations that will grow up around them will deprive the people of all property until their children will wake up homeless in the continent their fathers occupied."

Now is the time to reject this so-called Federal Reserve

---

*John Pugsley, *Common Sense Viewpoint*, vol. IX, no. 11, Nov. 1983.

System. There is nothing radical or kooky about this idea. There was no need in the past for a federal reserve system. Until 1913, our country had no trouble growing in power or might without a federal reserve system. Mighty empires arose in the past without need of any kind of federal reserve system. The mighty bezant, the primary source of power and influence for the Byzantine Empire, endured for 800 solid years without the aid of a federal reserve system. All those who ballyhoo the Fed should study history and realize that the Fed was created solely to protect and advance avaricious bankers and politicians at the expense of the public and that this Federal Reserve tradition has evolved into a vehicle to be used by those who wish to subjugate us to a system in which they are the controllers of our destinies rather than we ourselves.

The Fed is totally committed to preventing banking failures, even if caused by irresponsible, unprincipled lending practices, loss of the profit-making apparatus, and maintenance of the shadow government power base. In short, the Federal Reserve is not only a system by which to guarantee profits and credit but also one of the means by which to control the people. A free money is a free people. A tightly controlled money is an enslaved people. It's as simple as that.

As a footnote, we should understand that these descriptions apply mainly to the big, powerful, international bankers. Before we go out and lynch a few neighborhood bankers, remember that many of these folk are generally hardworking businesspeople who labor within the community to promote its economic well-being. They are probably subjected to the same amount of inequities from the elite higher-ups as are the nonbankers. It is actually the banking system itself and its controllers that are at the root of the problem.

Now that we have examined the nature and workings of the Federal Reserve System, it should be apparent why its abolishment is crucial to renewed economic health and freedom. We have discussed a return to the gold standard as another component of the solution to our economic problems, which leaves us with the third element of the solution: the repeal of the 16th Amendment, along with a reduction in both size and expenditures of government.

5
IRS, BOONDOGGLES, AND A CASE AGAINST GOVERNMENT CHARITY

As stated earlier, this book calls for the repeal of the 16th Amendment as part of the solution for our economic problems. We all feel the income tax squeeze once a year, so it's hardly necessary to convince American taxpayers of the undesirability of income tax. However, many Americans are unaware of the unconstitutionality of a federal income tax. We have become so inured to the annual tax bite that we tend to forget that it didn't always exist and, indeed, that the Founding Fathers intended that it never be used to oppress the people.

Perhaps one reason we so complacently submit to income taxation is that we are enveloped by government bureaucracy of so many types. Our government doles out funds to so many different individuals and groups that we have come to believe that an income tax truly is necessary to keep the coffers full. Who will pay for all of these government projects and charities if the flow of income tax revenues is cut off?

The answer is simple. To accompany a repeal of the 16th Amendment, we must reduce government budget deficits and spending, reduce size of government, and reduce governmental control of industry and individuals. The jungle of bureaucratic regulations is driving businesspeople crazy. The IRS has stepped up its attacks against the people, and now the Treasury Department, in conjunction with the Fed, is planning a currency exchange. President Reagan ran on the platform of getting government off the people's back and turning them loose to get America back on its feet again. You can judge by the quality of your life and by current events whether this campaign promise has been kept.

In this chapter, we will review the background of the income tax and the concomitant unchecked growth of government bureaucracy.

The power to tax includes the power to destroy. As the repository of this power, and considering its increasing abilities to attack whomever it pleases with relative impunity, the IRS must be dismantled. The Constitution has provided the means by which government can easily obtain ample funds to operate legitimate programs. No IRS would exist if the income tax did not exist.

The IRS, as well as the currency recall, will be viewed by future historians as instrumental in having brought about the degeneration of our government into a tyrannical, internationalistic, totalitarian entity. The most venomous serpent can be rendered harmless if its fangs are broken. In the metaphoric head of our government, many such fangs exist, the IRS being a major one. And if the people break these fangs, government will be returned to its proper position of limited power.

The IRS is not an independent agency as much as it is an all-reaching arm of the government. The government and international bankers continue to collaborate as power brokers. Bureaus like the IRS and maneuvers such as a currency call-in are related in the sense that they are designed to achieve the same goals: to augment and centralize the power coveted by the power mongers.

The IRS works on the principle of fear. If fear of the IRS did not exist, those citizens who presently offer (in)voluntary compliance would rebel. IRS horror stories abound, and gestapo-tactics must continue if the IRS is to maintain control. This is no way to run a government, especially when so many claim the freedoms that are enjoyed in our country cannot be found elsewhere. The IRS reflects the deterioration of our government into a power-stricken entity.

The IRS is also involved in the trend toward centralized world government. Examine the alleged ideological enemy of the United States, the totalitarian Soviet Union. Marxism, which the Soviets cite as their basic political philosophy, is based on 10 major platforms:

1. Abolition of property in land and applications of all rents to public purposes.
2. *A heavy progressive or graduated income tax.*
3. *Abolition of all right of inheritance.*
4. *Confiscation of the properties of all emigrants and rebels.*
5. Centralization of credit in the hands of the state by means of a national bank with state capital and an exclusive monopoly.
6. Centralization of the means of communication and transport.
7. Extension of factories and instruments of production owned by the State. . . .
8. Equal liability of all to labor. Establishment of industrial armies, especially for agriculture.
9. Combination of agriculture with manufacturing industries; gradual abolition of the distinction between town and country. . . .
10. Free education for all children in public schools. Abolition of child factory labor in its present form. . . .

These platforms are presented not to launch into a diatribe on Marxist politics, but to point out that certain philosophies, supposedly anathema to our system, are being incorporated into the American political system by the IRS. Although loudly speaking contrary goals, both the U.S. and the Soviet Union are moving toward the same totalitarian philosophies.

The IRS is especially effective on platform points 2, 3, and 4. An aberration of point 5 gives us the Fed. Agribusiness is found in point 9. Internationalism that abolishes distinctions among countries, let alone between town and country, fulfills the goal of the other half of point 9. Increased government intrusion into operations of factories and other industries, whether perceived to be good or bad, brings us closer to fulfillment of point 7. The only noble platform is point 10, which only proves that no system is 100 percent wrong.

The currency recall is not an isolated event. There would be no need for a recall if it were not for the existence of the underground and a desire to further government goals. The underground would not exist (at its present size) if it were not for the IRS. The IRS would not be here if it were not for the 16th Amendment. And the 16th Amendment never would have come into being if not for government's desire to increase its power and function. The more it taxes, the greater its ability to destroy those who oppose it. The more the government spends, the more it expands in power.

The federal government will spend three-fifths of this year's budget on socialistic, militaristic, and foreign aid giveaways. The American people have to get it into their thick collective head that the government has neither the right nor the justification to force tax money from hardworking people so that the government can give it away to its selected favorites. And Americans should not forget the state and city governments, which have joined the federal government in what they believe is their divine right to tax a certain portion of the population to death. The increasingly vast sums required to carry on inspired the 16th Amendment, which in turn spawned the IRS. The IRS has caused the underground to mushroom. The resultant need to tax and control, which the underground circumvents, has created the necessity for a currency recall.

It is important, therefore, to understand the IRS and its history. The currency call-in may not be an ongoing event, but the IRS is. And both ultimately serve the same goals and the same masters. Both are different steps in the evolution and emergence of a new type of international big brother.

THE IRS EMERGES

The 16th Amendment, creating the income tax, was ratified on February 3, 1913. Previous to that, the government had tried to tax income, but it had been overturned in the courts as unconstitutional. In order to get this amendment passed, its proponents swore that no taxes would ever be imposed on any portion of income that would be necessary to maintain a decent standard of living. In fact, it was emphatically declared that only large, unearned income would ever be subjected to this tax, except in the case of a national emergency such as war.

In 1916 the rates were as follows: 1 percent tax on the first $20,000 of taxable income and 2 percent at the $50,000 level. Exemptions were set at $3,000 for a single person and $4,000 for a family, which would be equivalent to $30,000 for a single person and $40,000 for a family today. The highest rate that was set was 6 percent at $500,000 ($5 million by today's standard). Even though the income tax is unconstitutional and required an amendment for its enforcement, not many people would care so much if its rates had remained at their 1916 equivalents.

After FDR took office, he imposed extremely burdensome rates on the people (90 percent during World War II). The tax also became enmeshed in the cost and price of goods. For example, when manufacturers are taxed, they must mark up their products in order to cover the tax and maintain the same profits. The wholesalers and retailers must do likewise. The tax actually becomes treated as a part of the cost of material and labor. The consumers who buy the product ultimately pay everybody else's taxes and must still pay their own "income tax."

On top of this income tax are levied city taxes, state taxes, and social security taxes. Then there is sales tax and other "minor" taxes. Beyond that, a large chunk of the tax dollar goes toward salaries and wages of the tax collector. We have additional taxes to pay to have our taxes collected from us. In other words, the cost of government goes up because it must create huge bureaucracies to collect taxes.

These bureaucratic workers perform no productive work whatsoever for society. We saw, in the example of the American Revolutionary War, how increased use of goods and services by the government is extremely inflationary. Hundreds of billions of dollars could be saved by the government each year if it did not spend this money simply to maintain itself through services that are absolutely unproductive and serve no useful function for society. To get the full impact of this, visit any government tax office and observe the rows of desks and workers busily depriving the private sector of goods and services through their work, without one whit of productivity. By reducing taxes, the government could reduce its own budget immensely.

The IRS is the principal bureaucracy formed to handle the tax matter. As with the Fed, the IRS extends its power beyond its designated area of responsibility and has also become a very powerful tool that is utilized to control the masses. Control of the poor is no problem since they are so dependent on the government and kept so ignorant that they pose no threat. Then there are thousands of tax-exempt and tax-subsidized organizations that, upon request, often bend or acquiesce to government demands out of fear of losing tax-exempt status. Most of these institutions would cease to exist if they lost their government largesse. Once they are on the dole, the government threatens them with loss of tax-exempt status if any dissidence occurs within their ranks. The super-rich (most of whom are part of the secret ruling elite in lesser or greater roles) keep a bevy of lawyers employed full-time to take advantage of all the loopholes in the Internal Revenue Code placed there for their benefit. For example, Paul Getty had a personal income of $70 million and paid an income tax of $.90 per $1,000 dollars. (This amounts to $63,000, .09 percent, or less than $\frac{1}{10}$ of 1 percent tax). Compare this to the hardworking middle-class person, who may pay up to 50 percent of what he or she earns.

The remaining middle-class producers must foot the bill for everyone else and pay a much greater proportion of taxes than their numbers in the population. This segment of the society cannot be bribed or bought off. Consequently, the IRS uses the threat of an audit to instill fear into their minds to keep them in line.

The print and audiovisual media, which are heavily influenced by official government statements, repeatedly drive home this point with scare-tactic headlines and full descriptions of the punishments meted out to noncompliers. This free-spirited middle class will be forced to waddle through 10,000-plus pages of IRS codes, spend billions to fund the IRS, spend tens of billions to have their returns prepared, and waste hundreds upon hundreds of millions of man-hours to perform the task of filing tax returns.

The IRS bureaucrats are no different from their brother bureaucrats at the Fed or any other bureau. They are not elected, and their identities are unknown to the electorate. They answer not to voters but to nebulous financial powers that have effectively created a shadow government in this country.

BOONDOGGLES AND OVERRUNS

And what is done with the billions collected by this IRS? It is spent on stupid government boondoggles like these:

- $21,000 to study the mating calls of toads
- $154,000 to teach mothers how to play with their babies
- $300,000 to build a good surfing beach in Hawaii

These are vastly dwarfed by idiotic expenditures exemplified by $1,000,000 extra per day for three years caused by a three-year delay in NASA's launch of the space shuttle (plus $689 million in interest payments), resulting in a total $1.2 billion cost overrun. It is given to fat cat politicians and bureaucrats who, for example, recently spent $4.8 million for chauffered limousines. Ronald Reagan's first inaugural ceremony was the most expensive in U.S. history and cost the taxpayers $12.5 million.

It is given away to foreign countries whose leaders use it to line their pockets and to wage oppressive wars of aggression. It is given to international organizations, many of which work behind the scenes to bring down American society and its way of life (we are all familiar with the recent stink over UNESCO). It is given to Third World debtor countries to pay off loans to greedy bankers who made them knowing full well that these loans are underwritten by the American taxpayers. This is accomplished through such agencies as the International Monetary Fund (IMF), which was recently handed an $8.4 billion gift from the American taxpayers by Reagan and the Congress. The IMF is demanding another $20 billion, and in all likelihood the U.S. Congress will capitulate because we are "obligated" to help the Third World.

Through taxes and inflation, the powercrats wish to break the backs of the independent-minded middle class, who are the last holdouts against a controlled socialistic society. Once this is done, everyone can look to "big brother" for peace and security.

The atrocities inherent in this system seem obvious, but you may ask, "If income tax were abolished, how would the government operate?" Well, you should understand that the income tax is a somewhat modern political creation and that there are many people who were alive when there was no income tax at all. That such a question arises so naturally actually demonstrates the inroads into our way of thinking that have been made by the socialistic power mongers in this country. What obligation does the taxpayer really have to support this self-serving, self-aggrandizing power? It has been said that government that governs least governs best. Is the ever-increasing size of government that we must pay for necessary or desirable?

We fought and won in two world wars without the existence of a department of defense. What is our military track record since the Department of Defense (DOD) was formed? We got nowhere in Korea, we lost in Vietnam, we were humiliated out of Lebanon, and it took weeks to capture the tiny island of Grenada from a handful of rebel resisters. And how does the

DOD spend its allotted tax dollars? The following are a few items of "minor" importance from a DOD spare-parts shopping list:

	Manufacturer Cost	DOD Cost	Markup
One Light Bulb	$0.17	$44.00	25,782%
One Machine Screw	$0.01	$37.00	369,900%
One Electric Plug	$7.99	$726.86	8,997%
One Hammer	$5.00	$435.00	8,600%

Has a bigger government made a positive difference? Or is it that we have been conditioned for so long to look toward the government for all our wants and needs that we subconsciously want a "big brother"? Are we willing to give up our freedom and independence for a false feeling of security from the government? As far as all this taxation goes, it is really unnecessary, because most of the government agencies are unnecessary, most of the government personnel are unnecessary, and most of the giveaways are unnecessary (and not only unnecessary, but in many cases unconstitutional). If you feel we must have big taxes to pay for government, there are still other alternatives.

A TAX ALTERNATIVE

One alternative to income tax, as proposed by Martin Larson, Ph.D., is a national transaction tax. Called the nation's foremost authority on tax avoidance, Larson has written over 25 books and innumerable articles on that and related topics. One of his books, *The Great Tax Fraud* (Greenwich: Devin-Adair, 1968), was a decisive factor in forcing through Congress the Tax Reform Act of 1969, which lifted a great deal of the tax burden from the shoulders of the middle class. In 1981, Larson outlined to Congress his universal trust plan as an alternative to the present system of Social Security and federal income taxation.

One of the frequent questions asked when we appear on radio or T.V. programs is what means of financing would be available to the federal government should the income tax be abolished. We have no hesitation in replying that other sources of revenue are available to meet any exigency, even if were were to concede—which we do not—that the federal government must continue to operate with a budget comparable to that of 1981–82 or even larger. We can easily point to an obvious alternative: much as we would dislike it and certain as we are that it would not be necessary, we say that a general transactions tax of 5 percent to be levied on personal services, the sale of consumer goods, and the exchange of all capital assets, including securities, would be infinitely more fair, economical, nondiscriminatory, productive, and far less onerous than the existing federal system of taxation.

In 1977, state sales taxes, which averaged 4 percent and were levied in 44 states, produced $83.8 billion. A nationwide 5 percent tax would therefore have produced about $125 billion; and had this been extended to the sales of real property, securities, and professional services, this sum would have been increased to at least $175 billion. By 1981–82, this would probably exceed $250 billion. It is therefore obvious that with the termination of certain unconstitutional federal programs, a general transaction tax of 5 percent would be ample for all legitimate activities carried on by the Washington government.

If a general transaction tax were to replace the present federal income tax, every person would pay his fair share and the Treasury would obtain the same income at perhaps one-third of the present cost to the people. However, great as the resulting economic benefits would be, these would be overshadowed by other advantages. At a single stroke, the uncertainty, the terror, the discrimination, the invasion of privacy, the universal imperative to cheat and lie, would be terminated.

The proponents of federal taxation declare that sales taxes fall most heavily on the poor and that only levies on large incomes can force the rich to pay their fair share. No greater lie, however, was ever concocted; the fact is that the rich become the super-rich because of the loopholes planted in the code for this very purpose and that they and a multitude of other favorites avoid at least $100 billion in federal taxation. Since taxes on production are paid by consumers in the form of increased costs and prices, they fall most heavily on those whose incomes must be expended largely for food, clothing, housing, and other basic necessities. It falls very lightly on those who have large unearned incomes or vast accumulations of wealth.*

THE UNCONSTITUTIONALITY OF AID

Dr. Larson also advocates elimination of certain unconstitutional programs to reduce government expenditures. What kind of programs could be eliminated? Perhaps the biggest and most obvious area deals with government handouts called "charity," "welfare," and "foreign aid." Nowhere does the U.S. Constitution authorize the government to levy taxes for the purpose of giving charity to other persons or other nations.

The following story, excerpted from *The Life of Colonel David Crockett* by Edward S. Ellis (1884), will provide a clear insight into the bane of governmental confiscation of wealth for the purpose of "charity."

One day in the United States House of Representatives, a bill was taken up appropriating money for the benefit of a widow of a distinguished naval officer. Several beautiful speeches had been made in its support. The Speaker was just about to put the question when David Crockett arose:

" 'Mr. Speaker—I have as much respect for the memory of the deceased, and as much sympathy for the sufferings of the living, if suffering there be, as any man in this House, but we must not permit our respect for the dead or our sympathy for a part of the living to lead us into an act of injustice to the balance of the living. I will not go into an argument to prove that *Congress has no power to appropriate this money as an act of charity* [italics mine]. Every member upon this floor knows it. We have the right, as individuals, to give away as

---

*Dr. Martin Larson, *How to Defend Against the IRS*, (Government Educational Foundation: Washington, DC, 1977) p. 206.

much of our own money as we please in charity; but as members of Congress we have no right so to appropriate a dollar of the public money. Some eloquent appeals have been made to us upon the ground that it is a debt due the deceased. Mr. Speaker, the deceased lived long after the close of the war; he was in office to the day of his death, and I have never heard that the government was in arrears to him.

" 'Every man in this House knows it is not a debt. We cannot, without the grossest corruption, appropriate this money as the payment of a debt. We have not the semblance of authority to appropriate it as a charity. Mr. Speaker, I have said we have the right to give as much money of our own as we please. I am the poorest man on this floor. I cannot vote for this bill, but I will give one week's pay to the object, and if every member of Congress will do the same, it will amount to more than the bill asks.' "

He took his seat. Nobody replied. Instead of passing unanimously, as was expected and as it no doubt would have but for that speech, it received few votes.

Later, when asked by a friend why he opposed the appropriation, Crockett gave this explanation:

" 'Several years ago I was one evening standing on the steps of the Capitol with some other members of Congress, when our attention was attracted by a great light over in Georgetown. It was evidently a large fire. We jumped into a hack and drove over as fast as we could. In spite of all that could be done, many houses were burned and many families made houseless, and besides, some of them had lost all but the clothes they had on. The weather was very cold, and when I saw so many women and children suffering, I felt that something ought to be done for them. The next morning a bill was introduced appropriating $20,000 for their relief. We put aside all other business and rushed it through as soon as it could be done.' "

Crockett went on to describe how, the following summer, in the course of campaigning, he encountered a man plowing a field and approached him for support. The farmer admitted he recognized Colonel Crockett but bluntly told him that he would not vote for him again, explaining, " '. . . you gave a vote last winter which shows that either you have not the capacity to understand the Constitution, or that you are wanting the honesty and firmness to be guided by it. . . . an understanding of the Constitution different from mine I cannot overlook, because the Constitution, to be worth anything, must be held sacred, and rigidly observed in all its provisions. The man who wields power and misinterprets it is the more dangerous the more honest he is.' "

When Crockett asked what his critic was referring to, the man replied that he was familiar with the bill that appropriated $20,000 to Georgetown fire victims. Crockett's protest that $20,000 was certainly an insignificant sum and that surely the farmer would have done the same thing in his place was met with this reply:

" 'It is not the amount, Colonel, that I complain of; it is the principle. *In the first place, the government ought to have in the Treasury no more than enough for its legitimate purposes* [italics mine]. But that has nothing to do with the question. *The power of collecting and disbursing money at pleasure is the most dangerous power that can be entrusted to man, particularly under our system of collecting revenue by a tariff, which reaches every man in the country, no matter how poor he may be, and the poorer he is, the more he pays in proportion to his means* [italics mine]. What is worse, it presses upon him without his knowledge where the weight centers, *for there is not a man in the United States who can ever guess how much he pays to the government* [italics mine]. So you see, that while you are contributing to relieve one, you are drawing from thousands who are even worse off than he. If you had the right to give anything, the amount was simply a matter of discretion with you, and you had as much right to give $2,000,000 as $20,000. If you have the right to give to one, you have the right to give to all; and, as the Constitution neither defines charity nor stipulates the amount, you are at liberty to give to any and everything which you may believe, or profess to believe, is a charity, and to any amount you may think proper. You will very easily perceive what a wide door this would open for fraud and corruption and favoritism, on the one hand, and for robbing the people on the other. No, Colonel, Congress has no right to give charity. Individual members may give as much of their own money as they please, but they have no right to touch a dollar of the public money for that purpose. If twice as many houses had been burned in this county as in Georgetown, neither you nor any other member of Congress would have thought of appropriating a dollar for our relief. There are about two hundred and forty members of Congress. If they had shown their sympathy for the sufferers by contributing each one week's pay, it would have made over $13,000. There are plenty of wealthy men in and around Washington who could have given $20,000 without depriving themselves of even a luxury of life. The congressmen chose to keep their own money, which, if reports be true, some of them spend not very creditably; and the people about Washington, no doubt, applauded you for relieving them from the necessity of giving by giving what was not yours to give. The people have delegated to Congress, by the Constitution, the power to do certain things. To do these, it is authorized to collect and pay moneys, and for nothing else. *Everything beyond this is usurpation, and a violation of the Constitution* [italics mine].

" 'So you see, Colonel, you have violated the Constitution in what I consider a vital point. It is a precedent fraught with danger to the country, for when Congress once begins to stretch its power beyond the limits of the Constitution, there is no limit to it, and no security for the people. I have no doubt you acted honestly, but that does not make it any better, except as far as you are personally concerned, and you see that I cannot vote for you.' "

Crockett realized that he had been wrong and discovered that he had been talking to Horatio Bunce, who, he said, " '. . . mingled but little with the public, but was widely known for his remarkable intelligence and incorruptible integrity, and for a heart brimful and running over with kindness and benevolence, which showed themselves not only in words but acts. He was the oracle of the whole country around him, and his fame had extended far beyond the circle of his immediate acquaintance. Though I had never met him before, I had heard much of him, and but for this meeting it is very likely I should have had opposition, and had been beaten. One thing is very certain, no man could now stand up in that district under such a vote.' "

Crockett agreed to attend a barbecue a few weeks later in order to convince his constituents of his newfound enlightenment. He gave credit for his speech to Bunce and garnered the renewed support of those gathered.

" 'Now, sir,' concluded Crockett, 'you know why I made that speech yesterday.

" 'There is one thing now to which I will call your attention. You remember that I proposed to give a week's pay. There are in that House many very wealthy men—men who think nothing of spending a week's pay, or a dozen of them, for a dinner or wine party when they have something to accomplish by it. Some of those same men made beautiful speeches upon the great debt of gratitude which the country owed the deceased—a debt which could not be paid by money—and the insignificance and worthlessness of money, particularly so insignificant a sum as $10,000, when weighed against the honour of the nation. *Yet not one of them responded to my proposition. Money with them is nothing but trash when it is to come out of the people. But it is the one great thing for which most of them are striving, and many of them sacrifice honour, integrity, and justice to obtain it.'* "

How much more like trash is the public's money treated today than in those days? The president and Congress will make fine speeches this year while they vote for a trillion-dollar budget, about three-fifths of which will go toward socialistic spending programs and foreign aid giveaways. These programs are turning America into a socialistic state despite reassurances by our political leaders that America is the greatest democracy on the face of the earth.

On Capitol Hill, there are big fears about the budget as talk of tax cuts and reduced spending fills the air. Yet, when recently given a real opportunity to cut spending in the form of a 10 percent pay reduction for the Congress, Congress voted the proposal down. Lower pay will not attract the high caliber of men needed to fill these important posts of responsibility, we are told. But scandals that regularly crop up in the form of page boy sex affairs, drug and alcohol abuse, and Abscam-type stings make a mockery of that statement. In other words, we need high-salaried government men qualified enough to expertly usurp public power and money for the purpose of redistribution to the selected favorites.

This book does not advocate abandoning or turning a deaf ear to those who are destitute or helpless. However, it should be clear that government taxation for this purpose is unconstitutional. And considering the misery caused by bureaucratic red tape, government involvement in these matters is often most undesirable.

According to the table below, Americans gave $65 billion in charity in 1983, 83 percent of which came from individuals, a figure that has climbed steadily every year on this chart. It is truly amazing that, in spite of the tax burdens that have been placed on the people, the public still gives such a huge amount of money in charity. This shows that charity and the administration of charitable causes probably can be left in the hands of altruistic humanitarian groups in the private sector, which could be vastly aided by generous and caring Americans once government tax burdens are lifted.

Charitable Contributions (in billions of dollars)

	1983	1982	1981	1980	1979	1978	1977	1976
Individuals	53.9	48.5	44.6	39.8	36.5	32.8	29.3	26.6
Foundations	3.5	3.2	3.1	2.9	2.2	2.6	2.0	2.1
Corporations	3.1	3.0	2.9	2.7	2.3	2.1	1.7	1.5
Charitable Bequests	4.5	5.5	3.5	2.4	2.2	2.6	3.0	2.4
Total	**65.0**	**60.2**	**54.1**	**47.8**	**43.2**	**40.1**	**36.0**	**32.6**

Compiled using figures taken from the *Statistical Abstract of the United States for 1985*, 105th Edition, U.S. Department of Commerce. These figures from the IRS are based on itemized deductions, corporate profits, and bequests and have been adjusted for nonitemized deductions and after having been compared with levels of the GNP, personal income, population, and publicly reported large bequests. The figures do not reflect directly unreported contributions such as anonymous donations or other types of unreported charity.

Not only is this forced charity a smokescreen for ulterior government motives—to influence the outcome of events or to dictate them outright—but forcing someone to give charity actually takes away the act of charity. In other words, government charity is very conditional and not an act of magnanimity or selflessness, which the word *charity* denotes.

By doing this, the government not only removes the personal satisfaction gained from giving, but also gives that money to causes to which the donor would never dream of contributing. This can be exemplified by tax money that is taken from antiabortionists to perform abortions or from pacifists to pay for nuclear weapons. Government charity for one group or another will only provoke confrontation between opposing groups.

There might be still those who do not feel persuaded by these arguments and who claim the billions given voluntarily amounts to substantially less than the government provides "charitably" and that this charity helps and reaches many who might otherwise suffer or be neglected without this government aid. Notwithstanding the previous arguments that, under our Constitution, it is not the government's position, duty, or obligation to provide charity, there are other considerations.

This book has already stated that the government's greatest proficiencies seem to rest on its ability to make people's lives miserable. Let's expound on this point.

Basically speaking, the government is run by its different bureaus. No one needs much explanation about bureaucratic red tape, and it would appear these bureaucracies exist for the sole purpose of blocking progress whenever possible, even to the point where high-ranking elected officials have become frustrated when dealing with these agencies. On top of that, official government policies themselves are at times impossible to comprehend.

For example, the government will spend huge sums to subsidize the tobacco industry while simultaneously spending equal or greater sums to try to convince the public not to smoke. It would be more logical simply to let tobacco farmers survive on their own in the free market than to have the government expend time, effort, and money to keep them in business and try to put them out of business at the same time. We have all heard how the government discards food into the ocean or pays farmers not to grow certain crops while there are those in other parts of the world starving. This will go on while taxes are being collected to send "charitable" aid abroad, often in the form of food.

Government charity also opens doors for individuals to develop new arts in cheating the public. For instance, it was recently reported that one government official of a foreign land was receiving powdered milk from abroad and giving only a token amount to the schools for which it was intended. He would pay off the headmasters and sell the rest to local merchants for a profit. There are also stories circulating that the recent event "Live Aid," staged to raise money to send to starving Africans, is seeing the fruits of its labors in the form of tons of food rotting on docks while government men are stealing whatever they can and selling it in the countryside. Theft is not limited to government men; it also includes common people who regularly cheat the government. For instance, food stamps are sold for liquor and other ineligible items. Welfare fraud stories are so commonplace that people are tired of hearing them.

The point is that big government will not, or cannot, be relied on to manage things properly. The political arena is the field of activity for power, not for charity. As a rule, humanitarians do not seek government positions but work instead in the private sector. Abuse of charitable funds may occur anywhere, but the odds are greatly reduced when dealing with private individuals or groups whose main objectives in life are to do social, humanitarian, or welfare work. When government gets involved, there will always be some ulterior motive related not to charity but to behind-the-scenes power struggles. Either domestically or internationally, so-called government charity is simply another tool used for political gain.

A logical argument may follow that international aid is, indeed, a political device used by us to gain allowances and access to defense bases and other favors in different parts of the world. Consequently, this country will dump billions into other countries with the result that our affairs become entangled in foreign embroilments. This aid, which usually comes in the form of military assistance, does nothing to promote peace and simply helps pit one nation against another. The result is that world anger gets pent up and unleashed in our direction. How is it that the U.S.A., the most so-called freedom loving and peace loving country in the world, is the target of so much of the world's terrorism? We may dismiss terrorists as irrational radicals, but it has been said that one man's terrorist is another man's freedom fighter. The Soviets and Afghanistan government may call Afghan rebels terrorists, but we refer to them as freedom fighters.

America cannot and should not expect to be able to solve the problems of the world by simply throwing money at that problem. It gets so carried away that foreign governments send representatives to the Congress to lobby for the most aid. Congress has become the clearinghouse for billions of American taxpayer dollars misappropriated for the sole purpose of influencing the outcome of foreign intrigues this country has no business being involved in at all. The effect is that, because of these power plays, we create a class of frustrated terrorists who not only direct their activities toward America, but also keep the entire world under a state of constant tension. It will be only a matter of time before some terrorist/freedom fighter shows up somewhere with a nuclear suitcase bomb demanding that some injustice be corrected. Since much of this hostility is directed at America, perhaps American foreign policy and "charity" are not always the altruistic causes they are touted to be.

America is involved in parts of the world where it cannot fathom or comprehend foreign religions, customs, or societies. It cannot force its way of thinking on other peoples. When it tries and the result is suicide car bombs, Americans end up wringing their hands in disbelief. If America is out to build a world empire and to conquer other people and countries, then let's go out and do it. If not, then our armies should not be extended beyond our shores. American foreign policy should be one of armed neutrality and "America first."

As far as real charity is concerned, if there is some country in genuine need of aid, then let us send trillions, not billions, if we so desire, but let it come from voluntary contributions. Huge sums of money are donated privately through telethons, fund drives, etc., despite the heavy tax burdens that are shouldered by people in general. Everyone is disposed toward giving charity in certain degrees, and there is no need for government intrusion.

The whole business of government interference in daily living is totally out of hand. Big brother will not be satisfied until it rules and regulates every detail of our lives. The power to steal money in the form of inequitable and unconstitutional taxes lays the foundation for this criminal arrogation of our civil liberties and freedoms.

What a tragic, ironic state of affairs we now find in America and her present-day tax system. The American Revolution began as a tax protest. The Founding Fathers, who were tax rebels themselves, literally pledged their lives and fortunes to their cause. What kind of revulsion might they feel today to see the freedoms they fought and died for not so many generations ago practically destroyed? Taxes were originally intended to be a voluntary matter, but through the aberration of the Constitution, those who withhold or protest unjust taxation (without pursuing the "legal" way to avoid taxes) are marked as criminals and thrown into jail. Americans must wake up and understand this action for what it really is. While there is still time, they must stand up and demand reforms from their legislators that will lift this growing yoke of oppression from the backs of the people. The income tax and the 16th Amendment must be repealed and forgotten!

6
LOSS OF FREEDOM, IDENTITY, AND NATIONAL AUTONOMY VIA PENDING CALL-IN

After the damaging policies of the Roosevelt era and at the end of World War II, the United States was still in a strong monetary position as it held over 60 percent of the world's gold reserve. The U.S. people had not wanted to enter any world wars and desired a policy of armed neutrality. But Roosevelt's European conspiracies dragged us into global conflicts and intrigues that, among other things, gave Russia half of Europe and made her the world power she is today. One of the most disastrous of these intrigues began in Bretton Woods, New Hampshire, in 1944. This was the site of the first meeting of the International Monetary Fund (IMF), the resultant strategies of which have set U.S. monetary policy to the present day.

THE U.S. LOSES ITS GOLD

The Bretton Woods Conference was dominated by John Maynard Keynes of Great Britain and Harry Dexter White of the U.S. delegation. Under the direction of White, a member of the Council on Foreign Relations and an undercover Soviet espionage agent, the U.S. delegation headed up and controlled the meeting. It was decided at this meeting that the U.S. gold position was too strong compared to that of other nations and that this imbalance had to be corrected (at the expense of the U.S., of course) by redistributing U.S. gold to other countries. It was resolved that currencies of all other nations except the U.S. would be relieved of gold convertibility, but that all nations had to maintain their currencies at official rates with parity to the dollar. Only foreign central banks would be able to redeem their dollars for gold.

The U.S. began to engage in grandiose military and foreign aid abroad. This resulted in a slow steady drain of our gold as dollars spent in foreign lands were cashed in by the foreign central banks. This effectively caused our gold to be transferred to other countries and gave the banking institutions of those lands control of the gold reserves. While the U.S. citizen was prohibited from owning gold, any authorized foreigner could step up to the Treasury window and cash in dollars for gold. Since these foreign banks got control of the gold, with every price increase of the metal their reserve went up in value, which allowed for greater inflation of their own money.

A gold crisis began to develop. In 1948 we held $24.4 billion in gold, and by 10 years later it had dropped to $19 billion. The Eisenhower administration responded with feeble attempts to stem this flow, but they were directed at the wrong targets. Eisenhower ordered some dependents of military personnel overseas to come home, and PXs in military bases abroad were instructed to limit sales of foreign merchandise. But the big military and foreign aid projects churned merrily on.

By 1961, foreign claims actually exceeded our gold supply. The Kennedy administration's response was no better than Eisenhower's. A few American offices abroad were closed, but aid to Vietnam and other trouble spots was stepped up. In the mid-'60s, the Johnson administration and Congress followed up by repealing the requirement that the Treasury keep gold reserves equal to 25 percent of the amount of actual currency circulated. This freed up more gold for foreign claims and allowed freer expansion of the domestic supply of money.

The government put pressure on businesspeople to curtail foreign investments by imposing higher taxes on the holding of foreign securities. Interest rates hit the highest levels in 40 years. The Treasury pleaded and coaxed foreign governments to keep their surplus dollars instead of cashing them in. Finally, the government promised to reduce and eliminate deficit spending. The last vestige of any real money was taken from the people when, in 1964, all silver was called in and our coin replaced with cupronickel slugs. This silver was being sold off by the Treasury in a frantic and futile attempt to keep the price of the metal down.

By 1968, our gold reserves stood at $10 billion, we were liable for three times that amount to foreign creditors, the domestic money supply stood at $200 billion, and all of this without a single ounce of free gold or silver to support it. The world markets went crazy as waves of furious speculation and smuggling swept through them. Emergency meetings were called in Washington, London, and Zurich. The British pound collapsed, after which, in March 1968, a worldwide gold panic followed. Desperate, the politicians and money managers rushed to embrace the neo-Keynesian philosophy that gold was a barbarous relic and an anachronism in our modern world of laser beams and spaceships. Federal Reserve Board chairman William McChesney Martin even went to the extreme of insisting we should pay out our gold to the last bar and that the American people would be better off once they had seen the last of it.

If the U.S. had retained its gold, we would not have found ourselves in an economic crisis. But what happened was planned at that historic Bretton Woods meeting 40 years ago. In 1944, the United States was the dominant economic and financial power on the planet. As the officially designated spokesman for the U.S., H. D. White was practically able to set the basic objectives of that meeting. The policies that were finally agreed on accomplished four major internationalistic objectives, which would tend to debilitate and remove America from her position of great strength:

1. Strip the United States of her great gold reserve by giving gold away to other nations.
2. Build up the industrial capacity of other nations, at our expense, to eliminate American productive superiority.
3. Take world markets (and much of the American domestic market) away from American producers until capitalistic America would no longer dominate world trade.
4. Entwine American affairs—economic, political, cultural, social, educational, and even religious—with those of other nations, until the United States could no longer have an independent policy but would become an interdependent link in a worldwide socialist chain.

And on September 30, 1963, President John F. Kennedy stated at a meeting of the IMF that this all came about not by chance but by design:

> Twenty years ago, when the architects of these institutions met to design an international banking structure, the economic life of the world was polarized in an overwhelming and even alarming measure on the United States. So were the world's monetary reserves. The United States had the only open capital in the world apart from that of Switzerland. Sixty percent of the gold reserves of the world were here in the United States. . . . There was a need for redistribution of the financial resources of the world. . . . This has come about. It did not come about by chance *but by conscious and deliberate and responsible planning.* [italics mine]*

As a bailout for the gold crisis, then Secretary of the Treasury, H. M. Fowler, went about pleading for the creation of a new IMF unit of currency to replace gold in the international marketplace. Out of this emerged the IMF paper gold,

---

*N. W. Hutchings, "New Money," *The Gospel Truth*, vol. 25, no. 3 (Feb 1984).

special drawing rights (SDRs), which could be used instead of gold to make international payments. Just review the events of the IMF conference of 1980 to see how far these SDRs have come: at that time, the IMF gave Third World debtor countries with the worst credit and in the greatest danger of default SDRs of up to 600 percent of their quotas for a three-year period. These SDRs have no real backing and are created out of thin air, so much so that OPEC refused to contribute to the fund. This was not the case with the U.S., which just gave $8.4 billion and promised another $20 billion of the taxpayer's money.

It seems that this particular bastion of the international bankers, the IMF, has been quite adept in fulfilling its purpose. Not only does it help prevent collapse of the international banking system, but it also is instrumental in bringing us closer to the modern-day goal of a cashless society, so eagerly sought by our new, would-be masters. If they could convince us that SDRs, electronic bookkeeping entries, credit cards, and the like are all we need, then total manipulation of the people could take place rather easily. With the great strides made by science in the areas of robotics, computers, and electronic gadgetry, totalitarian government becomes increasingly closer to reality. We are told that these mechanisms, once installed, will greatly advance and enhance our lifestyles, but they actually will be used against us. For example, we hear of the benefits of electronic banking, but we are not told how this new banking can keep total surveillance over our finances.

FREE ENTERPRISE vs. FREE TRADE

A few decades ago, American-manufactured goods were in great demand throughout the world and sold at a premium. American products enjoyed the reputation of high quality and good value for the price paid. Many, many companies, like Ford, GM, General Electric, Westinghouse, and others, built factories in foreign nations. Today, these holdings are practically gone. The markets have been taken over by Japan, Hong Kong, West Germany, and a few other nations. Even our domestic market has dried up to our own manufactured goods, and our balance of payments is growing way out of proportion.

Domestic markets are flooded with government-subsidized foreign-made goods ranging from automobiles to radios. We have been reduced to exporting raw materials like coal or timber and importing manufactured goods we are failing to produce ourselves. The one-worlders gleefully watch as American industrial might is decimated and transferred to other nations. Any talk of halting this loss of jobs and industrial capacity through such means as import tariffs is denounced as protectionism and unsatisfactory in a new, interdependent world economy. Americans are made to feel guilty and are told we must distribute our wealth and knowledge to other nations or must be responsible for world economic collapse and suffering.

At this point, you may feel that a pro-tariff stance is inconsistent with the philosophy of free trade or government noninterference with the marketplace. Government imposed import tariffs, or protectionism, carry with them the negative connotation of government obstruction of free market activities. Clarification of this point is necessary.

Before explaining import tariffs and their relationship to free trade, it should be pointed out that imposts, duties, etc., are one of the authorized methods laid down in the Constitution by which the government can collect money. Article I, Section 8 of the Constitution states: "Congress shall have power to lay and collect taxes, duties, imposts, and excises, to pay debts and provide for the common defense and general welfare of the United States. . . ." Section 9 states: "No capitation, or other direct tax shall be laid, unless in proportion to the census or enumeration herein before directed to be taken." Section 10 states: "No state shall . . . make anything but gold and silver coin a tender in payment of debts. . . ."

According to our Constitution, supreme law of the land, the proper and legal method for government to obtain revenues is through means such as import duties. Section 9 forbids an income tax or other direct tax unless based on the census. In other words, if the government needs money for some legitimate program, which it cannot obtain through such measures as imposts, it may lay a direct tax according to population, not income. What this means is a head tax—everyone paying an equal amount to add up to the amount required. And all this only can be done legally, using gold or silver coin. Of course, the 16th Amendment supposedly changed the definition of direct taxation according to income. While there are many who make very convincing arguments to prove the 16th Amendment still does not give permission to levy a personal income tax because of the government's own definition of what is income, rather than wage war in the courts or halls of government over the technicalities or language of the amendment, it is best to repeal the thing and be done with it once and for all. So we should keep in mind that most of those who advocate income tax while denouncing imposts as protectionist measures should read the Constitution and find out that imposts are exactly what is called for and should be installed immediately, and the income tax should be denounced and repealed. Now let's get back to the free trade question.

Though not implicitly stated, the term *free trade* should include the concept of *fair* trade. Trade cannot be free if one of the traders has an unfair advantage. Therefore, antitrust laws, securities exchange rules, etc., have come into being to prevent dishonest and damaging business practices from gaining prominence in commercial transactions. Government interference in the marketplace is often the source of unfair advantages that seem to favor one trade or industry over another. Many then logically conclude protectionism is merely another form of government intervention.

Others also observe that protectionist measures usually result in other nations retaliating with protectionist measures of their own, which causes strains in relations, hampers commerce and trade between the two traders, and so on. In the same way that many think the Federal Reserve System is part of the federal government because the word *federal* appears in the name, many will feel that, because the word *free* appears in the term *free trade*, free trade must be defended because freedom must be defended. The problems created by this so-called free trade go beyond the concept of trying to uphold a particular economic philosophy.

There are principles that take precedence over other principles. Priorities must be established. In this case, national fraud, injury, and survival take precedence over adherence to some ill perceived economic theory. One merely has to examine the advocates of modern-day free trade to ascertain the goal of free trade policies.

Perhaps the best place to start is with Karl Marx, patron saint of all present-day communist dictatorships. Karl Marx valued free trade as a powerful tool to foment social unrest and upheaval. Marx, speaking in Belgium on January 9, 1848, endorsed free trade as a means to wreck the economies of free-enterprise nations:

"Generally speaking, the protective system [of tariffs] in these days is conservative, while the free trade system is destructive. It [free trade] breaks up old nationalities and carries antagonism of proletariat [industrial workers] and bourgeoisie [small business owners] to the uttermost point.

"In a word, the free trade system hastens the social revolution. . . . Gentlemen, I am in favor of free trade."

Is it not strange that the father of Communism declares the protective system of tariffs is conservative while "conservatives" in the halls of U.S. government fight for free trade?

A corollary of free trade is free immigration and worldwide integration. In a time when most people are seeking out their roots and identity, internationalistic policies, as exemplified by free trade and noble-sounding terms such as *integration*, are creating a global hodgepodge and mongrelization of races, religions, cultures, languages, and customs. This creates the illusion of a global village and slowly negates and eliminates nationalism. This internationalistic blending is not intended to create harmony and brotherhood, but instead is meant to further merge and lump peoples together so that they will be easier to control under a one-world government. Internationalism opposes nationalism and unity based on race, religion, heritage, etc., to which people naturally gravitate and identify. This identification gives people a common ground on which to build their lives and adds a sense of purpose and individuality. Of course, to the internationalist, conformity based on these traditions creates nationalistic pockets of resistance and must be eliminated. As George Orwell once said, "Patriotism is usually stronger than class hatred, and always stronger than internationalism."

This is not to say that we must become racists, or supremacists, but there is no reason why different races, religions and cultures cannot peacefully coexist without needing to be blended into an indistinguishable jumble of people who have no clear-cut heritage with which to identify. After all, we are speaking of divisions that occur naturally in the scheme of things. In any event, even though destruction of national sovereignty and identity *is* one of the Marxist goals of free trade, we are straying from the economic consequences of a free trade policy.

The flip side of the coin on the free trade matter involves national self-sufficiency. Those who advocate free trade have helped shape domestic and foreign policies based on the false assumption that the United States is a have-not nation that must depend on trade with the rest of the world for many of its needs.

As a key motivator in this scenario, we find once again Harry Dexter White, communist agent and close advisor of FDR. White developed the idea that the U.S. could not be self-sufficient in the production of critical raw materials. Senator George Malone, populist Republican statesman from Nevada (1947–1959), who was chairman of the Senate Subcommittee on Minerals, Materials, and Fuels, exposed the mistake in this reasoning and proved that all the strategic minerals we need are in the ground but that government policy is to keep them undeveloped. Many modern scientists, geologists and engineers consider the reports produced by the Malone subcommittee to be the greatest ever put out by the Senate, in need, some 25 years later, of only minor statistical updating.

Reports from Malone's subcommittee are generally unknown and have been relegated to the Establishment's "memory hole." A self-sufficient America would remove this country's dependency on faraway lands and faceless multinational corporations. The internationalists in government keep this knowledge hidden from the general public so as to add fuel to the argument for free trade: after all, they ask, without free trade, how might we obtain supplies of critical materials and minerals that we lack?

According to Senator Malone, the belief that America lacks or has exhausted its supply of vital and strategic minerals and ores "is one of the greatest frauds and hoaxes ever perpetrated on the American people."

Granted it is still possible to argue about the exact definition of free trade. However, none can argue that free trade has not had catastrophic effects on our nation's industrial strength as well as on its survival capabilities.

The government supports a bailout of Chrysler or a Communist Polish government but demonstrates indifference toward the mass of foreign imports that have almost destroyed many of our most vital industries. Internationalists and free traders will have us believing that, to a dynamic economy such as ours, many of these basic industries are outmoded, especially since we are heading into a new era as a service economy. Can it be that shipbuilding, steel, forge, foundry, machine tool, textile, footwear, and clothing, as well as other industries, are obsolete? If the country is dependent on foreign manufacturers for these important products, how would we be supplied if sea lanes and other trade channels were cut off? As it presently stands, even our military depends on key basic necessities from foreign suppliers.

Free trade advocates proclaim foreign imports are beneficial because domestic industries will become more efficient and competitive. The real result has been the debilitation and destruction of survival industries and the loss of hundreds of thousands of jobs. Balance of payments have become so lopsided that further destruction is guaranteed, and now, for the first time since World War I, the mighty U.S. has become a debtor nation.

Probably the best example of the deleterious impact of free trade on one side and protectionism on the other can be demonstrated by our trade relationship with Japan. How is it that it is practically impossible to find a camera, VCR, radio, TV or other electronic device of U.S. origin? Almost everything is imported from Japan. How is it that it is possible to buy identical Japanese goods at a lower price in the United States than in Japan? Even our semiconductor industry has filed formal complaints, for the first time ever, against Japanese protectionist barriers, which hinder U.S. firm's attempts to penetrate that market. Instead our government encourages Japanese and other foreigners to establish plants in the United States and offers investment benefits and import concessions that place their U.S. competitors at a further disadvantage, not to speak of subjecting our industrial capabilities to the whims of foreigners. Many of these plants are assembly plants, which means the skills to manufacture parts for assembly are not required. The manufactured parts are imported. The effect of this is to leave only low-skill and unskilled jobs for Americans.

Legal action by U.S. manufacturers is excessively costly and usually requires years to resolve, which ultimately results in many business failures as well as the aforementioned loss of skills and jobs. In other words the U.S. manufacturer must bear the burden of an overvalued dollar, huge domestic budget deficits, which create adverse conditions in the marketplace, and foreign industries that are given subsidies not only by their own governments but by ours as well.

The Japanese prime rate as of summer 1985 was only 5.8 percent. For certain targeted industries such as auto, electronics, photography, and shipbuilding, the rate was even lower—2–3 percent. Japanese protectionist measures lock out any foreign penetration of goods outside of raw materials needed for production

Consequently, Japan manufactures 56 percent of the world's ships, both free-world and non-free-world. The overwhelming hold Japan has on this industry comes not only from its high level of subsidization but also from the high level of protection offered to supporting industries such as steel, forging, and metal casting. (The runner-up is South Korea, at 17 percent of world shipbuilding, for the same reasons: heavy subsidization, cheap loans, and protectionist measures.) By comparison, the U.S. produces less than 2 percent. The demise of American shipbuilding was caused by the abandonment of the Jones Act of 1920, which protected this industry for over 50 years. The Carter and Reagan administrations are responsible for dismantling this act.

The only major items of U.S. origins seen in the world markets today are military hardware, high-tech computers, and Coca-Cola. Foreign investments have been liquidated to forestall the monetary crisis this country must face in the near future.

A discussion of the wholesale destruction of vital and basic industries could go on ad infinitum, but it shall suffice to say that the internationalistic theory of free trade is the driving force responsible for these devastating conflicts. Better to espouse the concept of free enterprise than that of free trade so as to establish the difference between two similar-sounding but very different schools of thought.

THE CALL-IN TIME FRAME

So, by cashing in on our overseas investments, the government has managed to keep down inflation for the time being. In addition, high interest rates have caused foreign flight capital to seek refuge in the United States, temporarily increasing the money stock. But where does the government go next? The government, according to its own figures, is heading for more deficit spending in the next few years than it has engaged in in the entire history of the nation. Because of this, many observers expect inflation to be raging once again within the next five years. Somewhere in that time frame would seem to be an advantageous time for a currency call-in.

Purposes Served by a Currency Exchange

This call-in would be timely because it could serve many

purposes that currently need to be fulfilled or will need to be fulfilled in the next few years.

1. It could flush out the underground economy, which is presently estimated to be up to 30 percent of the gross national product (GNP). Those exchanging old for new in amounts, for example, over $500 or $1,000 might have to leave their name and Social Security number and explain to the IRS where the money came from. This action would fill IRS coffers from previously untaxed monies.

To control or destroy the underground economy seems doubly important in our current circumstances. First, the black market keeps money out of the hands of the tax collector, making a farce out of governmental rules and regulations. Second, it is a major obstacle in moving us toward a cashless society. As discussed in an article in *Business Week* in April 1985, this underground economy is made up of millions of generally upstanding citizens who do not report income in order to avoid paying taxes on it, in addition to the counterfeiters, drug dealers, et al. There are so many of these people, according to the article, that in 1984: "From $29 billion in 1960, the amount of currency in circulation increased four fold by 1981. Currency holdings last year amounted to $542.00 for every man, woman and child in the country, compared with $187.00 per capita in 1965. And even after adjusting for inflation, cash per capita reached levels almost matching those of the black market days of World War II."

2. A call-in also could be used to repudiate the national debt. Our dollar is worth about $.01 compared to a turn-of-the-century gold dollar. With double-digit and even triple-digit inflation a distinct reality in the very near future, an exchange of 10 to 1 or even 100 to 1 looks very attractive. With the uncertainties and volatilities of our modern world, an occurrence such as a Third World debtor default prevented by a 1980 Monetary Control Act type of bailout could send inflation through the roof. We can understand that the Fed will never allow the bankers to lose their profits or power base.

3. A new currency could also serve as a transitional currency ultimately to be replaced in the new hoped-for cashless society. The new transitional currency could be imprinted with computer code markings, magnetic codes, and metal fragments that would all facilitate the control and monitoring of our cash and its wanderings throughout the economy and the world.

4. This transitional currency could be used as the first international paper currency. The coming currency exchange is being coordinated with recalls in six other nations (more on this later in the chapter). Even though an issue of one standard currency for all these nations would be rather difficult to pull off right now, computer codes, magnetic markings, and the like would make them all appear identical to a machine.

To review, the authorities know the U.S. is headed toward a major devaluation of the dollar and hyperinflation. The huge black market has derailed government plans to consolidate power, and the international bankers fear a massive default by some foreign country that would cause the banking system to collapse. They have been able to avert a crisis through the IMF, give-a-ways, strengthening the Fed, and so on, and by temporarily maintaining high interest rates. This has served to postpone the inevitable by causing liquidation of the nation's overseas patrimony and by causing foreign flight capital to seek refuge in the U.S. This action has been financing the government but will soon run its course. In the meantime, the goverment has been trying to figure out how to tax the underground economy, which they know, if feasible, could wipe out the national debt, possibly create a surplus, and simultaneously strengthen their power base.

Government Leaks of Information

The time is ripe for a currency exchange! We have already examined the objectives that a currency exchange in the near future could accomplish, but there is still other evidence that a currency exchange is coming soon. Namely, the government has recently begun to leak stories that large-denomination bills will soon be exchanged in order to combat the criminal element that supposedly dominates the underground economy. It all started with articles about the illegal drug market.

Fighting Illegal Drugs

In order to prepare us psychologically for a recall of our dollars, the government began to leak stories that there were plans to exchange $100 and $50 bills to combat drug activity. On August, 23, 1982, for example, *The New York Times* reported that Roscoe Egger, IRS Commissioner, requested a ban on $100 bills, because they make up 40 percent of the total $125 billion in circulation, and most of that can be attributed to illegal activities involving drugs, gambling, and loan sharking. On December 5, 1982, *The New York Times* reported that the number of hundreds in circulation had grown 11.3 percent over the last year and, while acknowledging inflation, cited the underground economy as the main reason for the increasing demand. The article showed the currency breakdown in billions of dollars ($) as of September 30, 1982.

$1— 3.47	$20—42.53
$2— 0.68	$50—15.82
$5— 4.52	$100—57.38
$10—11.00	

A mere eight months later, Treasury Department statistics for June 30, 1983, show that total money in circulation increased by $12.38 billion, with 43.7 percent ($5.41 billion) of that increase in $100 bills. If we take May 1984 figures for total cash in circulation of about 170 billion and divide that by the U.S. population of 230 million, we come up with a cash hoard of $740 for every man, woman, and child in the country. An average family of four would have $2,960 in hiding. This is one of the nation's highest per capita rates of cash in history.

Where is all the money? The answer is that the money is circulating in the cash-and-carry underground economy.

In this country, the officials know that they must go after black market money if they wish to tighten their control and continue their current policies of spend, spend, spend.

Unfortunately this is where the government runs into problems. This black market underground economy is their own creation. The more they try to control the people and the more that people are racked by high taxes and inflation, the stronger this black market becomes. Therefore, the government must come up with a way to convince the public that an exchange is necessary for their own good. The way our government has chosen to do this is to purport to combat some alleged evil. In this case, the evil we must attack is drug dealers, who are supposedly the main handlers of this underground cash. But this is, a bogus contention.

According to studies done on tax avoiding, drugs are actually a small part of the problem, and the government knows this. Take, for example, studies done by Carl P. Simon of Michigan State University and Ann D. Witte of the University of North Carolina. Basing their estimates on a very, very conservative $380 billion of unreported income in 1981, they came up with the following figures.

LICIT ACTIVITY

Self-employment	$115 billion
Wages and Salaries	$ 80 billion
Interest	$ 20 billion
Corporate Profits	$ 18 billion
Rents and Royalties	$ 15 billion
Other Legal	$ 7 billion
Total	$255 billion

ILLICIT ACTIVITY

Drugs	$ 45 billion
Stolen Goods	$ 20 billion
Bribery	$ 15 billion
Prostitution	$ 15 billion
Fraud	$ 6 billion
Pornography	$ 6 billion
Gambling and Loan Sharking	$ 4 billion
Other Illegal	$ 10 billion
Total	$121 billion

These figures show that drugs account for a little over 10 percent of the total overall activity, while so-called total licit activity accounts for about 70 percent, with the self-employed being the greatest offenders at over 30 percent of all activity. A governmental attack on the underground economy is not so much an attack on drug trafficking as it is an attack on legal activity, especially the self-employed. This became even more obvious when, after announcements to recall $100s and $50s, the drug trade fearfully switched to $20s and $10s but the amount of $100s and $50s in circulation continued to rise. However, the government continued to claim to want to attack the evil drug dealers and even went so far as to introduce legislation to replace $100 bills or phase them out altogether. According to an article in the *Washington Post* on March 31, 1983, such legislation would also require those who exchanged more than $5,000 in the large bills to give their names, Social Security numbers, and addresses to the U.S. Treasury. The article stated that the IRS and the American Institute of Certified Public Accountants jumped on the bandwagon and advocated doing away with large bills.

The Second Tack: Fighting Counterfeiting

After planting such hints in the press, the government hired two independent survey teams to carry on a very quiet survey to test further public reaction to the recall. One survey was carried out by the University of Michigan under the direction of marketing professor Claude Martin. The other survey was commissioned to Market Facts, Inc., of Oak Park, Illinois, and Washington, DC.

The results of these surveys were not made public, but a considerable amount of information from them has been made available by Federal Reserve officials and in a report made to the members of the House Banking Committee on November 2, 1983. On that date, representatives of the Bureau of Engraving and Printing, the Federal Reserve Board, and the Secret Service held a meeting with the House Banking Committee and distributed a briefing paper written by the Treasurer of the United States, Katherine D. Ortega. The following is a transcript of that report:

CONGRESSIONAL BRIEFING
ADVANCED COUNTERFEIT DETERRENCE PROGRAM

KATHERINE D. ORTEGA
TREASURER OF THE UNITED STATES
U.S. DEPARTMENT OF THE TREASURY

Background:

The objective of the Advanced Counterfeit Deterrence Program is to protect U.S. currency from counterfeiting. The program was begun in 1978 by a Four Nation Committee on Advanced Counterfeit Deterrence (United States, the United Kingdom, Canada, and Australia) whose formation was impelled by the mounting threat of counterfeiting posed by rapidly improving technology in the field of reprographics. The United States was represented by the Bureau of Engraving and Printing, the U.S. Secret Service, and the Federal Reserve System.

The committee found the threat to currency integrity to be very serious due mainly to the introduction of improved color copiers, but also to substantial improvements to lithography in general. It recommended two approaches to counterfeit deterrence: covert and visible. The covert deterrents would be for machine use only, at Federal Reserve Banks. The visible deterrents would be used for commercial and personal authentication of currency used in everyday transactions. Individually, the other three member countries also are actively planning to use these approaches.

Evaluation of Threat

Following up the work of the Four Nation Committee, we retained the services of Battelle Columbus Laboratories to examine the counterfeiting threat as a way to understand its effect on the continued viability of the present design of U.S. currency. Battelle, a highly respected nonprofit research firm with broad experience in reprographics, worked closely in its analysis with the Secret Service, The Bureau of Engraving and Printing, and the Federal Reserve. Battelle's conclusions confirm the mounting seriousness of the threat, particularly as it derives from the proliferation of color copiers and the resulting mass dispersion of counterfeiting "plants" which will exceed the pragmatic suppression capability of the United States Secret Service. Battelle estimates 1987 as the threshold year.

AVAILIBILITY OF ADVANCED COLOR COPIERS CREATES NEW ENFORCEMENT ENVIRONMENT

1987		1992	
No. of Copiers	People with Access	No. of Copiers	People with Access
1,000–2,000	54,000–95,200	2,000–5,000	95,200–196,000

Locations

- quick print shops
- in-plant print shops
- others
  architectural-engineering firms
  research and development firms
  advertising agencies

Plans of Other Countries:

- Because of recent large-scale counterfeiting of its 20-pound notes, England is planning to introduce an enhanced design during the summer of 1984.
- In addition, it intends to redesign its 50-pound note during 1986.
- Canada plans to produce redesigned currency during the second half of 1985 for introduction in 1986.
- Australia is planning to introduce redesigned notes in the next 3 to 4 years.
- Germany is planning to redesign its currency during the latter part of 1985 or 1986; however, a final decision has not been made.

Results of Market Research Surveys

The ACD Program Steering Committee retained two survey research firms, the University of Michigan Survey Research Center and Market Facts, Inc., to evaluate public attitudes toward U.S. currency, its redesign, and proposed design alternatives. The following is a summary of their major findings:

- The public is generally satisfied with the appearance of U.S. currency, but would be in favor of a redesign if a sufficiently good reason—such as counterfeiting—were given as the reason for the change.
- People are generally favorably disposed toward the use of color in the currency, provided the colors are tastefully applied—not too bold or garish.
- The public is not opposed to security devices requiring transmitted or reflected light, but in general prefers authentication features that do not require a demonstrative verification procedure.

Conclusions

1. By 1987, the increasing sophistication of reprographics will permit counterfeiting on a scale that could have a seriously negative effect on public confidence in U.S. currency. Because the timing and magnitude of the threat cannot be determined with absolute certainty, the serious consequences of a miscalculation support the early implementation of deterrence measures that minimize the risks associated with counterfeiting.
2. The incorporation of deterrence features in currency can have a significant effect in reducing the level of counterfeiting by both professionals and amateurs. In order to have a viable defense against counterfeiting in place by 1987, action should be initiated to issue currency with proven features as early as 1985, if possible.
3. At present, there is high likelihood of a favorable public reaction to a design-enhanced currency. Indeed, 1985–1986 appears to be a window of opportunity for a currency

redesign program that could reflect most favorably on the U.S. Government. Beyond this time frame, however, counterfeiting is projected to increase substantially, thus, creating a greater risk of a difficult and costly accelerated transition program.

Plans

- The Bureau of Engraving and Printing and the Federal Reserve System are actively engaged in research and development of deterrent features to incorporate in U.S. currency to defeat this threat. We expect models to be fully designed and tested in 1984. The basic design is unlikely to change—rather, additional features and protection will be added to it. Public opinion will be tested again prior to format change and issuance.
- There have already appeared several articles in numismatic and other publications about this program, and more public interest may be generated over the next few months. It is our intention to discuss our assessment of the threat and plans for responding to it in only general terms until final decisions are made by the Secretary of the Treasury, who has authority to approve changes in currency design within the definition of the law.
- Congressional briefings will be held prior to any formal announcement.

The public opinion survey conducted by the University of Michigan revealed four major conclusions:

1. The public is well satisfied with our present currency and would permit a change only if it were to deter counterfeiting.
2. The public wants to be kept fully informed of any new developments. Much of the public, however, is more concerned with seeing that the government is doing the job it says its going to do than with the specifics or ramifications of tasks it undertakes.

3. The public opposes any visible or overt markings requiring any procedure for verifying authenticity that leaves an inference of suspicion. In other words, a merchant would not want to hold up a bill to the light to see if a watermark is visible.
4. Americans, having a great concern for the disadvantaged, and if changes were being made anyway, would not be opposed to incorporation of special features designed to help the disadvantaged, such as indentations that would help the blind for instance.

The Market Facts, Inc., research generally confirmed these facts. Market Facts interviewed 602 individuals in a random sampling and also singled out certain people who handled large sums of money, such as bank tellers, cashiers, etc. Their survey also included groups at shopping malls. These group sessions shed additional light on the feelings of the American public on paper currency. They are:

1. Few people had ever received or even seen a counterfeit.
2. If the color copying machines were as good as claimed, 10–15 percent of the population might be tempted to "experiment" with duplicating bills.
3. If changes absolutely had to be made, color changes, security threads, and an optical variable device would be most readily accepted.
4. The public is very concerned about continuing as much of our present basic design as possible.

Because of this last fact, the government is very sensitive to public opinion and plans to seek further input from the population and to continue to test new designs until it gets a final public approval. The government is also very concerned with preventing fears of a devaluation, which would undermine the value of the new currency as well as the old. It is imperative that the government avoid any type of widespread resistance to a new currency.

It is interesting to note that, in the Ortega report, the

government's main concern seems to be a new wave of counterfeiting. The report recommends that as early as 1985, and no later than 1987, installation of a new currency is necessary to stave off this new wave of counterfeiting. It states that 1985–1986 is the most favorable time frame, beyond which counterfeiting is expected "to increase substantially, thus creating a greater risk of a difficult and costly accelerated transition program." But recently, it has been reported that the conversion target date has been pushed to at least 1988. In the meantime, we have seen no dramatic rise in counterfeiting. This tends to undermine the argument made for the time frames mentioned in the report and especially for the need to deter counterfeiting as the reason for this exchange. The more time that passes, and as this new surge of counterfeiting fails to materialize, the more this argument is exposed as a cover for some ulterior governmental motive for inaugurating a currency exchange.

In any event, these surveys showed that most people opposed the whole idea of a new dollar, newly colored or otherwise, most likely because they somehow or other sensed an intended abridgement of their freedom. However, it was ascertained that, if a change was made in order to stop counterfeiting, they would favor it. As soon as the government learned this, it immediately abandoned its position of trying to prevent drug trafficking and adopted a new approach: that we must curb the huge counterfeiting threat that is facing the country.

Suddenly, the articles appearing in the nation's press began ignoring the so-called drug problem and instead focused on the counterfeiting problem. The *Chicago Tribune, The New York Times*, the *Washington Post*, and *USA Today* all carried stories hawking the new government line, describing the alarming menace we face from counterfeiters. There have been blatant incongruities in these stories as evidenced by some of the headlines of 1983:

"PINK BILLS NOT IN U.S. PLANS" (*The New York Times,* November 29, 1983)

"TECHNICOLOR GREEN BACKS?" (*USA Today*, November 29, 1983)

"U.S. CONSIDERS PINK, BLUE CURRENCY" (*The Chicago Tribune*, November 30, 1983)

"U.S. GREENBACKS ARE TO STAY GREEN" (*The New York Times*, November 30, 1983)

"CHANGES IN PAPER MONEY MAY INCLUDE NEW COLORS" (*Washington Post*, November 30, 1983)

"MONEY MAY BE COLORFUL BUT IT'LL MOSTLY BE GREEN" (*The Chicago Tribune*, December 6, 1983)

What these articles and others basically explained was this: Former Republican Congressman Ron Paul, of the 22nd district in Texas, who was a member of the congressional Committee on Banking, Finance, and Urban Affairs, had been shown by Katharine Ortega multicolored currency scheduled for release to the public. Alarmed by this development, Congressman Paul called a news conference in order to reveal this to the American people. He had not been allowed to take samples of the currency and had to be content to show artists' drawings of the new bills to reporters.

The next day, Treasury spokesman Robert Levine and Robert J. Leuver, Director of the Bureau of Engraving and Printing rebutted by saying that there were no "pink and blue bills" planned even though in the past it had been considered part of the ongoing effort to prevent the epidemic in counterfeiting that is anticipated in the near future. This alleged threat comes from new-generation color photocopying machines that have the technological capability to reproduce color very accurately. The articles mentioned that Congressman Paul is running for the Senate seat being vacated by Senator John Tower, subtly implying this was merely grandstanding on his part and there was no need for alarm.

Citing surveys of public reaction, Leuver was quoted as saying, "People don't want to change the currency. But if there is a threat of counterfeiting, they would like a change." He then described other features being considered, such as color tints in the background, magnetic threads, watermarks, and three-dimensional printing. This was stated in such a way as to have us believe that these measures are second-rate, but that it is what we will have to settle for since the public is opposed to any highly visible change in appearance. The articles then give some exaggerated time table for this exchange to be effected (1987 or 1988) and a grossly underestimated cost ($1 million) for new equipment and the like necessary for a different currency to be produced. (Note: The latest target date given for the conversion is 1988. Ron Paul was shown new currency printed and ready for release in 1985–1986. These are also the dates mentioned in the congressional briefing report. Even though the newspapers had no way of knowing the dates would be pushed back at the time of these articles, 1985–1986 was to be the time at which the new currency was to be released, and there was no reason to believe otherwise. Still, we find, although aware of the correct dates, the newsprint media "elected" to give exaggerated time frames for the release date.)

And finally, we are told that the members of Congress are being briefed on the matter and are requested to send recommendations to Treasury Secretary Donald T. Regan for a final decision.

It was no accident that the information leaked by the government to various newspapers contained enough contradiction to make the public disregard it altogether. In fact, further examination of these articles will reveal to what extent this information was intended to be misleading.

First, all these articles appeared on the back pages of the newspapers, which automatically reduced their significance, especially to those busy individuals who read only the main headlines and skim the articles. The articles also received very little space, which tends to make them obscure and reduced their importance even more. Most people probably failed to take note at all.

Second, those who did take note of them were met with headlines that focused attention on color changes. The real news is the other changes that are planned, but these were given second billing in the stories and not mentioned at all in headlines. These articles were very cleverly constructed: The reader's interest was piqued by the heralding of a new-colored money in headlines since, as the surveys had already revealed to the government, most people are opposed to a new color. Then the body of the articles revealed that a new color was never really a serious consideration but that, because a counterfeiting deterrent is needed, some minor "invisible" changes might be made—no cause for alarm. Thus, rather than questioning why the Treasurer of the United States would show a highly responsible congressman on the Committee on Banking, Finance, and Urban Affairs a new-colored currency only to have, on the next day, other high governmental officials deny any color changes at all, readers automatically questioned Congressman Ron Paul's credibility, and the real question was forgotten.

Indeed, all of these conflicting reports have been a carefully engineered smoke screen intended to confuse the readers about the real dangers of the other, "lesser" anticounterfeiting measures under consideration. Color changes to prevent counterfeiting really aren't an issue at all. Allegedly, color change was one method considered in the past to combat the threat of new-generation color copiers. If that were the case, how could changing from our present color to others fool the new sophisticated copiers? And how is it that in the same breath we are told there will be no color change but there will be background tints of different colors? Is that not a color change? If the copiers are as good as they say, will a new tint pose any problem?

Furthermore, the whole counterfeiting explanation for a currency exchange is simply another delusion advanced by the government. At a recent government meeting to discuss this problem, a Secret Service agent boasted that about 90 percent of all counterfeiters are caught before they ever pass a single bill. In a story carried by *The New York Times*, October 30, 1983, we are told that the Secret Service seized $5 million in California and Nevada in bogus $100 bills. It was called one of the nation's biggest cases. Not only was not one bill passed, but the manufacturing plant was found and shut down as well.

Of all the bogus notes that are manufactured each year, less than 10 percent ever get into circulation. According to the Federal Reserve Bank of New York, the Secret Service found and seized, before circulation, $16.5 million of counterfeits in 1970, while an estimated $2.2 million were passed to the public by counterfeiters; $45 million of bogus notes were seized in 1975, while about $3.6 million were passed; and $55.3 million of phony notes were caught in fiscal 1980, while $5.5 million were passed. These figures show that an average of less than 10 percent of all counterfeits ever make it to the street.

These figures do show that the number of counterfeits seized each year has increased, but that is due to inflaton and not so much to an increase in the number of counterfeiters. Any business, legal or illegal, has its overhead (machinery must be purchased, workers paid, etc.). Counterfeits are usually sold, at the lowest level of wholesaling, at one half the price or less of face value. Because of inflation, making profits commensurate to the risk involved requires larger quantities of higher-denomination bills to be produced and passed. Inflation has made the lower-denomination bills so worthless that counterfeiters won't touch anything under a $20. Consequently, many business establishments won't accept $50s or $100s.

The government is aware of this. Legal currency is printed by a very costly engraving process called the *intaglio method.* This results in an extremely high-fidelity, fine-line document, which, because of its visual excellence and unique, three-dimensional feel, is most difficult to counterfeit and is recognized worldwide as the premier method of counterfeiting deterrence. The government dropped the use of the intaglio method on $1 bills in 1981 to save on printing costs because the $1 note is of such low value that it posed no threat whatsoever in terms of counterfeiting. If it were not for the stiff resistance coming from the printer's union, the government would probably switch to lower-cost printing methods for other denominations as well.

We should also note that the few millions of bad dollars that do get passed are not enough to justify spending hundreds of millions for new equipment to make the changeover. Figures have been circulating that the Bureau of Engraving and Printing has spent over $200 million on this project so far. You don't go around spending $200 million to prevent the loss of a few million.

With this also goes the inane argument that counterfeiters upset the money supply with the infusion of bogus bills. But when $170 billion is in circulation, a few million dollars will have little impact (.003 percent of $170 billion equals $5 million). Better yet, ask yourself when the last time was that you saw or got stuck with a counterfeit bill?

The greatest obstacle to counterfeiters has always been insurmountable for them: the secret, unique, unobtainable paper that the "real" stuff is printed on. If we are to believe the government's story that the new currency is intended merely to deter counterfeiting through the use of color tints and a new paper of different characteristics, how is that any better than our present colors and already secret, unable-to-be-duplicated paper?

The paper is a high-quality 75 percent cotton and 25 percent linen paper with red and blue fibers embedded in it. It is manufactured by only one company, the Crane and Company of Dalton, Massachussetts, under a highly secret process. In reality there is very little that is secret about the way this paper is made. It was developed by Crane and the Treasury department under a joint effort and came into use in 1879. It used to be 100 percent linen, then 75 percent, then 50 percent, before it was made with 25 percent linen. The cotton used to come from old cotton shirts obtained with the help of rag pickers, who would also remove the buttons and bleach the fabric white. Since most shirts are now made with synthetic fibers and colors that won't react to bleaching, Crane has switched to buying new rag cuttings—small squares of virgin fabric—from different textile companies.

This cotton is mixed, in a three-to-one ratio with linen, added to water, and beaten by large machines into a fiberless pulp mixture. The red and blue fibers are added at this stage so that they will become an integral feature of the paper. A measured quantity of pulp is poured into special molds that will allow the right size and thickness to be achieved with the dried sheets. These molds permit excess water to drain from the pulp, leaving a damp sheet slightly larger than specified to allow for shrinkage. Then the sheets are carefully transferred, or "couched," to wool mats. At this stage the sheets and mats are stacked and squeezed under a press to remove the remaining water.

Next, the sheets of paper are peeled away from the mats and placed on large screens, the loft, to quick-dry. The faster paper dries, the more durable it will be, and special care is taken to ensure rapid drying time. These screens allow drying from both sides and produce a very durable, quality paper suitable for circulation as currency.

Any paper that is used to print on must be treated by a process called *sizing*, which prevents printing ink from spreading when applied to paper. Without this sizing, paper would act as a blotter, soaking up and spreading out the ink. Sizing is especially important for currency paper, which has some extremely fine lines printed on it. Most experts agree the sizing used is glue made from a gelatin produced by boiling ears, tongues, hooves, and other parts of slaughtered animals. Dry sheets of paper are dipped into a bath containing the dissolved sizing material and then removed to be dried.

The final step involves pressing the paper between highly polished metal plates. Heavy rollers flatten these sandwiched sheets to very specific tolerances. Most of the other steps of manufacture could be duplicated by counterfeiters except this one. This final pressing requires very expensive high-pressure rollers that are beyond the reach of amateur paper makers. Treasury specs for paper thickness call for 0.0042 to 0.0045 inch in a very uniform thickness almost impossible to achieve without these rollers. Consequently, most counterfeits will be found on paper whose thickness is uneven and will fall outside these boundaries. It is this final pressing step that, more than anything else, makes the currency paper a "secret, unable-to-be-duplicated paper." The final sheets are rectangles of 53.5 by 63.0 centimeters, just the right size to make 32 bills, 8 down and 4 across.

There are two interesting stories that circulate among

printers concerning this paper. Many printers believe that, in the same way the colored fibers are made part of the paper, there are also small dots, few in number, randomly scattered in clusters across the paper and, although appearing to be printed, are an integral part of the paper.

Another feature that is believed to be a secret characteristic of currency paper is a total lack of a special fluorescence that must be put, by law, into all white paper that is manufactured. According to this, all white paper, when viewed under a "black light," will reflect a violet to very bright violet color, depending on the amount of fluorescence in the paper. Currency paper, when viewed under this light, will reflect no color and will look dull or dead. Using this principle, manufacturers have produced counterfeit bill detectors with a small compartment into which the suspected bill is inserted and bathed in this black light. If there is any fluorescence, the bill is a counterfeit.

Two other features that are supposed to be contained in the paper are magnetic ink and small invisible holes that riddle the entire sheet and can be seen under magnification.

It was discovered, after a little research, that not all these stories are true. When viewed under magnification, there *are* small dots on the paper. However, you will find that most of these dots can be erased and are merely dirt spots. A very few tiny dots won't come off with an eraser, but these appear to be more like ink spots from "sloppy" printing, if you can call it that, because they are so few and they are so very, very small. They are also the same color as the ink.

It is true that under a black light paper money emits no bright violet color. But other types of noncurrency white paper can be found that reflect little if any fluorescence.

As far as tiny holes are concerned, if you take a crisp clean new bill and hold it in front of a strong light, looking at it with a 10X magnifier, what appear to be little white dots or holes can be seen. They are connected by white lines that resemble very nearly the cracks or crazing that can be found in the glaze on antique porcelain objects. Take note that these crazed lines and holes are barely visible and it takes a while of looking before they come into focus. In any event, if these holes are there, they will have to be viewed under a microscope, which would probably reveal a lot of other peculiarities as well. This can hardly be effective as a counterfeit deterrence if they can only be seen under a microscope, but most likely this is where the other story of the printed dots originated.

Another common belief among those in the print trade is that color copiers must, also by law, be manufactured with a 1 percent error factor built into them. This is done, it is claimed, so that these machines cannot fully duplicate a color and are therefore useless as counterfeiting machines.

This information was checked out with the Xerox Corporation Manufacturing Division. The chief technician there stated that, although he could not speak with complete authority for machines of any other company, Xerox color copiers did have a 1 percent error factor. This was not because of any law or government dictate, but was due to limitations of the technology currently available. In other words, state of the art has, at best, a 1 percent error factor.

This was also indirectly confirmed in a phone interview with a Secret Service agent in the counterfeiting division. When asked about characteristics concerning fluorescence, little dots, and color copiers, the agent was reluctant to confirm or deny any of this because of the secret nature of the paper and the need to protect these secrets. However, the agent did say that whoever was accepting this information as true was being misled. Later in the conversation the agent did confirm that the ink now used is magnetic. There was other information given, however, that was vastly more interesting.

When asked about the color copiers, the agent stated these machines posed no threat whatsoever. As a matter of fact, lying there on the desk in front of him were a number of bogus bills that had been picked up the day before, which had been made on a color copier. The agent called them "pure crap." Anyone who took the time to look could easily detect phony money made on one of these copiers. The agent felt the technology needed for these machines to do any kind of decent job is at least 30 or 40 years off. The agent commented that a lot of people just don't look and that you would be surprised at the really bad stuff that gets passed.

What is interesting is that Xerox technicians are 1 percent away from perfection, and the Secret Service person thinks they're 30 to 40 years off the mark. And this new technology, which will provide a 1 percent improvement, is what has the government shaking in its boots in fear of a new epidemic of counterfeiting. A 1 percent improvement over a process an expert calls pure crap is hardly enough to be concerned about.

There are two other major points the agent touched on. The first dealt with the proposed changes for the new currency. The agent revealed that it was only a week before our discussion that the people from the Bureau of Engraving and Printing came to discuss the new changes. This agent expressed his dissatisfaction over these bureaucrats as much as any civilian would. It seems this was the umpteenth time they had come to discuss the new changes, and every time they did they were talking about either red or blue or some other color, but they never could seem to make up their minds.

When asked about other changes and the target date, the agent replied that no one knows for sure because these bureaucrats change their minds every week. Color changes were always the central theme, and a target date of 1990 was the newest release date mentioned. The agent reiterated that, even though 1990 was mentioned, as well as color changes, you could never really be sure with these bureaucrats since they had changed their minds quite often already.

The other interesting point had to do with counterfeiting itself. The agent stated that, outside of Florida where some big drug deals go down and large sums get passed, counterfeiting is dying out. For whatever reason, there has been a decrease and it seems to be a dying art. The agent's opinion was that counterfeiting requires too much skill. Other crimes are much easier to commit. Special mention was made of counterfeit credit cards and credit card numbers that are much easier to make or get. Someone just hunts through trash cans for carbons of the credit card slips and uses the numbers on them for different scams.

These credit card crimes have nothing to do with stolen cards. But they do use stolen numbers. Anytime a card is used, three copies are made on the different sales slips, two of which remain with the sales clerk. Crooks will hunt through trash bins of prestige specialty shops, high-priced type department stores, or any other business establishment frequented by high-credit-limit credit card users. Thse carbons will reveal number, expiration date, and signature.

Converting a number into cash requires a few steps. This can be explained by the following example. The con man will call an airport and order tickets for pickup at the airline's ticket counter, using a stolen number. The tickets are ordered in a name other than the cardholder's. The con artist then shows up, with phony ID if needed, and picks up the tickets. The ticket then is sold by the thief as a discounted hot ticket. There are other angles as well, but this example should suffice.

Moving up one grade, you find, for about $1,000, operations that buy credit card pressing machines. Compared to making phony money, making bogus credit cards is a breeze. There's no fancy fine-line filigree work to duplicate. To get the most mileage from a fake card, the maker must get a real number with the highest possible line of credit. In this case, the thieves are interested in getting the largest cash advance permitted on the account number.

Obtaining numbers with the highest cash advance credit lines is accomplished in many different ways. One simple ploy involves posing as the bank and calling the intended victim. The con man tells the victim the bank has decided to raise his credit line to $5,000. The victim replies that his credit line has always been $10,000. The con man then claims there must be some type of computer foul-up and asks the mark to read off the number on his card so that it can be double-checked against the bank's records.

Another con involves hanging around those blue credit-card-only telephones and nonchalantly listening to credit card numbers as they are given to the operator. With a number, thousands of dollars of long distance calls can be racked up without anyone's ever knowing.

The problem all these crimes have in common is the great lead time enjoyed by the criminal. If an actual credit card is stolen, it will be reported immediately, and that card will come up on the "hot sheet" in 24 hours maximum. Illegal use of numbers, on the other hand, will not show up until an inflated bill is issued to the cardholder. This can run anywhere from two to six weeks. If the swindler doesn't get carried away, the number can be used for at least two weeks undetected.

This is a crime that has been reported to be rising to major proportions and one that the card companies are trying desperately to keep the lid on for fear that publicity will tempt people and increase its frequency. Since it is infinitely cheaper and easier as a crime to commit than is the skilled crime of counterfeiting, it is bound eventually to reach epidemic proportions.

This leads to some very interesting observations. The Secret Service's counterfeit division, from the looks of its success rate, has extremely capable law enforcement personnel. The agent in the phone interview stated that 90–95 percent of all bogus bills are caught before they ever hit the streets. This figure represents a success rate that is difficult, if not impossible, to improve on. Counterfeiting money is an art that is dying out and being replaced with counterfeiting credit cards, a crime that gives the criminal plenty of lead time and that the victim is helpless to prevent, short of giving up the use of all credit cards.

The government is not stupid. It knows these things. Everything is being done to push us into a cashless society where credit cards and electronic banking are king. Yet, this is where the greatest threats of counterfeiting and fraud exist. Never mind that it also gives the officials the most convenient way to record all our financial transactions. Seasoned undergrounders and tax evaders leave no trails, paper or otherwise, to be traced. Electronic business transactions attempt to bring that under control. And credit card fraud has to be one of the easiest and comparatively most lucrative crimes to commit, as well as one of the hardest for law enforcement people to control.

On the other hand, we have paper currency, and the art of counterfeiting is becoming extinct. In this area we have a group of expert professionals at the Secret Service turning in what should be an award-winning success rate and making it almost impossible to pass out counterfeit money. Yet, the government wants us to believe this is where the threat lies. This is an insult to the Secret Service as well as to the American public.

For the sake of argument, let's say we believe the government's story about these new-fangled color copiers. Let's say they're as good as claimed. Instead of spending untold sums to recall and issue new currency because of the threat posed by these machines, why not simply require all manufacturers to make, by law, machines that have a built-in 3–5 percent error factor. These are very sophisticated machines your regular neighborhood counterfeiter has no way of manufacturing. Machines with built-in error would discourage casual use by office workers to make bogus bills.

The companies manufacturing these color copiers are building them anyway, and making them a little less perfect should not add any burden or cost. If there is some industry that would require a copier with ultrahigh color reproduction qualities, it could purchase one under a special permit and restrict usage to certain employees with security clearances.

It would be infinitely cheaper and easier for the government to regulate color copiers than it would be to keep track of billions of pieces of little paper. This should also be considered in light of official statements that most of the proposed changes designed to foil sophisticated color copiers will have no effect on the ability of a skilled professional counterfeiter to continue the art.

This could be done in conjunction with different countries in the world so that better-quality or unregulated machines in other countries could not be used to make bogus money outside the borders. After all, the big countries in the West are having all these meetings because they're so concerned over what to do. Regulating copiers would benefit all the world's countries since any nation's currency could be jeopardized. And if some nation did not agree, still making bogus bills and trying to smuggle quantities large enough to be worthwhile would add another difficult obstacle to an already risky endeavor.

This whole line of reasoning is purely academic since we know that these machines cannot hope to make paper money duplication anywhere near what their advance billing gives credit for. And if somehow they can, we have some crack troops at the Secret Service that can quash any feeble attempt to do so.

More Confusion

We've examined how government leaks have tried to manipulate the public into accepting a currency exchange on some moral grounds: to stop drug traffic and counterfeiting. We've also shown that the information that *has* appeared has been presented in such a manner as to mislead, confuse, and delude the public. Well, the confusion still runs rampant. Newspapers, newsletters, and other print sources disagree widely on whether there will actually be an exchange, when it will take place, and what the exchange ratio will be.

For example, on August 6, 1982, *The Kiplinger Washington Letter* reported "Rumors about recalling the dollar—We're getting a flood of reader mail on this. Nothing to it. Baloney." And in May 1982, the *U.S. News Washington Letter* wrote, "Currency reform ahead? Don't you believe it. A few promoters have been mailing flyers that predict a 'new dollar' is coming next year. Won't happen."

Other newsletters reported the coming exchange with varying degrees of urgency. *Barron's* magazine ran a full-length article on the exchange in its April 2, 1984, issue and hinted that the exchange is not the innocuous anticounterfeiting measure that it is claimed to be by the Establishment, but concluded that it is not really that big a deal either, thereby leaving the reader ultimately confused.

Most other publications have taken a sort of middle-ground stance. None deny the event, but they feel it will be a one-for-one exchange intended primarily to flush out underground money that most likely will allow an adequate grace period to turn in old for new.

One newsletter, the *Economic News Review and Financial Digest*, is of the opinion that the exchange will not be 1 for 1 but 10 or 100 for 1 and presented an interesting plan to make money during an exchange using regular clad coins. The newsletter points out that there are 150 billion coins in circulation. After silver coins were recalled in 1964, a coin shortage developed. In the three subsequent years, the U.S. Mint was able to produce only 15.5 billion coins. During the 1976 coin shortage, the U.S. Mint, through a massive all-out effort, was able to produce 13 billion coins in one year. If a swift paper exchange took place (let's say 10 for 1) it would be quite impossible to do the same with the coinage. To exchange coinage would require the call-in and release of new coins of different sizes. A new coin of the same size but different face value would render the old coin a perfect slug. So a coinage recall would demand that new-sized coins be introduced. This would take many years for the mint to accomplish. Much of the economy is run on coins, and to change over all existing vending machines, video games, Laundromat machines, slot machines, coin changers, bank coin counters, newspaper boxes, postage machines, pay phones, parking meters, toll gates, ad infinitum, would also take many, many years and wreak havoc not only in the private sector but within city and state governments as well. Therefore, unless there was a new mintage, old coins would keep the same face value after an exchange as before the exchange.

The newsletter advocates obtaining and hoarding clad coins. The idea is that, if the exchange is 10 for 1, then all prices will come down to $\frac{1}{10}$ preexchange levels. For example a $1.00 box of cereal will be reduced in cost to $.10. Trading in an old dollar for a dime will still enable that person to buy a box of cereal, but to the holder of $1.00 in coin, 10 boxes of cereal could now be purchased.

In this type of exchange, some kind of price controls would also be necessary to prevent the shop owner from dropping the price to an amount higher than the $\frac{1}{10}$. In the example of the box of cereal, a shop owner could drop the price to $.12 instead of $.10, which would be equal to a 20 percent price increase. (It may also be suggested that, since there has been no talk of a coinage recall, this portends a 1 for 1 exchange.)

On the other hand we have the *Pick World Currency Report*, that claims the coming call-in is not a true reform and will be made 1 for 1. This newsletter is published by Dr. Franz Pick, one of the world's most venerated currency and precious metals authorities. Dr. Pick feels that this new currency really is just to deter counterfeiting, dismissing those pushing other explanations as fanatics having lurid imaginations intending to exploit the ignorant. He claims that the government would not give a two-year advance warning of an exchange but would do so in the same manner in which MPCs (Military Payment Certificates, which are used by the military in occupied countries instead of greenbacks) that had found their way into the black market are recalled. In complete surprise announcements, MPCs would be exchanged in a matter of hours.

Dr. Pick also points out that most of the world, especially the underground markets of totalitarian countries, operate on a de facto U.S. dollar standard. An exchange would be devastating to these nations and far outweigh any advantages to be gained. He also states that there already are many countries that use security threads and it is nothing new. Dr. Pick's observations are most interesting since in the December 1979 issue of *Silver and Gold Report* (SGR), he created quite a stir when he predicted that in 12–24 months there would have to be a currency exchange of 100 to 1. When SGR again interviewed him in June 1981 he claimed his timetable had to be pushed back for two more years because interest rates had been raised.

Dr. Pick has five degrees including Ph.D.s in currency

theory, law, and deflation theory from the University of Leipzig, the University of Hamburg, and the Sorbonne in Paris. His vast practical experience includes service as paymaster of the French Resistance during World War II during which he played a major role in currency intelligence and underground finance. He is considered one of the world's top experts in black market activity and his advice is eagerly sought by bankers and top officials from world corporations and governments alike. He has lived through the destruction of the Austrian krone, the Czech koruna, the German mark, the French franc, and the British pound; and sees the U.S. dollar going through the exact same movements. Dr. Pick's ability to see the inevitable destruction and recall of the dollar but his inability to nail down a date (he's been off twice now by about two years each time), points to the unpredictability of the times we live in. Even with the vast knowledge and expertise Dr. Pick possesses, he cannot foresee when the inevitable will take place.

It all comes down to not whether a reform will occur, but, when will it occur? So far the government has been running around lying to us, first about drug dealers and then about counterfeiters. They deny stories they leak for years and then suddenly reverse themselves and announce the stories are true. And they will be able to circumvent Dr. Pick's objections as easily as they have his timetables.

For example, does it really matter if the people have been given advance warning? After hearing a story over and over—like the story of the boy who cried wolf—it begins to lose its credibility. Besides, the underground economy *must* continue to operate. Can it hold back cash and store it for years in valuables such as gold and silver because it anticipates an exchange?

And to make matters worse, the American people have grown apathetic and nonresistant to forces coercing their lives. They think in the backs of their minds that it would never really happen, that people would revolt if it did; but, were there any revolts when the energy shortage was contrived and there were long lines at the gas pumps? Were there any revolts when people sat in front of their TVs watching huge oil tankers waiting but not allowed to dock, while simultaneously being told that the world was running out of oil and we must conserve? Were there any revolts when the price of gasoline was jacked up to $1.50? You see, a lot of people don't care or don't believe it. They are more interested in a six-pack of beer and watching Dallas in the Super Bowl. It's sort of like the bread and circus days of the Roman Empire.

And does the government really need to worry itself over the de facto use of the U.S. dollar as a world currency? It could go about its flushing of the U.S. underground while imposing strict controls on the movement of greenbacks out of the country. It could set a different exchange period for greenbacks outside the country to give more time for other people. Whenever a dollar that sits in your pocket loses value due to inflation it's like having an invisible exchange of dollars. If these other lands live with a dollar of declining value, what would be so rough about a real exchange?

And what about security threads? As will be explained in more detail later, the anti-counterfeiting recall is to be coordinated with six other countries which include Great Britain, Switzerland, and West Germany. The currencies of these countries already contain a security thread but they are still concerned with the threat of counterfeiting. What have they done—invent a new type of thread that is more counterfeit proof?

This rebuttal is not meant to attack Dr. Pick but to point out that in our present monetary straits, nothing is certain but uncertainty itself.

FURTHER PROOF THAT THE TIME HAS COME

Despite the widespread disagreement over the currency exchange, all we need to do to see that the call-in is inevitable and imminent is to examine the rate of inflation predicted for coming years.

An exchange simply *has* to take place because as the value

of the dollar goes down and the price of goods go up, we will eventually be dealing with figures that are too burdensome to manage. To get a handle on this, check these price increases for the last 17 years:

	1967	1984	
New Car	$3,500–$4,500	$10–20,000	(450% increase)
New Volkswagen	$1,800	$7–8,000	
New Home	$15,000	$75,000	(500% increase)
Gasoline	$.25–.35/gal	$1.40	(470% increase)
Gold	$32.00/ ounce	$400/ounce	(1,250% increase)
Silver	$1.00/ounce or less	$9–10/ounce	(1,000% increase)

According to the Office of Management and Budget, by the year 2000, the *official* Fed budget will increase 7½-fold to $7.5 trillion; the Bureau of Labor Statistics at the U.S. Department of Labor says public debt will increase 9-fold to reach $9 trillion; and the Federal Reserve Board puts the total credit market at 14 times today's figures, for $26 trillion. Unofficial estimates place these figures much, much higher. However, by just using these official projections we can get an idea what items of everyday use will cost by the year 2000:

Gasoline	$14/gal (20-gal fill-up = $280)
Man's Dress Shirt	$200
Automobile	$100,000
with A/C extra	$7,000
New Home	$1,000,000
Doctor's Office Visit	$450
Groceries (1 week, family of 4)	$1,200

Soda	$5/can
Milk	$18/gal
Bread	$10/loaf
Hamburger	$16/lb
Cigarettes	$11/pack
Lipstick	$40

Remember, these are conservative estimates. These figures have been estimated by simply taking the prices of some ordinary items and increasing them 10-fold. This is if we do not have extreme inflation caused by big corporate, city, foreign government, or bank bailouts by the Fed (which will invariably occur).

The number of bills a person would have to carry just to make it through the day would leave room in his pockets for nothing else. As a matter of fact, we would all have to carry handbags just to handle common everyday expenses such as pay phones, parking meters, and bus fare.

Congressman Ron Paul, in a series of radio interviews in May 1984 (a copy of the complete text is available from Southwest Radio Church, PO Box 1144 Oklahoma City, OK; publication number B-453, "The Coming Currency Exchange") said he anticipated a 1-for-1 exchange if the recall were to take place in the very near future. However, he felt that in 1985, 1986, or 1987 inflation would be 20–30 percent, and if an exchange were delayed to these later dates, a greater-than-1-for-1 exchange would become a very distinct possibility.

If inflation were to set in at 25 percent average per year until the year 2000, our new projections would look like this (previous projection figures in parentheses):

Gasoline	($14/gal)	$50/gal
Man's Dress Shirt	($200)	$710
Automobile	($100,000)	$355,270
with A/C extra	($7,000)	$24,870
New Home	($1,000,000)	$3,552,715

Doctor's Office Visit	($450)	$1,600
Groceries	($1,200)	$4,265
Soda	($5/can)	$17.75/can
Milk	($18/gal)	$64/gal
Bread	($10/loaf)	$35.50/loaf
Hamburger	($16/lb)	$57/lb
Cigarettes	($11/pack)	$39/pack
Lipstick	($40)	$142

As you can see, the figures start to look ridiculous, especially with talk of eliminating $50s and $100s. Why, just to send your kid to the store for a loaf of bread, a gallon of milk, and two packs of cigarettes would cost you $177.50. A 10-for-1 exchange would reduce this figure to $17.75, and a 100-for-1 exchange would put it at $1.75. An exchange of this type would allow inflation to keep going while maintaining figures the public could handle as well as disrupting the black market. The government could repudiate its debt and start all over. This would also provide an opportunity to install wage and price controls.

Those who are to ultimately decide what ratio exchange will take place are fully aware of these facts and figures. Just think how attractive it looks to them to enact a greater-than-1-for-1 exchange. The authorities have amply demonstrated their ability to lie, cheat, and steal with relative impunity. As their rapacious propensities increase, will they be content to allow an opportunity to pass, by which they can feed their insatiable power-mad egos yet another accession?

So, maybe there will be a 10- or 100-for-1 exchange, and maybe there won't be. But one thing is certain. It has got to come, and—sometime within the next five years will present an ideal time to do so—the sooner the better, as far as the government is concerned.

Another piece of evidence that the exchange is coming is that the government apparently is already prepared for it. Tucked into the side of a mountain in Culpeper, Virginia, is the Emergency Relocation Facility (ERF), whose purpose is to allow the Federal Reserve to carry on its duties in the event of some natural catastrophe or nuclear war. This agency contains a communication network and elaborate records storage facility, in addition to a store of 700 million bills of replacement currency of various denominations.

There is a unique department within this facility called "Special Projects." This Special Projects Department contains two divisions, one of which is the "Currency Sorter and Counter Division," which is headed up under Mr. John Stoides, officer in charge.

According to a phone interview with Mr. Stoides, the division is working on the development of a high-speed money counter, one with the capability to count and sort 72,000 bills per hour. The Fed presently owns a half-dozen or so high-speed counters that can sort and count 55,000 bills per hour. By mid-1983, the Fed will order 110 new machines, which will increase the Fed's capabilities by 2,200. According to Stoides, the procurement of these new machines will enable the Fed to count and sort every piece of currency in the nation in four days or less!

Mr. Stoides was working on another project in conjunction with the Treasury Department and was not at liberty to discuss it for security reasons. When asked if increased sort/ count capabilities and storage of a replacement currency is tied into plans to introduce a new U.S. currency in the near future, he responded by saying that the Fed had discussed, on a few occasions, redesigning U.S. currency. He added that one of the difficulties encountered by such a move would involve citizens of foreign and communist countries who "illegally" use U.S. currency in the black market and who hold it as a means of escape. These people would be disinherited by a currency conversion. He did note that a simple solution would be to let both new and old currency circulate side by side until the old could be phased out.

It appears that the Fed has installed the apparatus and printed the new currency. It now needs only to figure out a way to secure a smooth changeover.

That the Fed is so well prepared was borne out by two items in the January 1982 edition of *Common Sense Newsletter* in an article entitled "Good-bye Greenbacks." The first mentioned that bank employees across the country have noticed that new currency, which used to be delivered from the Fed in sealed transparent cases, so that it could be counted from the outside, is now being delivered in opaque cases and stored uncounted in a special corner of the vault. The second item reported that, after a bank vault robbery in Los Angeles, the manager couldn't tell a TV interviewer how much was taken and said that it did not matter because the thief *wouldn't be able to spend it yet!*

What's this? The Fed is spending time and effort to ship and store sealed cases of concealed bills that can't be spent yet, and at the same time buying counting machines that can count all the currency in just four days?

The Bottom Line

So far, the most authoritative and detailed information on the subject has been revealed by former Congressman Ron Paul of the 22nd district in Texas. Based on a number of radio interviews and other sources, the following points about the currency exchange have been made by Congressman Paul:

1. The new money will be issued by a central Federal Reserve bank in an effort to remove any last restrictions placed on it by branch reserve requirements.

2. The new money will have a different appearance; tints, bar graphs, and metal fragments or strips have been mentioned predominantly. These will be used by the banks to monitor the flow of money through the economy and through other lands. Free movement of dollars across borders will be restricted.

3. The new U.S. currency is being issued in conjunction with Canada, Japan, West Germany, Switzerland, Great Britain, and Australia, which will all utilize similar emendations in a probable effort to internationalize these currencies.

4. Even though the official stance is to deter counterfeiting, the flushing out of underground money, possible repudiation of the national debt, and the opportunity to subject the people further are more probable causes.

5. As it stands, the recall will probably be 1-for-1 but could

be a greater ratio, depending on the state of the dollar at the time the recall is effected. If, for example, the recall is made while there are high rates of inflation, say at 20–30 percent, a greater-than-1-for-1 exchange is likely to occur.

6. Contrary to long grace periods the government people refer to, there are strong chances the recall will be rapid, possibly occurring in 30 days or less. Millions and millions of Americans will find themselves in jeopardy for having hidden money not reported and may be indicted for tax evasion.

Some might argue the exchange period would have to be longer than 30 days. For example, there are many people with perfectly legitimate reasons that have money in places like safe deposit boxes who might be out of the country vacationing or on business at the time a recall is enacted. Affluent businesspeople or vacationers jeopardized by a quick recall, some of whom might hold high positions of influence in our society, could scream loud enough to effect change. Still, a swift 30-day-or-less exchange could be made with, let's say, special extensions to those individuals who find themselves abroad.

It appears there will be a trade-off as to how fast an exchange is desired in relation to how many toes the government is willing to step on. However, we should not underestimate the uncanny ability of the powercrats to foresee and circumvent problems of this nature. You can be sure that the high-salaried bureaucrats they employ to solve these types of contingencies will demonstrate they are more than able to rise to the occasion. The ingenuity that manifests from a bureaucrat when asked to sit up and speak by the master can truly astound.

A great example of this recently took place with an event that was completely overlooked by the public as well as most of the business community. By declaring that there had always been an error in bookkeeping practices, which they have now corrected, the Fed was able to expand the money supply by 5 percent with no indications of that expansion reflected in the official figures.

This expansion was actually a banking and political maneuver to allow a 5 percent increase in the money supply without ever having to report it. This was done to relieve pressure on the banks and the politicians and was accomplished with amazing ease—effortlessly done with the stroke of a pen. This example demonstrates the adroit skills possessed by bureaucrats who are usually taken for idiots.

7. Japan, Great Britain, West Germany, Australia, Switzerland, and Canada will begin their exchange previous to that of the U.S. They become bellwether nations, and, by monitoring their exchange programs, we can be tipped off to the date of our own coming exchange. Our exchange should come right at the end of theirs.

Japan has, in fact, introduced its new currency. In a special report on world currency put out by the Mitsubishi Corp. in its September 1984 *Tokyo Newsletter,* the new currency is described. It is smaller, has new portraits, large and distinct watermarks, intermediate color shades that are adopted in profusion, indentations in the lower left-hand corner for the convenience of the blind, and "special inks." What is in this ink that makes it special is not mentioned. Inks that are used in the production of currency have always been special. They are made with colors that are difficult to match and mixed with certain chemicals that cause them never to fully dry. It is possible these inks are the special magnetic inks, able to be encoded, we have been expecting. Right now, in the currency of Israel, there is a magnetic filament that is said to spell out magnetically, in Morse code, the name of the central bank. Could it be that, instead of a magnetic filament, technology has created a new ink that can take the place of a filament?

8. Those in control of the exchange program do not need any congressional approval to carry out this plan, and their continuing prevarications are all designed to keep Congress and everyone else in the dark. And, to make matters worse, the Congress, along with much of the population, considers monetary reform an irksome triviality.

9. The international banking cabal, as demonstrated by the Argentine bailout, is powerful enough to bypass the Congress and dictate government policy.

10. The policymakers are not concerned with any shock-waves that would be sent through world markets, including those of totalitarian countries that depend on the U.S. dollar as a means to preserving freedom.

With these points in mind, we look at other aspects of the current economic climate. Chapter 7 will show that, despite the appearance of newfound stability, the American economy is in probably the worst straits since the nation's birth.

7
THE ILLUSION OF STABILITY—EYE OF THE STORM

At this point it should be obvious that many stand to lose much of their wealth when the transition from old money to new money takes place. Up to one-third of GNP will come under attack by this move. And wealth is not the only thing that will be threatened; the exchange will also precipitate the greatest attack on our personal freedoms that this country has ever experienced. Already there are many subtle indications that the authorities are maneuvering for this onslaught. One example is that, under the most "conservative" administration in recent history, the IRS continues, unhampered, to augment its power and influence and has arrogantly stepped up aggressive assaults against people and business.

Add to this other factors that we have dicussed so far:

1. **Inflation is permanent**. Unless we make drastic changes in our economic system, inflation is here to stay. Inflation's tenacious grip is reinforced by:

- use of banking reserves other than gold, such as SDRs, notes, bonds, certificates, paper, etc.

- the Monetary Control Act of 1980 and current emergency banking regulations; a banking system (both national and international) that is financed by the American taxpayer, a system whereby weak, profligate, and unprincipled loans are guaranteed by the same taxpayers
- massive foreign aid, giveaways, bailouts, and huge military expenditures
- the unrestricted and irresponsible use of influence and power by special-interest groups clamoring for more and more
- a political system dominated by politicians who either are willing or are forced to engage in something-for-nothing schemes and handouts in order to buy votes
- a bureaucratic system that constantly expands in size and power; consumes greater amounts of manpower and goods; imposes wasteful, impractical, and contradictory regulations on business and the people; and is accountable not to the public or their elected representatives but to power brokers whose identities are generally unknown
- a foreign policy that is determined to place the needs and interests of America last, while placing those of foreign countries first (one-worldism). For example, in recent history, the U.S. has been abandoning friends while kowtowing to enemies. Sensing weakness, these nations increase their belligerence toward us while we seek to appease them with foreign aid. At the same time, we must increase our military strength to defend against potential threat
- a government in which the people are powerless to stop debt, deficit spending, and growth
- an economic system controlled by obdurate international bankers and multinational corporations that have no roots, pledge allegiance to no one but themselves, and use the American taxpayer to underwrite their global adventures
- a system of taxation whereby the producers are penalized with higher taxes and nonproducers are awarded handouts (welfare state)

- a huge, mounting national debt and the interest ($33.12 million per day) that must be paid on this debt (The government is desperate for increased revenues, and it plans to tax Social Security payments and previously untaxed pensions beginning in 1985. The debt ceiling was recently raised to an official $2 trillion. The real debt, according to the National Taxpayers' Union, using government figures, unofficially stands at $13.6 trillion, which includes the Social Security system's potential unfunded liability of over $5 trillion. *Not included in this figure is private, state and local debt.* This is a disgrace. If we take the official $2 trillion figure, about $8,500 of debt is owed by every man, woman, and child in the U.S. If the real debt figure of $13.6 trillion is used, however, approximately $58,000 is owed by every man, woman, and child in the country. It is obvious this debt will never be repaid. The government raises the debt ceiling regularly and plans to hyperinflate the debt away or attempt to eliminate a large portion via a tax increase and currency recall.)
- record-setting balance-of-payment deficits that continue to skyrocket with each passing month (This problem has finally pushed America into the debtor nation status for the first time in 70 years.)
- an uninformed, indifferent, acquiescent public that still favors large, expanding government and government solutions to social problems despite dismal failures in this area
- continuing government waste
- unsound paper money that can be manipulated politically
- a morally bankrupt and dishonest government

2. **A multipronged attack headed by a return to a gold standard, a repeal of the Federal Reserve Act and the 16th Amendment, equitable elimination of the national debt, outlawing of government deficit spending, and the reduction of size and function of government would go most of the way toward solving our current problems.** There must be a return to a morally just constitutional republic as laid down by the

Founding Fathers and a return to constitutional law. (Where there is a separation of powers, it is illegal to issue money other than gold or silver, all bills for raising revenue must originate in the House of Representatives; our present system of taxation is illegal, etc.)

Since it is unlikely that these things will happen, it is safe to assume that inflation has become a permanent feature of our present economic system. It would appear that nothing short of a complete economic or military disaster resulting in the destruction of the entire system would cause an abandonment of our present course.

So, we know that our freedom is in grave jeopardy, an exchange is coming, and inflation is permanent. With these major points in mind, all we need now is to examine the current political and economic climate to determine what course of action to take in order to preserve our wealth and freedom.

THE NATIONAL DEBT AND TAXES

Let us examine the current debt and tax problem. According to *The Spotlight*, December 17, 1984, in 1982 the interest paid on all loans was nearly 27 percent of the GNP. The figures given take into account all federal, state, local, and private debt and also consider unreported income from the underground economy. Foreign debt is also reflected in the calculations because reimbursement of any loans that default will fall on the American taxpayer. This type of action has already taken place in part through agencies such as the IMF.

Updating to 1984, *Spotlight* goes on to state that, because taxes and interest have risen so much since 1982, much more rapidly than disposable income, taxes and interest now undoubtedly amount to 60 percent of all personal income.

Deficit spending, the national debt, and interest on the debt continue to rise. Recent slowed economic growth, which has reduced the GNP, thereby reducing tax receipts, plus additional spending and the inability or unwillingness of Congress to make cuts in expenditures, add to the problem. "Temporary" debt ceilings become "permanent" debt ceilings only to be replaced later by other "temporary" and then again more "permanent" ceilings.

To visualize the grave problem we face from a runaway debt, examine the following graph, reproduced from Dr. E. L. Anderson's 1984 revision of his essay "Upright Spike." Note that both scales, years and dollars, are scaled arithmetic, with equal intervals between the dollar figures and the years. This represents a much more realistic picture than the "ratio charts," which are often presented to the public and distort the facts.

As Dr. Anderson points out, this chart shows that, if the current trend continues, the national debt is headed for almost an infinite figure in just a few years. Ironically, this is the case during what many consider the most conservative presidency of the 20th century. We now have the largest deficit that the U.S. or any other country has ever had, with a runaway budget of almost $1 trillion for 1985.

Anderson sees no change in this disastrous trend, pointing to the fact that, after taking 155 years from the ratification of the Constitution to reach $100 billion in 1942, the national debt has taken only 42 years to reach more than 15½ times that, to the current total of $1,824 billion.

Extrapolating, we can expect the national debt to double by the end of 1986 and to reach four or five times that figure by the end of 1987.

The dangers of this trend can also be seen in terms of interest payments and a 15 percent annual increase in the deficit. The following two tables are reproduced from the December 17, 1984, issue of *Spotlight.*

The Spotlight explains the tables as follows: "As a percentage of the GNP, the federal taxpayer debt has grown from 28 percent in fiscal year 1980, to an estimated 37 percent in 1985 and 39 percent in 1986. Ultimately, the interest payments on the federal debt will cause the U.S. economy to collapse. The government borrows to pay the interest, with no thought of ever repaying the debt itself. The result, realistically, is that the federal debt will rise to about $322 trillion by the year

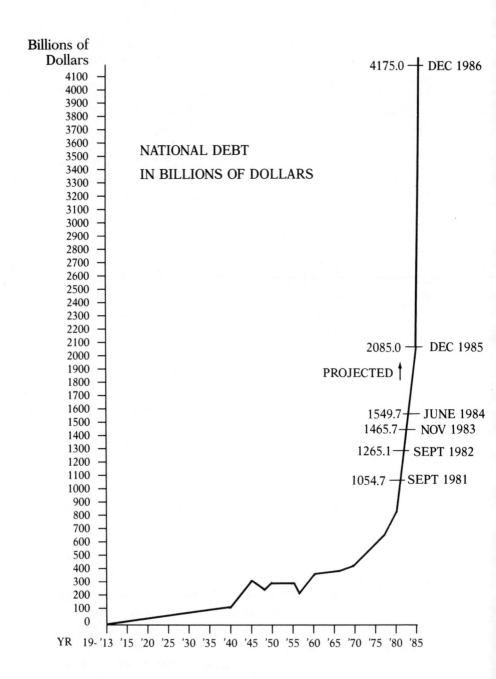

Billions of Dollars

NATIONAL DEBT
IN BILLIONS OF DOLLARS

4175.0 ── DEC 1986

2085.0 ── DEC 1985

PROJECTED ↑

1549.7 ── JUNE 1984
1465.7 ── NOV 1983
1265.1 ── SEPT 1982
1054.7 ── SEPT 1981

YR 19- '13 '15 '20 '25 '30 '35 '40 '45 '50 '55 '60 '65 '70 '75 '80 '85

Chart from Dr. E. L. Anderson's 1984 revision of "Upright Spike" as reprinted from *The Spotlight*, 300 Independence Avenue, SE, Washington DC, 20003.

2000, if our form of government lasts that long. The interest on this federal debt will be, for that year alone, $111 trillion (Table A). This projection is based on interest rates rising to 30 percent. It is not unlikely the scenario will be even worse. With interest rates going from 10 percent to 40 percent between now and 2000, the federal debt would hit more than $608 trillion by 2000 and the interest payment for that year alone would hit $208 trillion (Table B). This is without even being pessimistic. It is possible America could become like Israel today, which has an inflation rate of 800 percent and growing. Should that be the case you would have to stop thinking in terms of trillions of dollars and go to quadrillions or quintillions of dollars. Your cup of coffee at the corner cafe could cost you a million dollars."

TABLE A*
15% Annual Increase in Deficit

Year	Federal Debt Trillions	Additional Deficit Billions	Interest On Debt Billions	Interest Percent
1983	$ 1.500	$ 225	$ 172	10.00%
1984	1.897	284	243	11.17
1985	2.424	363	344	12.35
1986	3.131	469	487	13.52
1987	4.087	613	691	14.70
1988	5.391	808	984	15.88
1989	7.183	1,077	1,409	17.05
1990	9.669	1,450	2,027	18.23
1991	13.146	1,971	2,934	19.41
1992	18.051	2,707	4,273	20.58
1993	25.031	3,754	6,264	21.76
1994	35.049	5,257	9,246	22.94
1995	49.552	7,432	13,743	24.11
1996	70.727	10,609	20,573	25.29
1997	101.909	15,286	31,022	26.47
1998	148.217	22,232	47,124	27.64
1999	217.573	32,635	72,118	28.82
2000	322.326	48,348	111,202	30.00

*Reprinted with permission of *The Spotlight*, 300 Independence Ave., S.E., Washington, DC 20003.

TABLE B*
15% Annual Increase in Deficit

Year	Federal Debt Trillions	Additional Deficit Billions	Interest On Debt Billions	Interest Percent
1983	$ 1.500	$ 225	$ 172	10.00%
1984	1.897	284	256	11.76
1985	2.437	365	379	13.52
1986	3.181	477	559	15.29
1987	4.217	632	827	17.05
1988	5.676	851	1,228	18.82
1989	7.755	1,163	1,836	20.58
1990	10.754	1,613	2,764	22.35
1991	15.131	2,269	4,196	24.11
1992	21.596	3,239	6,427	25.88
1993	31.262	4,689	9,939	27.64
1994	45.890	6,883	15,521	29.41
1995	68.294	10,244	24,485	31.17
1996	103.023	15,453	39,027	32.94
1997	157.503	23,625	62,862	34.70
1998	243.990	36,598	102,332	36.47
1999	382.920	57,438	168,372	38.23
2000	608.730	91,309	280,015	40.00

Note that these tables are based on the somewhat optimistic projection that interest rates will rise from 10 to 40 percent by the year 2000. We will undoubtedly see high double-digit inflation and interest rates in the very near future.

THE LIQUIDITY CRISIS

Another huge problem ready to explode in the face of the banking system is the liquidity crisis. Today, it seems everyone has his or her money in money market funds. These funds promise the highest interest rates, combined with instant

---

*Reprinted with permission of *The Spotlight*, 300 Independence Ave., S.E., Washington, DC 20003.

access to funds whenever needed. It is not possible to take depositors' money, lend it out so that it can generate revenue, and offer depositors' access to that money at any time desired. It is impossible to offer the depositor instant liquidity while this money must circulate in order to generate more money. The system works on the premise that not everyone will show up at the same time demanding liquidity (fractional reserve banking). Right now this is working, but what happens when some crisis precipitates a rush of depositors demanding their funds all at once?

The banks are teetering on the edge of total collapse. They are overextended in loans to Third World countries that have no hope of ever being able to repay those loans. Many of these loans were made based on the expected income from the sale of petroleum. With the present world oil glut and the drastic drop in the price of crude oil, these countries are helpless and angry about the stranglehold the international bankers have on their economies.

Of particular interest, though it is receiving little press coverage, is that the oil-rich country of Saudi Arabia is on the verge of economic collapse. The oil glut has cut Saudi oil revenues from $110 billion in 1981 to $41 billion in 1984, against which the Fahd regime spent $63.8 billion.

Because of its decision to finance Iraq's war with Iran, King Fahd was forced to withdraw $26 billion from foreign bank accounts in 1984. After shelling out $132 billion to Iraq in the last five years, there is no end to the war in sight, and Iran has vowed to fight until it topples the Iraqi government. Considering Iran's zealous fanaticism, that nation most likely will fight until it achieves this goal or destroys itself in the process. This will cause a steady drain of Saudi funds that will push Saudi Arabia closer to the brink of collapse.

The Saudi Investment Bank (a Chase Manhattan subsidiary) and six other private banks are staggering under annual profit losses of more than 75 percent. The Saudis have withdrawn $165 billion from foreign reserves. Tipped off that King Fahd planned to withdraw another $50 billion in 1985 alone, the banks scrambled and demurred at this demand by invoking complicated contractual agreements. In other words, the banks just don't have the money.

This lucid example of a bank liquidity crisis demonstrates what could happen if some dilemma caused a rash of withdrawals from domestic banks. We could have a modern-day bank run, an event we are told cannot happen anymore. In one sense, this is true because depositors will be told to wait patiently, while in the back rooms the paper money will be printed up—the losses being passed on to the entire population via inflation.

The Saudi problem is a very serious one for the Reagan Administration. David Rockefeller has informed VP George Bush that only massive U.S. government intervention can stave off a total disintegration of the banking system. President Reagan is in a quandary because he has been advised that not only would such an intervention bring an end to Reaganomics and American prosperity, but that the high taxation and inflation necessary to save the banks also would polarize the nation and probably bring about violent social unrest.

In the meantime, the Saudis have been dumping tons of gold, along with the Soviets and South Africans, to pay their way until they can pry funds loose from the banks. This is helping greatly to keep the price of the precious metal down. When the Saudis run out of gold, they will again be at the banks' doors, demanding their money. The banks are expected to sidestep these demands once again. The banks' refusal to honor their commitments will cause a drastic response by the Saudis, which could jeopardize the already fragile liquidity predicament the banks must face.

As of January 1985, the price of OPEC oil was set at a shaky $28 per barrel. Many producers of oil (about two-thirds of the world's oil is non-OPEC), notably Nigeria and Mexico, are suffering from severe economic problems and desperately need oil revenues to stay afloat. Nigeria is selling all it can pump for whatever price it can get, and Mexico, which constantly undercuts OPEC prices, is contemplating increasing production by 200,000 barrels or more per day if its economy slips any further.

There are many Saudi competitors for world oil dollars besides Mexico and Nigeria, including Libya, Britain, Norway, USSR, and the United Arab Emirates. In the meantime, Iran has been selling oil at $23 per barrel. The bankers have admitted that the price of oil cannot drop below $25 per barrel without causing a major banking crisis.

A triple effect is being felt by many Texas banks, whose revenues are tied to the price of oil in the $27- to $29-per-barrel range and cannot survive lower prices. If natural gas prices come down to compete with oil, independent oil and gas companies would be severely weakened, which would bring additional downward pressure on land prices in the U.S., which is already suffering from low farm prices. This in turn would mean heavy losses for hundreds of banks.

Since this writing, the price of oil has dropped into the $15 per barrel range. It will be interesting to note what kinds of fallout will occur if the price stays in this range. Most likely, some smaller or very weak banks may be sacrificed and allowed to fold, while bigger banks will see the Fed step in and save the day. As stated already, rescue moves like this will have an inflationary impact.

The government has promised the public that no banks will be allowed to fail. There was a great increase in the size of the FDIC's troubled bank list in 1984, and bank failures throughout the country have been making headline news. Of course, what this means is, through inflation, there will be mass transferal of wealth from the citizenry to the banks.

At this point, you may be saying, well, inflation is down, stocks are up, interest rates are good, the dollar is strong, the economy is growing, tax cuts and reform are coming, unemployment is decreasing, a spending freeze has been called for, and America is enjoying a renewed world leadership position. How can the outlook for the future be so negative?

THE DELUSION OF REAGANOMICS

The answer lies with Ronald Reagan. The whole thing is resting on the illusion of stability Reagan is so adept at projecting. He has a somewhat charismatic personality and the uncanny knack to walk through the muck and come out smelling like a rose. Nothing sticks. He is able to tell the people the right things at the right time even though his actions betray his rhetoric. It can be said he is a very capable actor playing, extremely successfully, the greatest role of his life.

Reagan is responsible for the renewed patriotism and reversal of the national malaise experienced in recent times, especially under President Jimmy Carter. His economic policies, dubbed *Reaganomics*, have caused a turnaround in our economy and promise to take us to new heights. It is this Reagan euphoria that temporarily staves off collapse, until the next great stopgap measure, the currency exchange, can be implemented.

Let's examine how Reaganomics works. President Reagan recently declared he will impose a "freeze" on spending. He tells us, though, that Social Security will not be affected. This serves to allay the fears of the elderly, the disabled, and others who depend on Social Security. Then he states that interest on the debt cannot be altered. As he speaks, there is a degree of remorse but courage in his voice as he leads us to believe his bold new measures will pull us out of another mess. He is able to convey this persuasively as he acts the part beautifully. We become convinced as he declares that even defense spending is subject to cuts. In reality, this is not the case.

Social Security payments will not be cut but were taxed for the first time ever in 1984. Checks continue to go out, but the government will take back any Social Security it pays that puts you above certain income levels. Cost of living increases (COLA) also have been sacked. Increases will be made in the coming years, but what good will increased payments be when the value of currency is rapidly disintegrating? Would $1,000 a week in Social Security mean anything if a loaf of bread costs $100?

The interest on the debt is also sacrosanct because payment goes to the bankers. A great portion of this interest goes to the Federal Reserve System, which at year end reverts back to the government in the form of an excise tax. Therefore, a large portion of the interest payment is merely another government tax. No wonder the debt must be serviced. It is a source of revenue for the government.

And where is the freeze on the billions that go into foreign aid that will be increased. We pour countless sums into Japan, Europe, Central America, Africa, Israel, and the Middle East. Meanwhile, at home, services go down while taxes go up. The populace must tighten their belts, programs are slashed, farmers are cut off, austerity measures must be invoked, but foreign aid is increased, along with military buildup.

What about the much-touted tax reforms we so eagerly await? The president has sent out the cry that changes must be made to simplify the tax system and that loopholes must be eliminated. What he speaks of is an increase disguised as a cut, depite his adamant denial of this fact. He tells us that with the coming reforms tax rates will be reduced but that ultimately there will be an increase in revenues. Shuffling figures, which ultimately results in more, not less, revenues, can hardly be construed as reform. The reform alluded to merely deals with getting everyone to pay his or her "fair share." The trouble is, what David Rockefeller's, J.P. Getty's, Armand Hammer's, or John Q. Public's fair share is is anyone's guess. *Fair share* is a meaningless doublespeak phrase the politicians sling at the public. The public then chimes in: yes, yes, everyone must pay a fair share.

One so-called answer to this fair share question is the different flat tax reforms that are grabbing the public's attention. But the flat taxers play the same word games. That is, increase revenues and call it a reform, eliminate some deductions while complicating the rules and call it simplification, and maintain multiple brackets and call them flat. In fact, a family of four with a 30,000 per year income itemizing deductions would find they would be paying more in taxes under the different flat tax proposals than in our present system.

Lots of big talk centers around getting businesses to pay their fair share. The press constantly reminds us that many major corporations pay nothing each year. The problem is that, as previously stated, any increase in business tax will result in an increase in the price of goods or services to the consumer. Business has long had to treat taxes as part of the basic cost to produce, and a tax increase will simply increase preprofit expenses.

True reform means reduction in spending, size of government, budget deficits, debt, *and* taxes. The aggregate whole of tax revenues must come down. We should not settle for more taxes paid by a redistribution of the tax burden as a way of getting everyone's "fair share."

Ronald Reagan and Reaganomics are merely exercises in word juggling. Reaganomics has probably worked more in part because of the big drop in the price of oil and energy than for any other reason. By scrutinizing President Reagan's tax reform, you can see the real goal of this word jugglery. What his plan really proposes is to attack small independent businesses and entrepreneurs and create banks as the only safe haven for money.

For instance, tax deduction for overnight travel will be limited to two times what the government daily allowance for the same expenses would be. On the surface, this seems fair until you realize that government people get reduced rates at hotels, drive in government vehicles filled with cheap subsidized fuel, and eat in subsidized cafeterias.

Reagan also wants to change the depreciation schedule so that accelerated deductions are no longer available. The proposal will limit interest rate deductions allowed for investments and entirely remove tax investment credits that many businesses use to subsidize current business strategies. This will result in businesses shying away from purchasing big-ticket items. The consequences are that companies and especially independent entrepreneurs will lose incentives to be growth-oriented and will cut expansion (and may cause some marginally weak companies to close down completely).

Middle-class Americans will be hurt by limits that will be placed on the amount of interest deductions allowed on itemized returns. There will be no tax investment credits. Many items will no longer be deductible, and interest expense deductions will be limited to the taxpayer's primary residence.

The most important "reform" will be elimination of the "loopholes" that allow tax shelters to exist.

Most of these loopholes, which allow *certain* shelters to exist, are actually business deductions and not some elaborate esoteric tax-shelter scheme that is available only to the super-rich. Their repeal are designed to affect mainly independent middle- and upper-class producers. As a matter of fact, many of these situations involve what are commonly referred to as the "poor man's tax shelters." Esoteric tax shelters requiring huge *minimum* investment sums, like $200,000 or $300,000, are beyond the investment capabilities of most middle- and upper-class producers, and it is these types of shelters that will continue.

On the other hand, mourning the loss of certain deductions or "shelters," while it seems elsewhere the text attacks the loopholes in the Internal Revenue code, is not inconsistent. That's because the whole idea of deductions and playing games with the code to reduce taxation should never exist in the first place. This is because the income tax should not exist. If by hard work, ingenuity, personal risk, and sacrifice, a person gains monetary rewards, that person should not be penalized by a graduated, unjust, and illegal tax.

When most of us think of income taxes as unjust, we think in terms of how to get someone else who pays less to pay more. This book thinks in terms of how to get *everyone* to pay less or nothing and to preserve, in the meantime, whatever the system provides in the way of tax reduction. In other words, if someone pays $10, and someone else pays $5, this is unfair, and government will play on the envy of people who will demand the closing of loopholes so that everybody pays $10, or his or her "fair share." The result will be that government, by fooling the people into thinking the system now has been made fair because everyone is paying the same $10, instead has gotten a tax increase.

If this book seems to attack loopholes that are far beyond the reach of the common folk while defending those that the ordinary people can take advantage of, it has nothing to do with paying a tax that should not exist in the first place.

Neither the poor, nor the rich, nor the super-rich should pay an income tax. The problem is that the aforementioned actions to destroy certain loopholes are designed to bring a certain segment of the society to its knees while allowing an elite group to thrive.

Depreciation and write-offs are the main advantage of most tax shelters. Elimination of these advantages will cause most shelters as they now exist to become practically worthless. Those who have been able to protect their assets in the past by investing in such shelters will find that now, not only will they lose a portion of their investment capital, but they will also get a second kick by having to pay on their losses in the form of a lost deduction.

To illustrate, let's say an investor is involved with real estate that carries a negative cash flow. Interest that was previously deductible now will not be. Above that, there will be an erosion of investment value due to the negative cash flow, and the investor will now pay taxes on interest as if it were positive cash flow or income. If you are involved in these types of investments and tax shelters, the net result is that you will be paying more taxes.

Historically, when taxes go beyond the 50 percent level, armed revolution occurs. By using his great speaking abilities, orator Reagan has us believing that tax simplification and reform are coming. The reform he speaks of, however, involves having some people pay a little less and having other people pay the same or more, which only redistributes the tax burden. True, it will be simpler to file a tax return, since there will be fewer deductions and hence fewer forms to fill out. But this is hardly tax reform.

The real goal is to drive the society into a temporary cash-rich situation. In that situation, the only safe money haven will be cash investments at the bank. By maintaining high interest rates, cash continues to flow into the banks. The price of hard assets such as gold and silver is being forced downward. The strength of the dollar is being upheld artificially to keep wealth flowing into dollars. A strong dollar, poor prospects for precious metals and hard money assets, high interest rates, reduced inflation, instant liquidity, destruction of tax shelters via tax reform, etc., are all measures designed to help create this cash-rich situation. *When these devices are in place, the currency exchange will take place.*

THE TRADE DEFICIT AND ANTIGOLD POLICIES

These measures are causing great alarm among many economic pundits. For example, the strong dollar is causing record balance-of-payments deficits (see the following graph). The largest one-month trade deficit in seven years, $11.4 billion, occurred in March 1985, one-third of which was with Japan. A recent study showed that the strong dollar has caused a loss (export) of 2 million jobs, a 15 percent rise in imported goods, and a 15 percent decrease in exported goods. American industrial might is being decimated and exported. This serves the internationalistic goal to deindustrialize America and turn it into a service economy totally dependent on foreign goods.

This crippling of industry and dependency on foreign-made goods comes at a time when the cry for a stronger national defense is being heard throughout the halls of government. The hardest-hit industries, most of which are smokestack industries such as the steel industry, are dying quickly. How this country will have a stronger defense when a vital defense industry such as the steel industry is being destroyed escapes logic.

These measures are certainly alarming when viewed for their long-term effects, but are also viewed by the present administration to be very desirable in achieving the short-term goals necessary to set up an unwary public for an exchange.

Another indication of the impending exchange and the desire to create a cash-rich situation is reflected in the present heavy antigold policy of the Reagan Administration. This includes, both currently and pending:

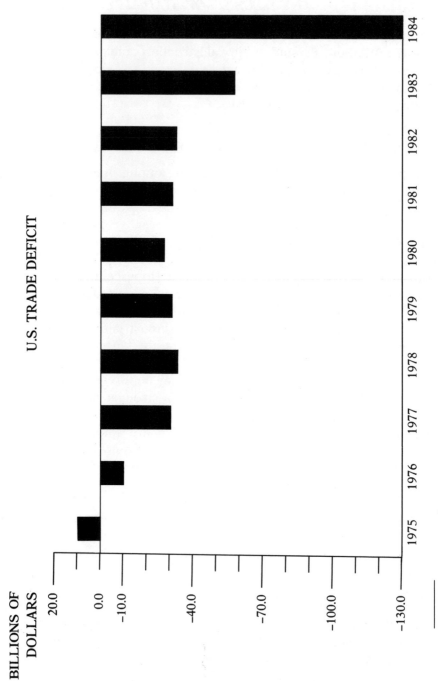

U.S. TRADE DEFICIT

BILLIONS OF
DOLLARS

Source: *Economic Indicators*, Published by Joint Economic Committee, U.S. Government

- requirements that sales of all metals be reported on IRS form 1099 B
- abolishment of capital gains treatment for investments in gold, silver, rare coins, gems, and stamps
- A total ban on importation of Krugerrands and prohibition of investment in South Africa
- requirement that name, address, and Social Security number be submitted to government by the precious metals buyer at the time of purchase

Two other areas where oppressive government crackdowns are in progress are:

- Treasury Department requirements to report large cash transactions and checks sent abroad over certain amounts
- expansion of powers to collect information about foreign financial transactions

Interesting to note is the hubbub in Washington over present-day apartheid policies in South Africa. In the name of racial and social justice, the U.S. government has banned the importation of Krugerrands and is expending much energy in order to discourage investments in South Africa. The government couldn't care less about social or racial justice. If it did, it has plenty of Indian reservations and ghettos across the country that could use racial and social justice. Its real goal is to discourage ownership of gold, especially the very popular Krugerrand, and investments in gold-related stocks of South Africa. So we hear that these investments will be banned to bring pressure on the government of South Africa to change its internal policies. Strange, though, that when these bans are called for they apply only to gold.

There are other minerals, such as chromium, manganese, vanadium, platinum, and diamonds, for which vital U.S. industries, including the defense industry, must rely almost completely on South Africa for its free-world source. (Other sources are Soviet and Communist countries, which are undesirable as suppliers.) Bans on these materials would bring things to a grinding halt. Therefore, bans on importation of these items are never mentioned.

Accordingly, bans of the nature discussed could possibly backfire. If gold production from South Africa were to stop or slack off, the price of the yellow metal would rise dramatically. The same holds true for other industries there. If investments are curtailed and goods boycotted, it will simply mean shortages and higher prices for us and increased economic hardship for those who are the victims of apartheid.

A little background information on South Africa's present troubles is in order. Heavy pressures on South Africa are coming, not just from the U.S., but from European nations as well. France's President Francois Mitterrand recently recalled the French ambassador there and is expected to call on the United Nations to bring economic sanctions against South Africa. If this comes about, South Africa will expel 1.5 million foreign workers, which will destroy the economies of Zimbabwe, Botswana, Mozambique, and Malawi.

If the UN decides to get tough and send in troops, it most likely will sustain staggering losses. South Africa has the ability to field 200,000 highly competent fighting men in less than 24 hours, with 2 million more over a two-week period. There is also a very distinct possibility that thousands of pro–South Africa volunteers would flow into the country, and she has the wealth to hire mercenaries if needed.

South Africa has a tradition of fierce fighters, as Imperial Britain found out during the Boer Wars, when it took the British three years to win, with great difficulty, the tiny Orange Free State and the Transvaal. What many fail to understand is that there have been whites in South Africa for over 350 years and they have nowhere to go, much in the same manner that white and black Americans would have nowhere to go if their conscience began to bother them and they decided to give America back to the Indians since the Indians were here first. In other words, the whites in South Africa would be fighting for their lives, backs against the wall, and would fight to the death. South Africa has possessed atomic weapons since the early '70s and, if forced to use them, would cause a nuclear war, resulting in the death of not only the whites there but also the blacks that we are supposedly trying to "save."

If boycotts come and the supply of Krugerrands is threatened, Krugerrands could possibly take on a numismatic value. If South Africa were to retaliate and purposely hold back on gold production, the gold markets would have wide and wild fluctuations, which would be to their advantage. And even if sanctions are enacted, there will be many countries that will ignore sanctions, especially when they are being paid in real money—gold. Sanctions don't work against the Soviet Union, which is much more oppressive than South Africa, because the Soviets pay in gold.

Those nations that maintain a boycott would dicover that bans and boycotts don't work when they result in increased economic hardships and austerities for the boycotter. You don't cut off your nose to spite your face, as the U.S. found out when grain embargoes were brought against the Soviets.

On the other hand, if measures designed to cripple the South African economy do work, then the whole country, and *especially those who suffer from apartheid,* will feel the results of a lower standard of living. It is obvious a move such as this is just another political expedient.

As a side issue, the elected officials know they can harvest some cheap votes from minorities and others, provided they make enough noise, regardless of what the outcome is. The main thrust, however, is to discourage ownership of gold.

On a final note, this is one area where we do not hear the free trade advocates pushing for "free" trade. If the consumer is king, as the free traders say he is, then the government should stay out of bans and boycotts. We deal with extremely repressive Communist countries, including the Soviet Union. American industrial might is going to hell. And the free traders scream that protectionist measures are government interference in the "free" marketplace while no one even makes a whimper in regard to the economic havoc that will be caused if sanctions against South Africa are effected.

The exchange that was announced for 1985–86 has been

pushed back until at least 1988. This will give plenty of time for the new tax plans to be implemented and set firmly in place. In the meantime, the dollar will be made to stay strong, interest rates will maintain a favorable position, and precious metals will be made to look like unwise investments. The new tax plan is a major part of this strategy, and the exchange will be delayed for it.

The latest news has it that the new currency will most likely have a hologram on its face. The American Bank Note Co. of New York City has received $1.6 million to research the printing of holograms on currency. The hologram proposal was made at hearings before the House Consumer Affairs and Coinage Subcommittee on June 18, 1985. Pending before the subcommittee was H.R. 48, the Currency Design Act. Amazingly, the Treasury Department has stated the holographic seal cannot prevent counterfeiting. It can only prevent copying bills on duplicating machines. It has also stated that it has a number of other security measures under consideration, which would be hidden or covert, one or more of which will be incorporated into the new currency.

The exchange must be maximized to the greatest extent possible since its repetition is unlikely to recur in the near future. The destruction of tax shelters will cause large sums of money to flow slowly into the banks seeking high yields with the advantage of mobility in the form of instant liquidity. Other investors, hesitating because of doubts cast on inflation hedges such as real estate and precious metals, will gravitate toward dollar-denominated investments, not really sure of what action to take until those doubts are dispelled.

High on Reaganomics, temporarily unsure of what to do next, but still with the thought somewhere in the back of their minds of collapse, all will be pushed into instant access money markets, T-Bills, etc., where they plan to get good returns but sit wisely poised for a fast switch should the economy begin to sour. Too bad the only fast switch will be the one the powercrats pull when they fast-switch the currency. The fallout will be tremendous. Debt reduction will come fast but on the backs of those who put faith in government promises, namely their greenbacks.

This is perhaps the last great stopgap measure that will postpone economic collapse. Hundreds of billions of dollars in the underground will be flushed out. Wealth that otherwise might have been put into tax shelters, gold, collectibles, real estate, and the like will be tied up in dollars. Flow of wealth out of dollars back into hard assets will be restricted by oppressive laws and a new currency that can be tracked and traced. Because much of the population will accept the new currency because of the alleged need to crack down on counterfeiters, gamblers, and drug dealers, they will realize too late these illusory problems were never an object of concern as was the reduction of their personal freedoms.

It is amazing how much of this actually rests on the complacency Ronald Reagan has been able to install into the public consciousness. If you don't think he is an essential part in this plot, consider this example of his unique powers to project confidence when collapse is so imminent.

Gold has been called the *anxiety factor* in terms of world events. When there is calamity, war, distrust, economic demise, or any type of social strife or uncertainty at all, populations shift their assets into gold. Gold is recognized universally as a freedom and wealth preserver. Many events that have occurred in the last four or five years of Reagan's tenure would have caused the price of the yellow metal to soar under normal circumstances. The bombing of Marines in Lebanon, the invasion of Grenada, the Falkland Islands war, the downing of Korean jetliner 007, and other events would have caused the price of gold to be $1,000, $2,000, $3,000, or more if they had happened under Jimmy Carter. The point is that Ronald Reagan projects confidence, stability, and strong leadership, whereas someone else, like Jimmy Carter, who lacked the ability to project these qualities, would have had everyone heading for the hills.

We are facing a perilous situation. Reality will soon force us to swallow some bitter medicine. It is said that a spoonful of sugar makes the medicine go down. Well, in this case, a spoonful of Reagan makes the nation go down. Ronald Reagan has become the Pied Piper of Washington as he leads us obliviously down a path fraught with dangers. He may be able to continue to tap his charismatic powers to perpetuate this false air of stability until he leaves office. But who do we have after that? George Bush? Howard Baker? Jesse Jackson?

To summarize: Barring any unforeseen catastrophe, there will be continued strength and stability in the economy and the dollar. Inflation will seem to be under control and there will be a major thrust to get people out of gold, silver, and other hard-money assets and into dollar-denominated investments. All manipulative powers will be employed to drop the price of gold to a targeted range of $200–$250. (This will be difficult, as it seems $300 gold and $6 silver have become psychological barriers that are hard to break.) Antigold legislation will be pushed through, using South Africa as a scapegoat. Tax reforms will result in increased taxes and the loss of tax shelters, causing a temporary shift of wealth into the banks, money markets, Treasury debt securities, etc. Motivated by frantic greed, the thought of high returns with instant liquidity will create an investment mecca at these money institutions. The dangerously explosive situation of banking failures, budget deficits, liquidity problems, international debt crises, etc., will be smooothed over with Reaganese charm, and he will be the deciding factor that keeps the whole thing together until events align so that the exchange can transpire. He will convince us that our liberties and economic freedoms are threatened by counterfeiters and undergrounders who are undermining the system while the powercrats do a cakewalk up the path of increased government control and oppression.

If the exchange and its contemporaneous tactics work according to plan, a relief valve will have been provided, defusing the explosive and crisis-ridden condition that is presently characteristic of the economy. Whatever magic powers Ronald Reagan has left will not be known because by then he will be on his way out of office. There appears to be no one else on the political scene who will be able to step in at the next election to fill the presidential shoes of Reagan, the "Great Pretender." It could be very likely that at that point in time the whole mess will explode into hyperinflation, terminating in a totalitarian state or a revolutionary downfall for the present ruling class, the latter being the less likely of the two.

The exchange can come at any time and is not dependent on the complete alignment of external factors such as business cycles, destruction of tax shelters, and depressed metal prices. Public access to information like that in this book could change the dates of an exchange. An element of surprise must be there to catch the public off guard. So if, for example, everyone is waiting for tax reform to precede the exchange, the powercrats could alter their plans. All the factors point to an exchange in the time frame described, but that can be modified at any time. One positive note is that, if there is a loud enough public outcry, strong pressure could be exerted to abandon the exchange program altogether.

As has been stressed throughout this book, knowledge is the greatest weapon the public can wield. Many individuals feel that even the fundamentals of economics are beyond their ken. They think that only the economic "experts" that they read about can predict, or even recognize, trends in today's economy. Not true, as we will see in Chapter 8.

8
SHIFTING INTO THE
SURVIVAL MODE

The last item to cover in our review of the current political and economic climate is an explanation of how business cycles operate. An understanding of these cycles will give you just about as much knowledge as the newsletter economists who try to impress us with their ability to predict future economic events.

Even though the system of cycles still dominates the business world, we are rapidly approaching a period when these cycles will no longer be applicable. In addition, mob psychology, blatant government intervention, and unforeseen calamities can suspend the forces that push these cycles on their "regular" paths of movement. Still, we must understand the way these cycles function to comprehend today's markets fully. With this last key in place, we will be able to chart different strategies by which to survive the coming debacle. We can then examine how the death of these cycles should enter into our plans and calculations.

It is important to perceive that these business cycles are mainly reactions to government manipulations and meddling in the marketplace. Huge efforts are made to create the appearance that things are going well right around presidential election time. The government maneuvers interest rates and the money supply, which causes cyclical swings in expansion, inflation, and recession.

In the last two decades, the key to investment success has lain in being able to analyze accurately what point has been reached in the cycle, take into account current events, and make the proper investment based on those facts. Though not foolproof, following the cyclic trends generally has resulted in gain.

Successful investors also, of course, had to guard against inflation, which operates constantly. Even though there is a specific phase in the business cycle that is called the *inflationary phase*, inflation never really goes away. The inflationary phase is merely a phase during which the degree of inflation is sharply increased. Inflation never subsides to the level where it was previous to its rise. The result is that each inflationary bout leaves the dollar's purchasing power a little more drained than before. This abradant force is responsible for the slow destruction of the dollar.

Taxes are also a constant. To beat the tax racket somewhat, investment strategies had to stress long-term investments. Long-term capital gains (profits made on investments held for at least six months and a day, a period that used to be one year and a day) result in profits being taxed at lower rates. At this rate, a maximum income tax of 20 percent is paid, whereas short-term gains are taxed at the full "ordinary" rates. The other common angle used to beat out taxes were tax shelters or investments that create paper write-offs. As reviewed in the last chapter, if the government has its way, this maneuver has seen its last days.

To give an example, let's say you purchased a long-term Treasury bond that payed 13 percent annually. This seems to be a favorable return. But take another look. If you are in the 50 percent tax bracket and paying another 10 percent on state income taxes, your return would drop to 5 percent. And taking into account a 5 percent inflation rate, your return would be reduced to zero!

Over the long haul, most of these dollar-denominated investments provide little if no return and usually result in a negative return. Most of the time, they simply allow you to lose wealth slowly. Most investors park their funds in T-bills, etc., because at certain junctures the business cycles make nothing else look good. The philosophy then becomes to stay as liquid as possible in order to make fast moves when advances in the cycles begin again.

THE THREE STAGES OF THE BUSINESS CYCLE

The three major stages in the cycles are the growth phase, the inflation phase, and the recession phase. These stages are reactions to external manipulations of the credit markets.

The Growth Phase

The growth phase begins at the bottom of a recession. The government feels it must do something to get the economy going, so it begins its cure by pumping more and more money into the economy. This is accomplished through action of the Fed, which lowers interest rates by aggressively purchasing Treasury debt from commercial banks. The credits thus received by the banks enable them to lend out more money based on their new "thin-air" reserves.

Interest rates go down, bank customers spend their newly borrowed dollars, and the economy gets pumped up with a shot of new money. Prices of raw materials stop falling and go higher, stocks take off, and business investments increase. Business borrows heavily, its operations expand, and more people are put back to work. Prices of goods and services fall temporarily as the competition increases (as exemplified by price wars).

Consumer spending also mounts. Loans are made for large purchases, home improvements, and vacations, and many start family businesses. The economy seems to glow with health, and things look peachy-keen. This sets up events for phase two to come into effect.

The Inflation Phase

Phase two, the inflation phase, often comes into play in a quiet sort of way. Interest rates still seem low enough, and many businesses will start to make unwise decisions. Some will decide to build factories and buy equipment to keep up with demand. But growth in the money supply now begins slowly to bid up the price of goods and services. Production cost increases, from new machinery, equipment, and so on, filter down the production chain until they hit consumers. The Wholesale Price Index (WPI) and Consumer Price Index (CPI) begin to show an almost insignificant but steady rise. Capital spending begins to drive up loan demands, and interest rates rise.

The inflation mechanism is now in progress. Unrestrained growth in the money supply will continue to drive prices higher and lead to hyperinflation, if unchecked. The Fed steps in, raises interest rates, and cuts the supply of banking reserves. Business can no longer borrow at cheap rates to maintain inventories or support new operations. All the unwise decisions become evident, and there is a fallout of weak businesses. Thousands of marginal businesses go bankrupt. Unemployment figures grow as layoffs intensify. Consumers reach their borrowing limits and delay large purchases. A recession is born.

The Recession Phase

Phase three, the recession phase, swings into motion. The Fed induces recession by cutting back on the money supply by way of stringent reserve requirements, higher discount rates, and confined open-market policies. This serves to prevent runaway inflation, but at the expense of business and investment opportunities. The result is an anemic business environment that results in sharp price drops for raw materials. Stocks retreat, and precious metals are weak. Remaining businesses survive by way of mass layoffs and slashed inventories. Consumers pay down their debts, and prices fall off while the whole economy flounders. Finally, when the entire condition becomes too severe, the Fed will ease credit and begin the cycle all over again.

INVESTMENT STRATEGIES

Timing is the most important element when investing according to cycles. If you know what part of the cycle the economy is in, you should be able to determine which investments to stress and which ones to avoid. The general strategies are as follows.

Phase One: Growth Stage

Best Investments—securities, penny stocks, common stocks, growth stocks, mutual funds, industrial commodities, business investments.

Marginal—real estate.

Poor—hard assets, cash and interest-rate vehicles, gold and silver bullion, mining stocks, rare coins, collectibles, foreign currencies, bonds, T-bills, money market funds.

Phase Two: Inflation Stage

Best Investments—hard assets; all inflation hedges; commodities; precious metals, bullion, and coin form; mining stocks; real estate; rare coins; collectibles; foreign currencies.

Marginal—money market funds.

Poor—cash and interest-rate vehicles, securities, bonds, T-bills, stocks other than mining stocks, mutual funds, business investments.

Phase Three: Recession Stage

Best Investments—cash and interest-rate vehicles, money market funds, bonds, T-bills, real estate bargains.

Poor—hard assets, securities, precious metals, rare coins and collectibles, foreign currencies, stocks of all types, mutual funds, business investments.

There are no sharp lines separating the different stages, but rather gray zones where stages overlap each other. It is during these gray periods that investors should shift their investments.

These gray areas, or subphases, provide windows of opportunity for investors. Since they usually last for about three months, there is enough time for making smooth transitions. For example, in the overlapping subphase between the growth phase and the inflation phase, a shift to hard assets would be prudent. When the inflation stage is winding down into the recession stage, the overlapping subphase would be the time to move into cash and interest-rate investments. And the overlapping recession and growth phases would be the time for transfer of assets into securities.

One minor exception to these rules involves real estate and rare coins, which often hold their value in contrary markets much better than paper assets. Because of the constant effects of inflation, many investors will hold on to their coin and real estate investments through several cycles.

RECOGNIZING THE PHASES

One problem that plagues investors is the inability to recognize these phases at the times of their peaks and valleys. Many will not realize that the end of a bull or bear market has been reached and will think changes in prices are merely "minor" market corrections.

Another mistake is to hold on too long in hopes of catching the exact tops and bottoms of the cycles. Many times the markets react in a volatile manner due to unusual or unforeseen incidents, thereby catching the observer off guard. The highest peak or lowest dip is lost while there is a wild swing in prices, which never "correct" back to near where they were. The big motivator in that scenario is the investors' greed, which makes them hold out too long. The big boom or bust may have just taken place, but the investor didn't hear the boom or just felt the bust.

One way to overcome the inability to recognize cycles is to understand that they typically last two to four years, usually centered around presidential elections. They can be monitored by observing when the Fed contracts or expands the money supply. It is more than coincidental that right around election time interest rates are low and the Dow-Jones industrial average is peaking.

When the Fed begins to pump money into the system as described in the recession cycle, the economy will begin to move toward the growth cycle, taking between six and nine months for a recovery to commence. In about two years, the growth stage will begin to peak conveniently around election time. Shortly thereafter, the inflation stage takes over, ultimately dying in a recession roughly two years later. The purpose has been served. The cycles are manipulated so that all attempts are made to have the growth stage in full motion at election time in order to make the incumbents look good.

Elections are not always a surefire way to plot these cycles, however. Mob psychology and sudden calamitous events can also distort cycles to render them temporarily impotent. And for reasons that will be discussed shortly, the cycles are becoming increasingly psychotic. Thus, the very best indication of cycle movements is to watch the expansion and contraction of the money supply by the Fed. Major moves on the part of the Fed will signal a new shift in cycles.

THE PROS AND CONS OF DIVERSIFICATION

Before it is explained why this knowledge of cycles will soon be obsolete, there are a few other points that should be understood when entering the investment world. One point involves diversification. Most economic strategists recommend that the investor diversify; that is, "Don't put all your eggs in one basket." The reason is that one major error can easily wipe out investors who have concentrated all of their assets in one basket. Such strategists suggest a more defensive or conservative approach by keeping, say, 60–70 percent of assets in investments pertinent to a particular strategy and spreading the remaining percentage among other investments. One rule states never to put more than 25 percent of your net worth into any one investment. In this way, if you make an error, you limit damage to your portfolio to that one vehicle.

Diversification also requires that you diversify even within one category of investment. For example, if you pick your own stocks, you should buy a number of issues so that one poor performer won't drag down the whole portfolio. Or a precious metal portfolio would include a little silver and gold coin, a little bullion, and possibly some platinum or palladium to round things out.

There is, however, another and perhaps more dynamic school of thought that states, "Put all your eggs in the right basket, look over that basket, and watch that basket grow." This maxim confronts a major problem with diversification. Our society, especially in the investment world, has become so complicated that it seems you need a college degree or years of study before you can perform even the simplest of tasks. The tendency to complicate matters seems to prevail at all times in history. It is the price we pay for "sophistication." This tendency once led the early American author and philosopher, Henry David Thoreau, to make the comment "Simplify, simplify, simplify." Rather than heed the sagacious, we take the opposite view and state, "Complicate, complicate, complicate."

The propensity to complicate has debilitated and obfuscated our potential to arrive at easy, simple, and proper decisions. Because there are multitudes of investment vehicles that are surrounded by myriad intricate rules to manage, diversification would necessitate that we immediately become geniuses in many different areas. The result is that the diversifier dissipates his energies in a dozen different directions. This problem becomes amplified when you consider the actual amount of time anyone has with which to follow so many diverse investments.

To illustrate, how many have the time to diversify properly when choosing their own stock? How many stocks can the part-time investor follow? In fact, this is so difficult that mutual funds came into existence to answer the need for expertise, which most lack, and a method by which to satisfy this urge for diversification.

Diversification is a defensive strategy that usually results in the investor's breaking even or losing. A poor performer will pull down the better performers when averaging the entire portfolio. It would be better for the investor to become expert in a few fields rather than try to learn a little about many fields. It has been said that a little knowledge is dangerous. Better to have a lot of knowledge about a few items than a little knowledge about a lot of items. In other words, be a specialist.

The principle of putting all your eggs in the right basket was one that was expounded by one of the most successful and famous multimillionaires ever, Andrew Carnegie. Diversification should be limited to having a small amount on reserve in a low-risk investment so that if a problem develops there is something to fall back on. The key to this strategy is to *have knowledge before acting*, then to invest in your strong suits and make them work hard for you. Wealth seekers must be on the offensive, not the defensive. The security sought by the diversifier will be illusive. There is no such thing as security, only opportunity. You may work 20 or 30 years on the job, feeling secure until the plant shuts down or you get laid off. You get a chance only if you take a chance. Shrewd investors are always on the offensive, ready to jump at opportunity *based on their knowledge.*

The only time you might consider diversifying is when diversifying within your chosen field of expertise. The purpose of this diversification is not to be on the defensive but to be on the offensive in different fronts within that field. For example, in a precious-metal portfolio, you may have some junk bags of silver, gold, and silver bullion coins; gold and silver bars; maybe a little platinum; and coins of numismatic value. You might also have some mining stock and some futures or options.

Each of these specific vehicles serves slightly different purposes within the field of precious-metals investment. Diversification within a narrow range allows a concentrated offensive to be carried out in the many different battles going on within that field of activity. You can expand or contract the amount of encounters within that narrow field and yet be comfortable because the same basic knowledge of precious metals will be active within that range. *Remember, the key to success will lie with the knowledge possessed.*

THE IMPACT OF TAXES AND INFLATION ON INVESTMENTS

Another pitfall to beware of is counting earnings before they have been put through the inflation and tax wringer. One example of this was given already. To drive home the point, let's assume you're an imaginary investor and give you 10 years with which to build a fortune, starting with $100,000 in capital. For this purpose, we will list projected average 10-year returns based on the opinions of "experts" in each category:

Gold, silver, collectibles	15%
Rare coins	25%
T-bills	10%
Money market fund, mutual fund	13%
Real estate	10%
Stock market	10%
Bonds	15%
Bank savings account	8%
Commodities	25%
Personal business	15%

We will put you into a 20 percent tax bracket, which includes state and local taxes. The inflation rate will average 8 percent per year. These averages and figures are not necessarily accurate and are based on educated guesses. They are also arbitrary and reflect a relatively stable economic climate. Of course we know better, but these figures are being used just to make a point.

You decide to play it safe and put half your money into a savings account. You put $30,000 into a business, and the rest is spent in non-income-producing areas. The breakdown and 10-year return are as follows:

$ 50,000	Bank account	$107,946
5,000	Vacation	0
10,000	Auto	0
5,000	Charity	0
30,000	Business	121,367
$100,000		$229,313

Not bad, you think. You have been able to enjoy life and build your fortune at the same time. Now let's account for taxes and inflation. If you figure in the 20 percent tax for 10 years on the 8 percent earned on the savings account, earnings are reduced to $92,979. Assuming that your business takes advantage of the tax benefits for a business, there is no tax loss on the $121,367. Adding these two figures gives you a net return of $217,724. Still seems like a nice figure. But now take the hidden plunderer of wealth, inflation, at 8 percent per year, and the figure is reduced to $93,109. As you can see, the tax and inflation wringer left you with a loss of $6,891.

Let's say you have decided to be more aggressive in your approach, and you invested this way:

$ 5,000	Bank account	$ 10,795
30,000	Mutual fund	101,837
25,000	T-bills	64,844
25,000	Money market	84,864
10,000	Auto	0
5,000	Vacation	0
$100,000		$262,340

In this case, you decided to put more into slightly riskier investments. You put less into a savings account and gave nothing to charity. You purchased an auto and still took a vacation. You also seem to have done better. After we adjust for taxes, you are left with $211,198. Inflation of 8 percent reduces this figure to $91,740. Not so good. You have actually earned a lower amount than through the less aggressive strategy of the first investment plan.

This should suffice to illustrate the unseen wringing effect of taxes and inflation. Never count your dollars until they have been put through this wringer.

You might ask, then, how it is possible to make any money on investments. Well, a basic flaw in the previous two strategies brings us to another investment rule. That is, in the beginning stages of investment, you must forgo non-income-producing expenditures. Surplus assets used to purchase goods that give the appearance of wealth but provide no income or do not increase in value merely sap the investment strength of the beginning investor.

Investment funds must circulate, so to speak, in order to generate profits. The stronger they are and the faster they circulate, the more that will be generated. As the funds go by, a little may be skimmed, but the large portion along with reinvested profits is left intact to circulate and grow. Later, when wealth has been achieved, you may indulge. At that time, provided you don't go crazy and squander your entire earnings, you can enjoy and be frivolous.

The general rule then is to make the maximum use of funds and hold off on nonproducing expenditures until they can be afforded without causing danger to the portfolio. Sacrifice and invest in things that increase in value. Make your money work hard in the beginning; then you can pamper yourself later—not vice versa.

As an example, let's take a look at a third strategy. You are on the offensive, investing within your range of expertise, and have forgone luxuries. Your investment portfolio looks like this:

$ 5,000	Money market	$ 16,973
25,000	Gold and silver	101,139
30,000	Rare coins	279,397
25,000	Commodities	232,831
15,000	Mining stock	38,906
$100,000		$669,246

If we take the $669,246 figure and reduce it by the amount paid in taxes, we get a total of $464,022. Taking into account the 8 percent inflation, we end up with a total of $201,563. This is a gain of $101,563, which is a world better than the other strategies, which did not account for the inflation and tax wringer.

These examples may be simplistic and even unrealistic in the sense that there are many other variables that have not entered our calculations. There are many other pitfalls of which you must be cognizant. However, the importance of having to account for funds that must first be passed through the inflation and tax wringer and the need for sacrifice in the beginning stages have been served by these examples.

BE OFFENSIVE, NOT RECKLESS

The third basic requisite for success, being on the offensive, must be qualified a bit. Being on the offensive does not mean being reckless. It requires more risk than acting in a conservative manner, but it is essential if wealth-building returns on investment are to be effected.

Most investment counselors recommend so called safe investments, which are low yielding, because of the need to cover their own shortcomings. Camouflaged under the garb of protecting or preserving assets, these investment counselors lead investors to believe they still will come out on top. They don't bother to explain the consequences of the tax and inflation wringer. Defense must be there, but it should take forms different from the traditional defensive tactics.

As stated earlier, one line of defense is not to be reckless. Look before you leap. This requires knowledge and experience, which the beginner may lack. So caution should be present, but the fear to act should not.

A Three-Step Plan for Success

Learning more about the importance of being offensive, take a look at the following simple three-step process for success outlined in the following three rules. They are:

1. Formulate a plan. Set concrete and attainable goals; define objectives; set realistic time tables; reevaluate goals periodically; review progress; fine-tune strategies as needed; be flexible but not capricious; be optimistic but not naive; put your plan in writing and look at it regularly; carry a mental image of your goals; think big not small; don't make assumptions (check it out).

2. Get knowledge. Do research; read books; attend lectures and seminars; talk to experts; listen to tapes; study the successful and follow in their footsteps; study the failures and avoid the same blunders; join groups and exchange ideas; cultivate business and like-minded associates.

3. Do it. Take charge of your own affairs; be organized; gain experience and expertise via on-the-job training; start slowly to gain confidence; after getting your feet sufficiently wet, go for it; recognize opportunity and take it; be humble, avoid pride and arrogance, but be confident and resourceful; work hard; make sacrifices; incorporate persistence and determination but avoid stubbornness or unwillingness to admit errors; don't be afraid to be different from others if it means success (in other words, don't join the march of the lemmings); associate with positive thinkers; avoid negative thinkers; be vigilant for greed and anger; exercise caution but not fear; be confident; see plans to the end (many game plans are lost on the one-yard line); don't fear failure (failure can be a great teacher).

Leveraged Debt

Now, to get back to being on the offense. Part of an offensive strategy is debt. Of course this means the right kind of debt. Taxes and inflation require that high rates of return be present to negate their eroding effects. These high rates are difficult to obtain through ordinary channels, but they can be had if you are willing to take on debt. More specifically, this particular type of debt is called *leveraged debt.*

It works like this: Imagine that you want to buy 200 shares of stock in XYZ Mining Corp. Shares are selling for $10, so $2,000 will purchase the 200 shares. A $1 increase in the price of the stock results in a $200 dollar profit or a 10 percent gain.

Now, what if you were to make half of your $2,000 purchase using $1,000 from a bank loan? The same $1 increase in the price of the stock would result in a $200 gain. But in this case you have used only $1,000 of your own money and still have a $200 gain. The result is a 20 percent return rather than a 10 percent return (minus the interest for the loan).

If the stock were to go to $20 per share and the full $2,000 were your own money, you would realize a 100 percent return. But if you were leveraged for $1,000 and the price of the stock went to $20 dollars, you would have a return of 400 percent. The return on leveraged debt can be quite dramatic.

The great pitfall is that a heavy loss could occur just as easily. If the stock were to drop $5 in price, you would experience a 100 percent loss of money. The trick is to know how to buy properly (which can get tricky). The risk is obviously greater in a leveraged investment, but the returns are much more dramatic. Risk is reduced proportionate to knowledge and expertise.

This technique of leveraging is popular among creative real estate investors. If they can bring a property under their control for 10 percent or less (even zero percent) down, and can have a positive cash flow from rents, after the debt is paid they will own 100 percent of the property. This is not as difficult as it sounds, but it is not a simple matter either. It requires dedication of time plus sacrifice to do the proper research and to acquire the proper knowledge to make the right buys. A creative real estate investor might sift through 100 sellers before finding the right one that fits the necessary prerequisites. Nonetheless, there are many creative real estate investors who have amassed a fortune through a careful, methodical search for the right properties that could be properly leveraged.

Ten years of expertly leveraged debt will buy a lifetime of debt-free financial independence. It requires only the right knowledge and expertise, which are tools that are within the range of all investors, provided they make the effort to acquire them. In other words, learning when to go into debt and when to stay out of debt is not such esoteric stuff that the ordinary investor cannot learn it. It is uncommon, though, because few will take the pains to master the essence of this principle.

To expound fully on the subject of leveraging would fill a book in itself. Indeed, most of the points above have been made in only an abbreviated manner. An in-depth study of these elements goes far beyond the capacity of this book. The fundamentals have been presented to alert and inform you of these powerful techniques.

Keeping Control

A final point to be considered concerns control. There may be many well-meaning but inept (and even dishonest) people ready to step in and "work for your benefit." To surrender control of your investments to these people will invariably result in the loss of your investment just as fast as ignorance of inflation, taxes, leveraging, compound interest, etc., will. Many of these characters make money on commissions and fees, whether they fail or succeed. Even the big investor with an in-house organization existing for the specific purpose of managing his investments must carefully oversee and guide the entire operation. *Never relinquish control of your portfolio.*

There are pitfalls and disadvantages to be avoided in all investment areas, and more detailed knowledge is needed when you plan to make a decision. For example, you might decide to buy numismatic coins, but you have to be careful of overgrading and counterfeits. Or you might want to buy real estate, which is highly illiquid and immovable. These areas will be dealt with in a more comprehensive fashion later on, when investment strategies specifically dealing with the exchange are discussed.

It would be impossible to present personally tailored strategies in a general treatment of the subject such as this. You would have to consider age, amount of money available for investment, tax bracket, number of dependents, need for cash flow, occupation, debt owed, assets, and many other personal factors.

Everyone's personal position is unique, and what may be a good investment strategy for you may not be right for the next person. Study your own position, educate yourself on different strategies, seek advice as backup counseling, but take charge of your own finances and make your own decisions. Be prudent and cautious, but do not fear to act. Armed with the proper knowledge, you will gain confidence and learn the ropes quickly. Remember that no one else will watch your investments as closely or be as interested in them as you.

THE DEMISE OF BUSINESS CYCLES

Now we can return to the subject matter of cycles and their imminent death. Most newsletters and popular economists make their predictions based on cycles. Many had predicted high prices in precious metals and other hard-money assets for 1985. This was based on the expectation that the inflationary cycle would have come into position. Many of these people have had to recant and uncomfortably explain that the prolonged sustenance of the growth cycle has caused a delay of their prophecies.

There would appear to be two factors these soothsayers have failed to take into consideration. One is the very nature of cycles themselves. As stated, cycles are not some naturally occurring independent phenomenon. They are reactions to actions, the actions being those exerted by the manipulators. And until these meddlers actually make a move, there are no reactions to predict. This means you can be wrong at any time.

The logical question that follows is: If cycles are the reactions to manipulations, what is the goal of the manipulators? The common answer is that manipulation of the economy is "necessary" to control inflation and recession. (Even though the opposite, that manipulation *causes* inflation and recession rather than prevents them, is true).

The real motivation behind the current set of maneuvers that have caused an extended growth cycle is the need to forestall the inflation phase. In other words, the growth phase would be the most advantageous cycle during which to enact a currency exchange. Because there has been a need to postpone the exchange, there also has been an attempt to postpone the inflationary cycle.

An inflationary stage would negate many of the benefits that will otherwise be available for the exchange. A recessionary stage would be the least desirable time. A growth phase coupled with the talk of tax reform and the other doublespeak mentioned could temporarily drive a chunk of the underground economy aboveground and many others into a cash-rich situation. Most investment experts are aware of the underground but are accustomed to dealing with the aboveground, which they feel accounts for 80–90 percent of the total economy. Not fully comprehending the size (around 30 percent and growing) and importance of the underground as a source of revenue, and considering it to be made up of largely illicit activity, they neglect to give it the proper importance in their calculations.

The second factor the economists have failed to recognize is that lately the business cycles have had anxiety attacks. They are more severe in magnitude, and their duration has been shorter. The cyclic waves are becoming more overlapping and distorted and are fast merging into an indistinguishable hodgepodge.

Let's return to our analogy of the human body. Health in the human body is reflected by a normal temperature of 98.6 degrees. High temperature indicates disease. The social body indicates a normal temperature when there is economic stability. The social body indicates illness or a high temperature when there are wild fluctuations in prices, money values, etc., and general economic instability.

The business cycles are a product of economic instability. In the '50s and '60s, when things were relatively calm and the social body stable, investment strategies were simple. You could put money into a savings account, buy some U.S. bonds, and purchase common stock, which, when kept in a buy-and-hold strategy, would easily put you well ahead of the cost of living.

In the '70s and '80s, the social body began to run a temperature. The simple strategies of the earlier decades were no longer applicable and, if employed, would assure you of a quick death. Fluctuations and swings in prices, etc., caused the system to evolve into one in which the orderly observations of these swings, or cycles, could keep investors ahead in the game. The temperature the social body is running has now progressed to a point where it will pass from a slight fever of 100 degrees to the danger point of 104 or 105 degrees.

A temperature of this magnitude within the human body induces delirium. It is not possible to predict what wild emotions a person in a delirious state will display. He may jump up or lie down. He might scream or lie there mumbling. He will writhe in pain, break out in a sweat, shout obscenities; any number of frenzied actions might be possible.

This condition of delirium is fast being approached by the social body. The cycles will become increasingly convoluted as there are greater degrees of economic manipulation. These manipulations will escalate to radical interventionism. Human talents and ingenuity will switch from industry, research and development, and entrepreneurial pursuits to a concentration of energy on the quest for economic safety and survival.

There will be successive and contradictory emergency measures in rapid sequence. The rules will be changed without regard for the players, in the middle of the game. A flurry of edicts, as has been demonstrated amply in the past, will only aggravate the condition. Emergency measures will be responsible for accelerated chaos. The business cycles will be worthless and as obsolete as are the strategies of the '50s. The only techniques or strategies with any value will be those that ensure survival. Black market or white market, aboveground or underground, whatever it takes to persevere will be the order of the day.

Again, it seems that the specific goal of the manipulators is to forestall inflation so that the exchange will be more effective. This is emphasized by an unusually prolonged prosperity or growth cycle in a period of time that the cycles have become erratic and will soon be defunct.

The evidence is all around us. The economic foundation of the country has developed great cracks. The edges are crumbling, and any large jolt could cause the whole structure to disintegrate. The anomaly of the situation is that in the midst of such precarious uncertainties we are experiencing a great calm. The economy seems healthy, the dollar is strong, inflation is licked, Reagan is great, and so forth. It would appear that we are sitting in the proverbial "eye of the hurricane."

The dilemma comes in trying to predict when the eye of the storm will pass over to leave us in the midst of a raging storm. These cycles are still effectual, and their end might be years away. The currency exchange is one move that could easily push back collapse of the cycles five years or more. Then again, it might just be spitting into the wind. This is because the system has never had to face the enormous amount of debt, debt interest, and deficits that it will in the immediate future. The sheer weight of this debt will eventually crush and destroy the system.

Tighter control of the flow of money and a siphoning of the power of the underground could very well tip the scales back into the favor of the present system. If it does, investment strategy based on cycles will still be the only fairly reliable method available for predicting market changes. If the exchange and other bandage-and-baling-wire quick-fix methods are not quite enough, then it could be we are looking at "the last train out," in terms of a "final" opportunity to discard cycle strategies and switch to a survival mode, when in the coming inflationary cycle crisis pushes us into hyperinflation. How to purchase a ticket on the last train out will be dealt with in the following chapters.

In conclusion, business cycles are the only decent method we have to know how to position ourselves in the investment world. These cycles are in their last days, the exact time of their death being hard to predict. High double-digit inflation is ready to come in the next inflation phase and, with the enormous debt problem, is ready to erupt into hyperinflation. Tax increases alongside an exchange could fend off such an attack and buy some more time. Then again, it might be too late for remedial measures. If the cycles die, then the afore-mentioned investment tips will die alongside the cycles. If this happens, the economy will switch to a survival mode, and the only valid strategy will be one that ensures continued exis-tence. These strategies will be detailed in the following chapters.

9
UNDERGROUND FINANCES: CATCH THE BIG BOYS OR BURY THE LITTLE MEN

Now that we understand that a currency exchange is inevitable, and that preparation for it has been made on many fronts, we are ready to discuss what individuals can do to survive and profit from it. In this chapter we will review both measures taken by the underground economy in the past to protect its wealth and general guidelines that you can follow to preserve your investments and savings.

INNOVATIONS OF THE UNDERGROUND

If the call-in were to involve a simple crossover from old currency to new, the job of protecting your wealth would be relatively easy. In fact, the members of the underground economy have essentially been doing just that, for the most part unchecked, for years. On the next few pages are lessons that can be learned from their experiences in the underground.

One viewpoint is that, with the two-year advance notice given, the biggies in the underground have had ample time to defend against a changeover. Apparently, conversion of cash into gold coins or bars holds little appeal for them since their resale to brokers or dealers would require reporting of the transaction to government authorities. Instead, the more astute undergrounders have parked their greenbacks in U.S. dollar-denominated traveler's checks issued by foreign financial institutions located outside the continental United States, far beyond the jurisdiction of Washington.

A question arises as to what might be the consequences of buying such traveler's checks denominated in a currency of a country that is also planning a currency call-in. This should not pose a problem unless one of the countries were to devalue its currency. If there is no devaluation, then exchange rates between currencies are already set at their individual level of purchasing power. Since it appears that the countries involved in the currency call-in are staggering their call-in timetables, the different rates of exchange between currencies will be easy to monitor. If you are concerned or uncertain about this, then it just might be best to avoid buying traveler's checks issued by these countries altogether. There are plenty of countries in the world to choose from other than the seven involved.

The Caribbean Connection

According to another theory, the big-time pros in the underground have been preparing for the exchange using a different tack. Namely, anyone can get on a Caribbean cruise ship heading toward a bank secrecy island (no custom searches boarding or exiting) with a bag full of cash and deposit the money in a Swiss branch bank. The offshore bank then ships the cash back to the U.S. and receives the appropriate credit. This takes place every week. These banks do not report who deposited the cash and they can wire the money anywhere in the world.

Money Orders from Domestic Banks

The really big boys of the underground that are awash in cash have a variation on that theme. Though drug dealing is not the largest part of the underground, large amounts of cash are concentrated in the hands of a few dealers, and they use this alternate method. Because of the cash-only nature of the business, even small deals can require millions of dollars to be used for outright buys, as deposits, or for operating capital. Boarding Caribbean-bound cruise ships can be very time-consuming as well as risky.

A suitcase with $1 million in $20s weighs over 100 pounds. Such suitcases can become unwieldy and can easily be spotted by trained officials. Big launderers have stopped going directly to Caribbean banks and have turned to domestic banks where big cash flows go unnoticed. Working in teams, launderers, or smurfs as they are sometimes called, go to different banks to purchase cashier's checks or money orders. To avoid banking laws, the MO amounts must be made out for less than $10,000. Amounts above this figure, by law, must be reported to the authorities.

The checks or MOs are deposited into the account of a shell corporation or dummy front company licensed by any one of a number of bank and tax haven countries in the Caribbean or elsewhere. No reports are filed because the transactions are under the $10,000 limit.

The money is then wired to the country where the account is held. Bank secrecy laws in these countries prevent any public, private, or government agencies from finding out who owns the account, and from getting information regarding activity within that account. Since there is no way to trace the money, it is now "clean." The money can be held in the account or wired anywhere in the world. It can come back to the mainland into the account of another front company to be used to buy land, buildings, etc., or wired to a bank in the country where the next drug purchase is to be made.

Laundering Trends

With the large volume of activity—including money laundering, migration, and general influx of wealth—between the U.S. and Latin America, and because of the close proximity of

Florida to Latin America, Florida has become the center of bank laundry activity in the U.S. Bank laundering of cash is a global problem, though, and includes countries such as Germany, England, and Switzerland. Drugs are not the only illicit activity in need of laundry services. Others include diverse operations from IRA arms deals and gambling and prostitution rings to Mafia-owned hotels, farms, and office buildings.

According to an article in *Business Week,* March 18, 1985, launderers don't use only banks. Before being caught, launderers involved in the chain of pizza parlors serving as Mafia drug drops in the early '80s made cash deposits of $4.9 million at Merrill Lynch, Pierce, Fenner & Smith Inc. and $15.6 million at E. F. Hutton & Co.

And the recent bankruptcy filing by Deak and Co. because of drug laundering problems shows that banks are not the only institutions eager to service the launderers. There is also the "licit" laundering required by people who must live under extremely oppressive governments, where the only way to survive is through the black market and concomitant laundering services.

One of the big roadblocks to laundering is the $10,000 rule. In the past, banks were lax in reporting transactions of this size. As one bank official described, it would be almost impossible to get work done in some areas if reports always had to be made.

Nonetheless, officials have increased enforcement of the law and have handed out more and stiffer fines to banks disregarding the rule. The smurfs have countered by using a few different techniques, other than that of keeping deposits under $10,000. Some don't play around; they directly bribe bank officials. Others buy stacks of cashier's checks, which are deposited at other banks. The most sophisticated operators use Panamanian shell corporations that don't provide any useful information or they create legal retail outlets with large cash flows and get a legal exemption from having to report the large transactions.

After the money is safely deposited, it gets wired to Panama or the Grand Cayman Islands, where the secrecy laws shut the lid on trace attempts. The money is then clean, and the launderers get paid their usual 3 percent commission.

Until recently, the drug trade money that poured into Florida, especially Miami, from Latin America was too much for greedy bankers to turn down. Hungry for money, Miami bankers soon turned that city into the "Wall Street" of the drug world. It was a common event to see couriers standing in line with duffel bags, cardboard boxes, and shopping bags crammed with cash. Willing bankers realized laundering was the easiest method to improve "cash-in" figures and gain status with higher-ups.

Smurfs have cleaned up their act lately. Because of the crackdown on the $10,000 rule, deposits have dropped to $7,000 and even $5,000 to prevent suspicion. The smaller deposits require more couriers working more banks, so they increase efficiency by keeping in constant touch by using beepers and telephones. They have also started projecting a corporate image by wearing suits and using leather brief-cases. And they will change addresses constantly to avoid detection. Smurfs can also be any assortment of people, as a group of grandmothers acting as couriers in a recent West Coast bust proved.

Smurfs avoid big busy banks and long lines. Consequently, little smurfing goes on in New York City. If the Federal Reserve banks take in more money than they send out, it is presumed that laundering is taking place. The following is a list that appeared in *Business Week*, March 1985, showing where laundering, based on Federal Reserve figures, seems the hottest. Positive numbers indicate more money in than out.

| City | **Millions of Dollars** | |
	1980	**1984**
El Paso	$ -78	$ 612
Jacksonville	1,157	1,394
Los Angeles	-136	374
Miami	4,676	5,263
Nashville	297	422
Philadelphia	-102	625

| San Antonio | 458 | 645 |
| San Francisco | -166 | 1,172 |

Many banks have begun to monitor in-cash flows. They will sell cashier's checks only to regular customers and have installed computer systems that turn out daily lists of transactions of $10,000 or more. Some banks have objected to government intrusion and are concerned with lost profits resulting in their customers' invasion of privacy. Bankers complain there is no way to tell dirty money from clean money. Carrying it in for deposit in paper bags is no more an indication of dirty money than leather briefcases are an indication of clean money. Besides, many banks resent having to use police powers against their customers.

A large bulk of deposits from Latin America consists of clean dollars escaping hyperinflation and political instability. Purchase of dollars in Latin America is for self-preservation, considered to be as important as the purchase of food. Supplying information on customers to authorities, where the result ends in no violation of laws or no laundering is found to be present, is beginning to create an air of distrust for banks, not to speak of the gross invasion of privacy. This has caused many banks and private citizens to complain loudly about government infringement of freedoms and privacy.

The government doesn't care about freedoms or privacy and is introducing new legislation to monitor international bank wire transfers. Recently, exempt lists (from the $10,000 rule) have been sequestered from banks for scrutiny.

Big international banks in Switzerland, London, Toronto, Hong Kong, the Cayman Islands, and Frankfurt do not monitor transactions and have stated that they plan to keep it that way despite pressures put on them of late by the U.S.

Some bank officials have expressed indignation with the American government's arrogant insistence that their country's (banking) laws are immoral or unjust because they do not align with what the U.S. government thinks they should be. Many U.S. officials can't realize they are dealing with sovereign nations that happen to have a different world view of privacy and freedom than they do and are no more appreciative of foreign imperious demands than U.S. officials would be if a German or Swiss official came to the U.S. and dictated to our government what it must or must not do. And even if these banking centers were to abandon their policies of discretion, upstart banking and tax havens would be quick to take their place. As a matter of fact, any sovereign state with a landing strip and building could accommodate a laundry system.

New havens that have recently sprung up are in the Turks & Caicos Islands in the West Indies, Channel Islands off the coast of France, Vanuatu in New Hebrides, and Nauru in the Pacific. For example, in Nauru, it takes only a few days to charter a corporation, which can be done very easily and anonymously through the mail. Then there are always places such as Bulgaria and Libya, which are more than willing to offer privacy and safe haven for laundering activities.

The ultimate result of government crackdown will be that the average citizen will lose more privacy and freedom. The government will be able to intrude under the guise of tracking illegal activity. It has been said that locks keep only honest people out. A determined thief will not be thwarted. The same consequence will result from new laws that invade and disregard individual freedom and privacy. The honest citizen will suffer while the real culprits merely move and adjust their operations to circumvent the law.

Perhaps the real objective is to condition the public to accept the new traceable currency. The Treasury Department alluded to this when a spokesman recently announced to the media that all efforts to stop crime have failed and that success will come *only by going after the cash trail left by undergrounders.*

Gambling

Another practice used by some undergrounders to legitimize money, short of opening a cash business that acts as a front, has been to go to casinos in gambling towns like Atlantic City. Two or three conferates buy chips of, say, $5,000 each. One casually plays blackjack, or another game, while the others go to a show. When they return they give their chips to their cohort who remained behind. He turns in all the chips for cash that he has "won." He can tell any IRS spotter (if there are any) on the floor that he won while playing. If the spotter claims to have been watching him and not to have seen him win big, he claims that he won most of the chips, went out to dinner, returned to play a few more rounds, and decided to cash in. The spotter must have observed him when he returned to play a bit more after dinner when he didn't win much. Or he can just hang around the tables for a few days and then turn in the chips. An odd quirk is that the IRS requires winnings to be reported as income on tax returns, but does not allow losses to be deducted. It seems that, if you lose, you lose, and if you win, you still lose.

Turning Cash into Stock

Those in the underground with a lot of cash to launder might also take a step that could actually be used by any store owner, manufacturer, or other individual who is working "off the books": to constantly and immediately turn any cash into stock.

For example, newspaper reports claim that a kilo of cocaine presently wholesales for around $50,000. With a stash of 20 kilos, which will fit into a large suitcase, a coke importer could store $1 million. Two suitcases equal $2 million. A retailer or manufacturer could take any surplus cash and do the same by increasing inventories of finished products or raw materials as the cash comes in. Knowing his own situation intimately, he can easily balance his cash flow against overstocking for short periods of time until the exchange actually takes place. The point is that storing wealth in objects of value that you are familiar with in your business dealings, and which you can even make profits on later, is wiser than letting wealth sit in a paper money whose immediate future is in real jeopardy.

Gold, Silver, Gems, et al.

Undergrounders with surplus cash might want to store wealth

in objects of real worth to ride out an exchange. Gold and silver are obvious choices, but any object of value that offers anonymity is acceptable. Those who have huge amounts of cash could concentrate on objects such as gems, which are small, easily hidden, and very valuable.

HOW TO PROTECT YOUR WEALTH

Even if you were caught off guard holding large amounts of cash, it might be tedious, but you could probably exchange money in small amounts at the banks day after day until all of your money was exchanged. But things will be a bit more complicated if the exchange is greater than one-for-one. In that case, the actual purchasing power of the currency could be altered. This would give officials the perfect excuse to enact wage and price controls, rent controls, and so on. There have also been some rumors that a few Swiss banks are not as secretive and are cracking under pressures by Washington to reveal their business. Even without that, because we are dealing with a fiat currency, its value can be manipulated and set according to government dictates. Therefore, those who take actual wealth and store it in illusory government promises, i.e., greenbacks, place themselves in a precarious position. They subject control of their wealth to the prevailing political winds in Washington. You can judge this for yourself by the degree of trust you have in the government. After all, our present currency has value only because the government says it does. In other words, the currency is only as good as the government's word. You decide how good that is.

As far as this book is concerned, wealth should be stored in real, tangible objects having intrinsic value, in a private safe place. Properly stored precious metals and coins fall into this category, and the disadvantage of having to deal with brokers who must report their activity is not a real problem. This book does not encourage the breaking of laws, but it must be remembered that the black market is the government's own creation. If the government insists on tying the hands of legitimate dealers with stiffer reporting regulations, it will simply create another black market operation that deals in gold and silver coin and bullion. Holders of bullion or coin who have obtained their earnings in the underground will merely continue to do their business there.

The more government seeks to impose its sanctions on the people, and the more the people become accustomed to operating in the underground to escape this oppression, the easier, more guilt-free, and more widespread this activity becomes. When the government responds with even tougher sanctions, it accelerates its own demise. Historically, the people can be pushed but so far, and then revolution occurs. It is amazing that each new regime, not matter how onerous, somehow or other thinks it is different from its predecessors and mighty enough to elude a revolutionary fall.

The most the government can hope to accomplish in the short term is to flush out all the money so it can start over and maybe catch a few big boys who are unprepared. The black market will continue as strong as ever. The real battle will come later, when, after having installed a new currency that can be traced and tracked, the underground seeks new ways to circumvent controls and avoid detection.

The government's two main goals are to shake up and flush out the underground and to install a new currency that can be tracked. This will make this currency unique in that it will be the first time in the history of currency exchanges that a paper money capable of carrying secret messages on it will be introduced to the public.

In all probability, most people will be caught unaware when the exchange is announced and will be at a loss as to what to do with all that unreported cash they have stashed away. These people will most likely take what might be called a "spend it or lose it" approach. They will rush out and buy furniture, clothing, appliances, automobiles, gold, silver, and jewelry and take vacations. A spending spree of great magnitude will cause prices to shoot up while there is a scramble to gobble up whatever goods or services are left in the marketplace. Merchants in a position to exchange old for new at the banks without any problem stand to make a killing by stockpiling now when prices are relatively low and then selling during the binge.

For the benefit of the "spend it or lose it" people, there are two general investments that can be made: those that have descending value and those with ascending value. Examples of descending-value investments are autos, furniture, clothing, and appliances. Examples of ascending-value investments are real estate, collectibles, art, gold and silver coins. Those who are astute will endeavor for investments of ascending value, which are as free as possible from government scrutiny and have the most liquidity. These ascending-value investments negate the eroding effects of depreciation and inflation while the descending-value investments do not.

Greenbacks have always been a descending-value investment. They are backed by nothing and buy less each year. They are subject to controls and manipulation. Holders of wealth stored in fiat paper leaves their fortunes exposed to involuntary confiscation—indirectly through inflation and directly via a recall or currency reform. (Include taxes, which are supposed to be voluntary.) This involves IRAs, Keoghs, CDs, bonds, bank accounts, T-bills, and basically any type of dollar-denominated investment.

For these types of investments to be of ascending value, returns must be higher than the inflation rate and taxes. To get favorable rates, you must pledge your dollars for long periods of time. During this time, taxes and inflation rates could and do change. As a matter of fact, a constant headache that plagues investors deals with the government's inclination to revise tax and investment laws every six months. The Congress delights in repealing new laws, especially at the most crucial times. If you are very shrewd, you may be capable of watching your investment carefully so you can thwart the confiscation of your wealth through taxes and inflation, but you will be helpless against the threat of a currency reform. Besides, after accounting for taxes and inflation, these investments usually leave very little in the way of growth.

There are better long-term investments, such as precious metals, real estate, and collectibles. Even though at present investors appear to be doing well with dollar investments, and items such as gold and silver seem to be dead, don't be fooled. We are merely experiencing a lull before the storm. The bubble will soon burst as new waves of inflation are looming on the horizon, and these dollar-denominated investments will be left by the wayside. We might say this is a golden time to buy, as many of these non-dollar-denominated investments can be had at bargain basement prices. This is due to cyclic lows in the prices of many of these items, the lingering effects of the past recession, and other cyclic market factors. You should set yourself above the crowd and follow the smart money, which always buys when everyone is selling and sells when everyone else is buying. It takes guts to do, but the rewards are the greatest.

For those individuals who seek simply to preserve their assets, it is sufficient to buy the proper investments and engage in a sit-and-hold strategy. Short-term fluctuations in price can be ignored. Because we live in an atmosphere of uncertainty and speculation, those investors who wish to parlay their wealth must follow cyclic highs and lows. They must buy low and sell high. As previously stated, the general rule is to buy when everyone else is selling and sell when all others are buying. For example, right now precious metals are at a low cycle point. Buying now and selling in a year or two when the cycle swings the other way will bring returns far more dramatic than the few percentage points presently offered by CDs, T-bills, and the like, which all are so involved in at the moment because they think inflation is dead.

Granted, to do this you must watch the market carefully and remain informed. You must also avoid greed that brings the temptation to wait a little longer to catch the lowest and the highest points of the cycle and thereby miss them altogether. The real tragedy is that this greed, gambling with your wealth, and other iniquities are the direct result of a government that has installed a cheating system of economics and currency. The common man is forced to fight fire with fire, and the ensuing competition becomes a battle of whose baser nature will prevail. In other words, government policy is directly responsible for the general decay of morals that is slowly overtaking the society. We can see how a return to a gold standard would force honesty in government and help to reverse this destructive trend.

Probably the best investment vehicles for protection against a call-in and inflation right now are rare silver and gold coins. They are free from government snooping if purchased privately or from independent coin dealers, are liquid, and are an outstanding inflation hedge. Even without inflation, they offer excellent appreciative possibilities due to shrinking inventories caused by greater numbers of collectors entering the field. In addition, gold and silver coins are one of the most reliable and historically successful methods of protecting wealth from inflation, recession, depression, war, turmoil, and economic collapse. They are easily stored, hidden, and transported. Gold coins are especially immune to the ravages of time, and they offer anonymity and privacy. (For the benefit of more sophisticated investors, the next chapter will provide specific strategies for using the cycles to invest.)

However, the ease with which we are now able to obtain some of these items could change. For the ordinary citizen it is a question of preserving wealth, but for the government the name of the game is control and power. Yes, the government is concerned with money, but since it already controls its issuance, it can get all it needs to operate. Its real concern with money, then, is related to power. Therefore, whichever way investors flow with their capital, the government will be standing there with roadblocks, asking questions.

If too much flows into an area where there is presently little government control, then the government could stage a "crisis" and set in controls to bring the "crisis" to an end. This is not new. FDR used this when, after having declared a bank emergency, he confiscated the American public's gold held in the banks when safe deposit boxes were allowed to be opened only with the officials standing there.

A modern-day banking emergency or crisis could be used to:

- freeze all bank accounts, both business and personal
- ration withdrawals of cash or require reporting withdrawal amounts over certain limits
- prohibit "hoarding" of cash
- prohibit the transfers of checks

- register all sellers and buyers of coin
- introduce new taxes
- make a currency switch
- universalize the use of the Social Security number as a national ID number
- impose wage-price controls

In other words, if investors began a rush on buying gold and silver coins, the government would enact controls to monitor and register all those people and their activities. If all the action was in flea markets or swap meets, the government would figure out a way to crack down there, too. But, as stated before, governmental attempts to control the marketplace will be met with greater surreptitious activity.

Right now, some places and items that individuals could deal in with relative privacy and anonymity are:

- discounted jewelry and other costly items from pawn shops
- antiques, art, and other collectibles
- gold and silver coins
- high-quality discounted goods at flea markets and private parties

In conclusion, the pros in the underground need little advice. They know the ropes and have long been prepared. The unprepared foolish ones that have ego problems and think they are too powerful to fall down will soon get an education in humility. As for the uninformed, they will scramble to salvage whatever they can when the announcement to exchange is made. If they are wise, they will endeavor for ascending-value investments that offer the greatest privacy and anonymity. The exchange will be an extremely disruptive event in the underground economy, albeit a temporary one. The real battle comes after the new currency is in circulation. If there is only one general rule to be gleaned from this information, let it be to get out of greenbacks and to store wealth in personally held objects of real intrinsic value.

10
THE ABOVEGROUND:
SAVE OUR SHIP

The last chapter explained how most of the big underground operators have been prepared and how most others who have unreported income might very well spend it or lose it. But how will the exchange affect the other 70 percent of the economy, which functions in the aboveground? One result is that every single solitary citizen will lose a little more freedom. But an important point to know is that almost every citizen deals in the black market to an extent. It's not that only 30 percent of the population operates covertly while the other 70 percent is totally in the open. The 30 percent underground is spread throughout the entire population.

THE SIZE OF THE UNDERGROUND

Throughout the book, the underground has been purported to be 30 percent of the economy and growing. There are those who might question such a high figure, having heard official estimates of 10–15%. The following analysis of the economy will demonstrate how this figure was arrived at.

For many years, the IRS simply ignored the underground, which has been the principal means by which people evade taxes, especially the technique of underreporting by the self-employed. In recent times, this segment of the economy has grown to be so huge that the IRS was forced to disclose formally, before congressional committees, the heavy losses the bureau has suffered at the hands of the underground. Recently, we've heard President Reagan making tough speeches about underground money and the need to crack down on it. The IRS candidly admits compliance is slipping and plans to attack recalcitrants with modern computers and tough audits. The IRS also admits the greatest obstacle to compliance is the widespread contempt for the Internal Revenue Code, which favors the super-rich and various tax-exempt entities while being grossly unjust to the average citizen. In a recent IRS study, which surveyed regular working-class people, 19 percent revealed cheating by either hiding income or inflating deductions. The small evader feels justified because of the lack of vigor exhibited by the IRS in demanding compliance by multimillionaires, who pay little if anything.

The IRS counters by saying tax reform is coming. Reductions in tax rates, the number of deductions, and the number and type of shelters should diminish contempt toward the system, and the tendency to cheat should decrease. No one in his right mind can understand how further limiting the ability to avoid paying taxes legally will induce compliance, and it is not hard to see this kind of action as a tax increase rather than a tax reform, especially when the common person will still face heavy tax burdens.

The IRS states that most taxpayers are careful to report income from wages, salaries, dividends, and interest. Noncompliance usually involves capital gains, where 41 percent of income is not reported, and alimony, of which 38 percent is not declared. In addition, the IRS states that just 78 percent of small businesses claim their true income, and it has become common practice to keep two sets of books—one for them and one for us.

The IRS has a "taxpayer compliance measurement project," by which the agency checks every line on 50,000 randomly drawn returns every three years. Through the information compiled by this project, the IRS believes it can prognosticate estimates of tax avoidance by the other 95 million who file. It also acknowledges that unreported income can be discovered only when there is some form of paper trail left behind. Seasoned evaders leave no paper trail of any kind.

And even if the bureau can match all payments of interest and dividends with reports made by corporations and financial institutions, there are still hundreds of billions that extend beyond the IRS's abilities to scrutinize. Although the agency has increased the severity of its audits, the actual percentage of audits has dropped from 3 percent to 1.5 percent. What all this indicates is that, because of its lack of solid information, the bureau is groping for answers and its estimates are undoubtedly erroneous.

The service claims that in 1981 $250 billion in earnings were not reported. This amounts to about 12 percent of all money legally earned that year. This does not include illegal income from drugs, gambling, prostitution, loan sharking, etc. As stated, because of its limited ability to ascertain information accurately on underground finances, this $250 billion figure is probably too low. The IRS also feels that, of the 20 million self-employed Americans who file, practically all underreport their earnings. This must certainly involve losses to the government at least equal to or surpassing those achieved by the subterranean economy.

If this is the case, then about $500 billion, or 25 percent of all legal income, escapes taxes. Add to this figure all monies that are earned illegally and that elude taxation because of loopholes and exemptions, and we probably will end up with a figure in the $700 billion area. This amounts to 33 percent of all reported personal income after taxes. It is easy to understand the anxiety felt by the government at the loss of such a sizable sum of money and the dire urgency it feels to round up all this cash.

So, the plumber who gets paid on a side job that goes

unreported as income on tax returns has been able to do this because cash is totally anonymous. The new cash, which attacks freedom, will partially lose anonymity because it will be traceable. The opportunities this opens up for the officials can only be guessed at.

One of the main concerns in the aboveground centers around the debt crisis. If the exchange can effectually flush out previously untaxed money and fill the government's treasury house, then the current economic system will have bought time. If it is not successful, and the debt crisis causes hyperinflation to become a reality, then the economy will shift into a survival mode, ultimately ending in totalitarianism or anarchy. The actions you take depend on whether you believe the system will continue or you believe it is gasping its last breath.

GENERAL INFLATION PHASE STRATEGY

Either way, the next phase of the business cycle that will be upon us is the inflation phase. At present, we are in a prolonged growth phase. The transitionary subphase between the growth and inflation phases is overdue. Or it may be that we are sliding, almost unnoticed, into this subphase; if we are, it is being stretched out. This is an example of the distortions of the cycles mentioned earlier.

Manipulative pressures are being exerted on the cycles to postpone the beginning of the inflation phase for as long as possible. Whether this can be accomplished until the newly revised 1988 target date for the exchange remains to be seen. Nevertheless, we should begin switching wealth to hard assets and other inflation hedges before the 1988 date, or, if that date is abandoned, whenever it becomes evident from major action on the part of the Fed that an inflation cycle will soon be initiated. What we do with those investments depends on whether we believe the cycles will continue or we believe we will enter a survival mode. In this coming inflation phase, high double-digit inflation will be all but unavoidable.

There will be only slight differences in basic strategies, the main difference being that, if things collapse into the survival mode, investments should not be sold. In other words, if this is the "last train out," we would not want to sell our ticket that is good for a seat on that train.

In a normal inflation cycle, two primary objectives will be the preservation of buying power and capital appreciation or profit, defined as increased economic wealth and purchasing power. Another consideration includes those who need income-producing investments on which to live. The list of best investments under the inflation cycle heading that appeared in Chapter 8 included commodities, precious metals, real estate, collectibles, foreign currencies, mining stock, all inflation hedges.

The phrase *all inflation hedges* requires a little more explanation. There are certain industries or companies that do well in an inflationary period that are not listed specifically because of certain factors that allow them to transcend the influences of the business cycles. These companies deal with inelastic objects where price is not a major factor. They are involved with items that are considered necessities and are able to pass on higher costs caused by inflation with little problem. There are also companies that have assets that inflation causes to go up in value, and they will retain purchasing power. (This really includes any type of company that is able to pass on higher inflationary costs.)

A case of this would be stocks in a food or drug company. For example, a diabetic who needs insulin will buy that drug no matter what the price. He cannot stop his treatments because inflation has caused the price of insulin to rise. The drug company that makes insulin, or any drug for that matter, should do well because people get sick and need drugs. Any type of health care company would likewise do well. People also need to eat. So stocks in a supermarket chain should do well. People also die and need caskets. Though not very glamorous, stocks held in a major casket company will have a tendency to do well. These examples are not intended to be morbid, suggesting that you should profit from the miseries of others. They merely point out there are certain necessities that transcend the consideration of cost and that companies that deal in these areas will be able to do well under inflation.

An example of an investment in an industry that has assets that would go up in value during an inflation phase would be oil stocks. Everyone needs energy in one form or another, whether it be for cooking fuel, heating, or cooling.

Nonetheless, individuals must remember that there are pitfalls in *all* investment areas. For example, if in the middle of a raging inflation you bought mining stock in the richest gold mine in the world, but the workers at that mine were to go on strike and stop production, the stock in that company could go down. Mismanagement, theft, scandal, death, and other events could also cause a company to go belly up even if it was in the midst of a boom industry.

THE AID OF A BROKER

Problems of this nature can be minimized with the aid of a good broker. This comes under the category of getting knowledge. Having a broker doesn't mean that you pick someone and just blindly follow that person's suggestions. Rules for success listed earlier state that you take charge of your own affairs but not to the exclusion of expert advice.

We are trying to function in a world that tries to "complicate, complicate, complicate." A good broker will help you to simplify things. He or she will carry what you lack. A good broker is a specialist, an expert, who, if on your side, will be invaluable. The broker has greater access to trade and industry knowledge that is very difficult to obtain otherwise and specializes in keeping abreast of any developments that could alter investment strategies. The president of our country makes all the decisions, but he takes advice from a staff of experts in his cabinet. That is the proper way to reach wise decisions.

Choosing a Broker

In most cases, whether you're a beginner or a veteran, you will find it difficult to achieve success without a broker. Not only is the broker necessary for the mechanics of buying and selling, but he or she will be indispensable in filling the gaps in your knowledge.

The general guidelines below can be used in choosing a broker of any type, from an investment broker to a real estate broker to a rare-coin broker.

1. Get opinions or recommendations from friends. People you know and trust can often recommend a broker with whom they have had a long-term relationship and who has satisfied them with performance and not just salesmanship.

2. Find out how long the broker has been in business. Experience is a good teacher, and the broker who has been in business a long time will have seen most of what there is to see. Longevity also indicates success.

3. Find out how long the broker has been at the same firm or location. Obviously, someone who jumps around from location to location might be unstable, unable to get along with others, or unscrupulous.

4. Learn how good the firm is. How effective and well established the broker's firm is reflects the kind of image the broker chooses to identify with. A firm that has taken long pains and efforts to create a solid reputation will want brokers who can further that reputation.

5. Does the broker want his clients educated? Good brokers want you to gain knowledge. If you get a bunch of double-talk intended to keep you in the dark, find a different broker.

6. Is the broker well informed? You want your broker to be a source of information. One who doesn't stay on top of things is no good to you.

7. What are the broker's personal credentials? Check the broker's background. Does he or she have degrees, certification, and other credentials?

8. What is the broker's reputation among peers? Is the broker well known as honest and reliable? Check to see if clients have registered formal complaints with groups or organizations that oversee the industry, such as the Better Business Bureau.

9. What are the broker's investment philosophies? There is more than one way to skin a cat. The broker's ideas about the market may be different from yours. Be sure your broker's investment goals or strategies are in accordance with your own, or you will find yourself locking horns.

10. Does the broker always tell you to buy, never to sell? Some brokers will want you to buy, then, after making their commissions, set you to drift off into oblivion, hoping not to hear from you again. What you want is the broker who thinks of the customer as number one.

11. Ask for a list of clients that can be contacted. There is no better way to get the inside info on a broker than to find out about him or her from those who have utilized his or her services.

SPECIFIC INVESTMENTS

Now let's look over a list of investments and examine their chief characteristics. (See chart.)

To prepare for the upcoming inflation cycle, our investments should obviously be concentrated in the category of inflation hedges. To fine-tune the investment strategy, you need to consider whether a cash flow is required, if leveraging is possible, and other factors. The perfect investment would be one that had an X in every column (except management) in the chart. Since this is not possible, the investments with the greatest number of Xs would be the strongest. Or, there could be fewer Xs as long as they were missing only from categories that are unimportant to your present strategy. Let's outline some basic strategies.

	Liquid	Stable	Leverage	Inflation Hedge	Deflation Hedge	Tax Shelter	Portable	Cash Flow	Management
Gold and Silver	X			X			X		
Coins	X	X		X	X		X		
Collectibles—Art, Antiques, Stamps		X		X			X		
Savings	X	X			X		X	X	
T-Bills	X	X			X		X	X	
Money Market	X	X			X		X	X	
Foreign Currency Denominated Investment	X		X	X			X	X	
Stocks$_1$ (Inflation-Cycle Stocks)	X		X	X			X	X	
Stocks$_2$ (Growth-Cycle Stocks)	X		X				X	X	
Mutual Funds	X	X	X				X	X	
Commodities	X		X	X					
Bonds	X		X		X		X	X	
Real Estate		X	X	X		X		X	X
Business, Personal		X	X			X		X	X

Income-Producing Assets

Suppose you were someone who must have an income-producing asset in order to live. Your strong suit would contain a powerful inflation-fighting income producer. Three investment areas where there is inflation protection with cash flow are foreign currency–denominated investment, inflation-cycle stocks, and real estate.

The strongest of these three could be real estate since it is also very stable and can be used as a tax shelter (a strong feature that is coming under attack via new tax laws). The major drawbacks of real estate are that it is highly illiquid, it is immovable, and it requires much management. Another pitfall for real estate comes in the form of rent controls and changing laws.

There are ways to avoid these particular problems (though they create another set of problems). Other than buy real estate outright, you could buy equities (stocks) that own or specialize in real estate investment. This negates illiquidity and management hassles but reduces control over the type of real estate invested in. Or you can buy into limited partnerships that offer a diversity of different properties. Again, new pitfalls are created in the way of long-term leases, demographic mix, agreements with partners, and illiquidity.

What it comes down to is that you should take on investments with problems that you are skilled in handling. For example, direct ownership of property might very well be the best way for you to own property if high liquidity is not a big concern and you are capable in management. Even if management isn't your strong suit, if the going gets too rough or you begin to expand, a qualified, reliable management company can be employed. Since no investment is perfect, it becomes a matter of trading off problems you can't deal with for those you are capable of handling. Everybody dreams of making an investment that can just be ignored and still keep the checks rolling in every month. Keep dreaming.

You may prefer to invest in the proper stocks or foreign currency. These investments provide liquidity and cash flow minus the management headaches. They are also portable, which real estate isn't. The drawback here is instability. Noneconomic factors, such as company mismanagement or governmental meddling, could cause a loss when there should be a gain. Close working knowledge can minimize risk in this area. This is an area where a good broker worth his salt can earn his keep.

All three of these investments offer leveraging, which the more aggressive wealth seeker can take advantage of. There are also other possible variations. Research into these areas, precise knowledge of your background and needs, and a good broker or counselor are the tools that will help you determine the best strategy.

Non-Income-Producing Inflation Hedges

The other group of inflation hedges falls under the non-income-producing category. For the investor who is not dependent on cash flow to exist, there are precious metals, coins, commodities, and collectibles. Again, there are drawbacks and advantages. Precious metals and commodities are highly liquid but not stable. All four are portable, but collectibles are not liquid and cannot be leveraged. There are many variations on these as well, and you must apply all the previously described techniques to build the proper portfolio.

As far as this book is concerned, the most important strategy is based on precious metals and rare coins. These investment areas are equally important to the investor who feels that the system will soon collapse and to the investor who feels we still have a way to go. Even if you feel the system will somehow or other buy time for itself, it is important to start *now* to build a precious metals and rare coins portfolio. If you think the end is near, then it is doubly important because this will be your ticket on the last train out.

The Best Choice: Rare Coins

At this juncture in American history, precious metals and especially rare coins, are an almost perfect double-edged weapon that can simultaneously combat inflation or collapse. The following table appeared in the *Wall Street Journal* in June 1983. It is based on 10-year returns of all the top investment vehicles and was compiled by Salomon Brothers Inc:

Salomon Brothers Inc.
Seventh Annual Investment Alternatives Survey
Average Annual Return (1973–1983)

Rank	Category	Rate
1	U.S. rare coins	25.7%
2	Oil	25.4%
3	U.S. rare stamps	19.2%
4	Silver	17.3%
5	Gold	15.5%
6	Farmland	11.7%
7	Diamonds	10.3%
8	Treasury bills	10.1%
9	Housing	9.2%
10	Consumer price index	8.5%
11	Old masters	8.4%
12	Stocks	7.5%
13	Bonds	6.6%
14	Foreign exchange	1.4%

According to this study, the top five investments that were able to produce real wealth-increasing returns (outside of oil, which is a commodity), are precious metals and collectibles. The top high performer, which is somewhat of a hybrid of precious metals and collectibles, is rare U.S. coins.

These top performers are all inflation-sensitive investments, which show that the trend in inflation is getting longer, more severe, and permanent. But rare coins are number one. Let's examine why.

Rare gold and silver coins respond to two driving forces. One comes from the bullion market, and the other comes from numismatists. When precious metals rise, the coins will rise accordingly. When precious metals fall, so will the price of coins. But not really. The price may come down, but there is more to rare coins than their bullion content. They have numismatic value. Numismatists create a demand for rare coins no matter where the price of bullion is going. Precious metals are difficult to locate and refine. And to find such metal in the form of a limited mintage coin is even rarer. New lodes of metals may be found, but coin mintages are fixed. If anything, they can only shrink (due to loss, destruction, etc.). So what we have is an object that has uninflatable intrinsic value because of the material it is made from and comes from an unexpansible supply of minted coins.

This situation creates a very thin market. Heavy investor involvement in a thin market can cause very large increases in the price of that investment. This is what happened in the last big gold and silver run-up of 1979–80. Coins and other collectibles skyrocketed in that panic market, yielding greater returns than even the fantastic increases coming from bullion. Of course if you bought $850 gold and $50 silver, you took a heavy loss, which is why you must buy when everyone else is selling and sell when everyone else is buying.

Dramatic losses were also sustained by coin investors who bought high. Some coins lost up to 75 percent of their value and have been in a flat market since. Coins, like all other investments, run with the cycles, and to buck contrarian buying philosophy, even with coins, is asking for trouble.

This rule becomes more evident in a panic market. It is even wise to stay out of panic markets unless you can be detached and logical and base decisions on cold hard facts. This is not the easiest stance to take in an emotional market, so that is why it might be best to stay out. If you do get involved, sell into a panic and buy coming out of a panic.

You would sell into a panic (provided you followed contrarian philosophy and bought low) because you have the goods everyone else is frantic to own before it's too late. Then you would buy goods coming out of the panic market because everyone is frantic to sell before it's too late. Selling into the panic will bring top profits, and buying out of a panic will bring bargain prices. At the end of a panic sell-off, many times the price of goods are driven lower than they should be and will readjust upward before leveling off. Don't worry about catching the exact tops and bottoms, or you might end up like the other panic participants.

While on the subject of wild booms and busts, be extra-careful to stay away from leveraged assets in wild markets. Don't go into debt to buy commodities. When the bust comes, you will find yourself in a pile of debt. Buy during the relative calm of a low cycle phase. Leverage beforehand to take advantage of a coming cycle phase. Don't procrastinate and desperately try to get in on the action once things start to take off. Again, you're just asking for trouble.

This is hard to do, but you have to subscribe to the contrarian school of investment thinking. Do the opposite of what other investors are doing. This thinking should also apply to the government. If the government is telling you one thing, believe the opposite. If it says the dollar is strong, get out of dollars. If it says gold is a weak investment, buy gold. If it says banks are safe, then you know banks are not safe. If it says there will be no currency exchange to flush out the underground, then understand the underground is its primary target. And if it tells you your freedoms are not in jeopardy, then you can be positive your freedoms are about to be sacrificed. In short, you must condition yourself to disbelieve all government certitudes and assurances or, as some state it, don't believe anything until it has been officially denied.

When you have leveraged yourself in anticipation of a cycle move, sell when nearing the peak of the cycle to pay off debts. Let the greedy and the procrastinators buy your debt while you take the profits. This way, when the prices of your income-producing investments drop, you will not die because of debt. It cannot be stressed enough. Buy low; sell high. Avoid emotional panics. Prevent your own greed from urging you to try to catch the exact tops and bottoms.

Coined Freedom

There is another factor that makes coins so valuable. Gold and silver coins have been referred to as "coined freedom." Why? Because gold and silver can take bullion one step further. Precious metals have emerged, in today's political climate, as more of a means to preserve wealth and escape government oppression and bureaucracy than as a speculative adventure. They hae become a survival factor.

Our freedoms have been taken from us so slowly that this usurpation has gone practically unobserved. Coins, more than bullion, can return and preserve those freedoms. Like bullion, coins are anonymous, transportable, easily hidden, liquid, and universally recognized; they possess intrinsic value that can't be destroyed; they are uninflatable; they retain value into the future; and they provide opportunity and privacy. Coins have these features in such a way as to make them more desirable than bullion. That is because coins put these qualities into a form that is immediately spendable or can be used for barter.

For example, in a hyperinflation a loaf of bread at the corner store might cost $100 or one silver dime. Silver stored in bullion form could not be spent or bartered with such ease. You would have to saw off a little piece, weigh it, and test it for purity.

Coins have been called "coined freedom" also because they will be able to ensure one of the most valuable commodities: opportunity. Opportunity in hand brings freedom. With gold or silver coin, you can go anywhere in the world and purchase whatever resources you need. Try that with paper money.

The following chart (compiled from several issues of *International Living*, Agora, Inc., 824 E. Baltimore St., Baltimore, MD 21202), listing some common world currencies and their value against the dollar's since 1981, shows how little opportunity paper money offers.

Currency	1981	1982	1983	3rd qtr. avg 1984	July 1985
Australia (dollar)	.87	.98	1.11	1.19	1.47
Brazil (cruzeiro)	93	180	577	1,995	5,990
Canada (dollar)	1.20	1.23	1.23	1.31	1.36
France (franc)	5.44	6.57	7.62	8.96	9.06
Greece (drachma)	55	67	88	116	134
Italy (lire)	1,137	1,353	1,519	1,800	1,900
Japan (yen)	221	249	238	243	246
Mexico (peso)	25	56	120	174	305

Spain (peseta)	92	110	143	165	170
Switzerland (franc)	1.96	2.03	2.10	2.44	2.50
U.K. (pound)	.50	.57	.66	.75	.74
W. Germany (mark)	2.26	2.43	2.55	2.92	2.98

There are disparaging contrasts in some of these currencies that demonstrate the ease with which they can be manipulated. These values reflect what has happened in four short years. How could paper money ensure opportunity when it is so easily subjected to political whim? The Roman Empire has long since perished, but one of its gold coins could, after 2,000 years, still purchase resources and opportunity anywhere in the world. This is coined freedom.

Many of you have traveled abroad. The first thing you do when reaching another country is to exchange currencies for local money. You may remember the first time you ever did this and how uneasy you felt with the new money. It looked like pretty-colored pieces of paper with numbers written on them. You knew they could be exchanged for goods, but somehow they didn't seem like real money—at least not like the good old American dollars that you are so used to. But you must remember that a foreigner coming to the U.S. will have the same feelings. Two thousand pieces of this paper equals one of that paper. Or 9.70 of these equals 252 of those. It becomes a confusing array of figures and colored paper. It's one Monopoly money versus another Monopoly money, a big game played on a global scale. But a one-ounce gold coin in any country would make immediate sense to anyone, anywhere. This is coined freedom.

The Gold and Silver Portfolio

Let's now focus on the way that investors should position themselves in relation to owning gold or silver. The first portion of the portfolio should be devoted to possessing physically at least one bag of junk silver coin for every member of the family. Junk silver coins come in bags of $1,000 face value per bag. They can be dimes, quarters, halves, and whole dollars. These should be kept in case of collapse to be used for barter to buy goods or services that might be out of reach for those attempting to use worthless fiat paper to obtain these items. These coins are purchased mainly for their bullion content and have little if any numismatic value. Their purpose is to provide spending money in the event of a collapse. They are also an investment because the price of these bags goes up and down in relation to bullion prices. They will be price discounted to bullion since they are not 100 percent pure. But this can be ignored since they should not be held for speculative purposes. They should be held for coined freedom.

Gold bullion coins should also be held for that purpose. The Krugerrand, which investors can buy in $\frac{1}{10}$-, $\frac{1}{4}$-, $\frac{1}{2}$-, or 1-ounce form, has been the most popular bullion coin to date and is readily accepted and recognized worldwide. Gold offers a more concentrated form in which to store wealth than does silver, so everyone should also hold gold bullion coin for spending money. If you are worried about having Krugerrands, gold Maple Leafs or Credit Suisse could be an alternative.

You will also want to hold some straight gold and silver bullion bars. These bars come in sizes ranging from $\frac{1}{4}$ ounce up to 1,000 ounces. The smaller the bar, the greater the premium paid over spot prices at the time of purchase. This premium covers refiner's cost, commissions, etc.

To give an idea of what it might cost to buy, here is a price list from a Midwest refinery issued in January 1985. Silver was listed at $5.97 per ounce, and gold was $299.50 per ounce.

Minted One Troy Ounce .999 Fine Silver Bars or Medallions

10–49	$1.50 over spot
50–99	$1.25 over spot
100–499	$1.05 over spot
500–999	$.95 over spot
1000 or above	$.75 over spot

Minted .999 Silver Bullion Bars

5 Troy ounce	$1.25/oz over spot
10 Troy ounce	1.00/oz over spot

Cast .999 Silver Bullion Bars

25 Troy ounce	$.90/oz over spot
100 Troy ounce	.65/oz over spot
1000 Troy ounce	.40/oz over spot

Gold Prices for Maple Leaf, Krugerrand, or Credit Suisse

1 ounce	$27.00 over spot
½ ounce	($.50 × spot) + $25.00
¼ ounce	($.25 × spot) + $15.00
⅒ ounce	($.10 × spot) + $12.00
10 ounces or more	10% discount off commissions

As you can see, purchasing the largest bars can save money on premiums. When buying these bars, try to get a nice mix. Even though you save money with the larger bars, the bigger they are, the harder they are to sell or barter. During the last gold rush, millions of ordinary investors had lesser amounts to invest in the smaller sizes, but the bigger and more costly the size, the smaller the market. This reduced liquidity to a degree since a greater effort had to be made to find an investor with more capital.

As a final note concerning gold and silver bullion coins, in a crisis, the smaller the coin, the better it is spent. If you find yourself spending larger coins, you might just be getting paper in change, which is something to avoid at all costs. The larger coins and bars should be purchased after you're in place with the smaller units. Buy small and build your way up.

The next part of the portfolio should consist of numismatic coins. These coins should be bought and held. They should never be sold. Like the bullion coins and bars, they should be bought for holding, not for speculation. The idea is that you are trading present paper for future money, future opportunity, future freedom. As much as possible, you should slowly, methodically, and constantly trade paper for metal, not vice versa.

Now, the goal of buying, holding, and never selling is not to take these investments to the grave with you. "Never sell" doesn't mean you will never, ever sell. If the next inflationary run-up ends because of the paper exchange and tax increases, coins will also follow cyclic movements and drop in price. There will be very dramatic and drastic price increases in the next inflation, and you might want to sell just a few of your holdings to trade for more coins after they have fallen in price. Depending on your investment strategy, you might sell off many coins, take paper profits, and repurchase more coins in the recession or growth phase.

This difference in strategy is not recommended but must be explained. In a "best case" scenario, the coming inflation phase will melt into a recession phase, which in turn will progress to a growth phase, and finally will revert to an inflation stage. If this happens, coins might very well take a beating, as they did after the last big inflationary run-up. Aggressive investors will not want to hold onto inflation hedges in the other phases.

In the last run-up, many investors jumped into coins, which caused many of them to reach astronomical price levels. After the panic died and the smoke cleared, coins, like gold and silver, bit the dirt. If the cycles remain intact, there will be many who feel justified in selling off their inflation hedges at the right time to take advantage of the next phases.

The reason this approach is not recommended is that these cycles are near the end of their existence. Even if they do go around once more, they will be very short in duration, and we will be back to an inflation stage before you know it. Depressed coin prices will also be back up before you know it.

There is just too much debt, deficit, escalating government interference, which the system has never had to deal with before. As explained, the present system actually cannot deal with these factors, factors that will bring about the death of the system and its transmutation into a survival mode. At this point, unique circumstances in the marketplace have put coins (and the other hard assets) into an affordable price range with relative availability. The smartest way to get involved in coins, collectibles, and other hard assets right now is to take a buy-and-hold position, and not for the purpose of speculation.

You hold for other reasons. These coins will become part of a retirement plan that will pale any IRA or Keogh that tries to come near it. These coins will enable you to meet any emergency contingency. They will allow you to offer your heirs a legacy free from government manipulation, confiscation, or destruction through debasement. This is another aspect of coined freedom.

You also want to have physical possession of your coins and bullion. Don't accept receipts for them and let someone else hold them. They might not be there when you go back to get them.

Now you might be wondering how you can take advantage of the coming inflation without compromising your survival portfolio. The answer is in paper. Buy and sell paper. Buy stocks in "inflation-proof" businesses. You might like foreign currency–denominated investments or real estate paper deals. Buy gold-mining shares or a commodities futures contract. You can buy and sell gold or silver options, options on gold-mining shares, or penny-mining shares. A penny-mining share can go up 10 or 20 to 1 when the price of gold is only doubling. You might want to go heavier on the silver than the gold. Silver has more dramatic percentage rises in price than does gold. The last time gold was near $900, silver was about $50. If these prices were reached again from today's prices of $300 gold and $6 silver, gold would have to triple in value, but silver would have to multiply by a factor of eight.

These paper deals can be leveraged and structured to take advantage of wealth-seeking principles. By following the correct strategies, you can reap nice paper profits and use this new paper to buy more coined freedom. In other words, if you want to make present money with gold or silver, you want to make it by dealing in gold and silver paper promises. You want to make future money, or coined freedom, by using the actual metals themselves. If there is a collapse, you will be paying debt with paper and using paper to buy whatever it can, if anything. You would go to your metals only if paper no longer will get whatever it is that you want.

The Coin Market

Let's get into a description of the coin market. As mentioned earlier, it is a mix of investor and collector. The investor doesn't give a hoot about mintage numbers, beauty, date sets, type sets, or historical value, whereas the collector does. If possible, an investor will buy and sell a coin in the same day if a healthy profit can be realized. On the other hand, come hell or high water, a collector cannot be persuaded to part with coins for any reason. A collector will even give price a back seat if it means the final completion of a set that he's worked for years to build. This is a big factor that keeps rare coins at a premium when other inflation hedges are falling.

During the last big run-up, many potential buyers stood on the sidelines, knowledge of the market being the great limiting factor. All these investors have since read about the tremendous profits that were made in rare coins. And when Salomon Brothers Inc. reports in the *Wall Street Journal* that coins are the number one investment, you can be sure there will be a lot of new faces in the coin market once inflation takes hold.

What many of these investors don't realize, again, is that the rare coin market is extremely thin. Heavy activity is going to make prices soar. It has been estimated that in the '50s there were about .5 million collector/investors participating in the coin market. This estimate rose to 14 million for 1984 and is projected to 25 million for 1985. One benefit of this is that all these new participants will create instant liquidity for coins. Dealers and investors in coin have the same problem: it is easy to sell quality merchandise but it is difficult to obtain. It is a seller's market, and this tendency will only increase in the future.

This is why the correct time to get involved is right *now!* Most investors are motivated by greed and fear, which are their biggest enemies. Actions based on these enemies are guaranteed to fail. The metals and coin markets are flat at the moment. Everyone is talking about inflation being dead, but no one really believes it. This talk will create a fear to act now when the time is proper. The greedy will wait for precise tops and bottoms, which few investors ever catch. The fearful will become greedy when prices have already shot up. The procrastinators will wake up at that time, too. They will all jump into the market when it's too late. When the bottom falls out, they will scramble, out of fear, to sell off before their losses become too great. Most people buy high and sell low. In the meantime, the shrewd investor sells into greed, buys into fear, and makes profits.

With greater numbers of collector/investors in the market, the unavailability of top-grade coins has caused many of these coins to price themselves out of reach for the common investor. What this should do is to create new areas for collector markets to emerge. Demand will cause previously overlooked lower-grade coins to command greater respect in the marketplace. There is tremendous pressure, and rightly so, by investors to obtain the best-quality coins there are. But there are just not enough of them to go around. And sources of this fixed supply can only decrease.

Because of this, the newcomer should not be afraid to invest in lower-grade coins. They are more affordable, and you can become educated in the market by dealing in these lower grades. When the opportunity arises, and it will, you can move with more confidence and purchase some high-grade coins. And your lower grades will also have increased in value. So even though the general rule is to buy quality, the best, heavy demand will make lower grades command respect.

The thinness of this market and greater awareness by investors of the value of collectibles will probably spill into other collector markets. Rare stamps (which are in the top five on the Salomon list), art, antiques, and other collectibles should benefit vastly from this new awareness.

The Advantages of Coins

What other advantages do coins offer? Privacy is one. The power mongers are after everyone, especially the underground, but not excluding the aboveground. The investor with the most visible wealth is first in line for governmental extortion. Coins offer a legal privacy from governmental eyes that is difficult to obtain in other investments. When it comes time for the powercrats to search for new pockets of wealth to arrogate, your coin portfolio will be safely hidden from sight. Coins bring the capacity to earn high profits in a low-keyed or unobservable manner.

Taxes are another advantage. Unlike dollar-denominated assets or paper profits, taxes are deferred until profits are realized at liquidation. And this tax will be at the lower capital gains tax rate rather than the higher ordinary rates. The only caveat to tax advantages is that tax laws change and so can the tax status of coins. What the boss-man giveth, the boss-man can taketh back.

This would be a good time to clear up misconceptions about IRAs and Keoghs. Since contrarian philosophy dictates that we believe the opposite of what government says, and since the government says these plans are a boon for the common man, these retirement plans should immediately become suspect. The primary objective for their creation was to aid the enfeebled banking system's liquidity dilemma and not to provide a tax benefit for the ordinary folk. The government wants us to believe that these plans are the best thing since sliced bread, but their creation is the result of a law that can be changed at any time in the future. Or, as the contrarian might repeat, what the boss-man giveth, you can be sure he will taketh back.

There are a few more tax angles left to discuss. If you live in an area that borders another state or can get an out-of-state mailing address, you can have your purchases shipped to you and avoid sales tax. This is an annoying tax that can start to add up. Or, if you live near a state, such as Delaware, that has no sales tax, a short trip there will be worth the effort.

Another tax break comes if you use your coins for barter in a like-kind exchange. An exchange of this type is treated as a nontaxable event. Also, no personal property taxes are levied on numismatic portfolios, as they are on real estate or stocks. Presently, there are no registration requirements for buyers or sellers of coins. But once again, it holds true that what the boss-man giveth. . . .

One last unique feature of numismatic coins is their portability. Millions of dollars in rare coins can easily fit into a small briefcase. The present regulations state that persons leaving the country with over $5,000 must be reported to the authorities. A $1,000,000 portfolio could easily be under $5,000 face value of rare coins, and to customs agents rare coins just look like small change.

The Pitfalls of the Coin Market

Now, let's detail pitfalls and limiting factors in the coin market. There are three major pitfalls to watch for: grading, counterfeiting, and storage. The biggest reason many investors who wanted to, but didn't, enter the coin market in the last big run-up was their lack of knowledge. Knowledge is the key to avoiding the pitfalls.

Choosing a Coin Broker

There is a whole lot to know about coins. This an area that takes years to master. But that should not prevent anyone from getting started right now. This is where choosing a solid, reliable dealer will get you over the first hurdles. You can start reading books and newsletters, join clubs, etc., and your broker can help you while you play catch-up with your knowledge. Apply the same rules to choosing a coin broker as you would to any other dealer, with the addition of these rules:

1. Will the broker give and honor a return privilege? This is mainly for coins that are purchased by mail-order. A money-back, no-questions-asked guarantee is essential. Of course, the coin must be returned in the same condition as it was sold.

2. Is your dealer willing to have ANACS grade his or her coins? ANA (American Numismatic Association) provides a grading and authentication service and will issue papers attesting to the coin's qualities. There is some controversy in the industry over ANACS (ANA Certification Service) grading procedures, and there may even be some scandal involved with kickback, bribes, etc. The ANA does use very sophisticated technology to check for counterfeits and altered coins. So far, controversy surrounds grading (which is subjective), but no one seems to be disputing their ability to spot fakes. A dealer who will not submit to an ANACS certification should raise doubts in your mind on his sincerity. A note of caution: beware of counterfeit ANACS papers sold with coins from an unscrupulous dealer.

Grading

Grading is the first big pitfall to watch for. The major problem is overgrading. In recent years, the most popular system for grading uses the numerical grading system. Coins are broken down into three main categories: circulated, uncirculated, and proof.

In the circulated grade, we have these designations (descriptions taken from *Red Book—A Guide Book of United States Coins*, Western Pub. Co., Inc., Racine WI):

About Good (AG-3)—Very heavily worn with portions of lettering, date, and legends worn smooth. The date may be barely readable.

Good (G-4)—Heavily worn with design visible but faint in areas. Many details are flat.

Very Good (VG-8)—Well worn with main features clear and bold although rather flat.

Fine (F-12)—Moderate to considerable even wear. Entire design is bold with overall pleasing appearance.

Very Fine (VF-20)—Shows moderate wear on high points of design. All major details are clear.

Choice Very Fine (VF-30)—Light even wear on the surface and highest parts of the design. All lettering and major features are sharp.

Extremely Fine (EF or XF-40)—Design is lightly worn throughout, but all features are sharp and well defined. Traces of luster may show.

Choice Extremely Fine (EF/XF-45)—Light overall wear shows on highest high points. All design details are very sharp. Some of the mint luster is evident.

About Uncirculated (AU-50)—Has traces of light wear on many of the high points. At least half of the mint luster remains.

Choice About Uncirculated (AU-55)—Barest evidence of light wear on only the highest points of the design. Most mint luster remains.

Uncirculated coins, which show no trace of wear, and are designated *MS*, which means "MINT STATE," are graded thus:

Uncirculated (MS-60)—Has no trace of wear but may show a moderate number of contact marks, and surface may be spotted or lack some luster.

Choice Uncirculated (MS-65)—An above average uncirculated coin which may be brilliant or lightly toned and has very few contact marks on the surface or rim.

Perfect Uncirculated (MS-70)—Perfect new condition, showing no trace of wear. The finest quality possible, with no evidence of scratches, handling or contact with other coins. Very few regular issue coins are ever found in this condition.

Proof coins are designated in the same fashion as the other two categories. The term *proof* does not indicate wear or condition but a method of manufacture. Examples would be Proof-60, Proof-63, and Proof-65.

Again, the big pitfall lies in overgrading. Grading is subjective, and, if a coin can be bumped up a grade, it will often command stiff price increases. To illustrate this, the following is a price list of a few Unc. Morgan Dollars that are very popular among collectors:

Date	MS-60	MS-63	MS-65
1880—O	$65	$136	$1,200
1884—P	57	82	600
1887—O	50	87	815
1890—O	60	97	1,375
1902—P	54	95	1,150
1921—S	41	82	950

You can easily see how overgrading can result in wide price differences for certain coins. There are many deceitful ways in which to bump grades higher. One is the almost irresistible urge to sell the AU coin as an MS coins. This could be an honest mistake on the part of a new, inexperienced dealer or the action of one who has larceny in his heart. One way to tell the difference is that a novice will both undergrade and overgrade. A crooked dealer will overgrade everything.

Four ways to avoid overgraded coins is to ask for ANACS papers, get a third opinion, deal with a reputable dealer, and learn grading yourself.

ANACS may have gone through some changes, but the certification is at least something to go on. There are also other organizations that grade coins if you feel uncomfortable with ANACS. Getting a third opinion can help. If you have a friend who is knowledgeable, bring him or her along. Dealing with a reputable, well-established dealer can prevent most hassles, especially when you take the time to learn grading yourself. The most basic tool you'll need is a magnifying glass. You can also buy books on the subject and join local coin clubs that offer hands-on training courses.

Counterfeits

The next great pitfall is counterfeiting. Counterfeits usually crop up with the rarer coins. Many are done expertly and, in fact, are so well done that the counterfeiter, taking pride in his craftmanship, will very inconspicuously put his trademark on the coin (which can be seen only under magnification). There are three basic types of counterfeits. They are coins that are altered, cast, or die-struck.

An altered coin is a coin that has been tampered with to appear like another coin. This usually involves the addition or deletion of dates or mint marks. Typically, a coin of the same type will be machined or brushed down to change its date or mint mark to that of one which is very rare.

Sometimes coins are altered by a method that is referred to as *whizzing*. Whizzed coins are worked over with brushes or dipped in acid to "upgrade" the coin from a lesser to a higher grade.

Cast counterfeits are easier to detect than their die-struck counterparts. A cast counterfeit is a copy of a copy and often lacks the fine detail of the genuine die-struck coin. Under a magnifying glass, many of the cast counterfeit's features will be blurred and grainy, whereas the genuine coin is sharp and clear. Although disguised, the fake will have a seam on its edge if it is a nonreeded coin. On a reeded coin the edge will have no seam, but the reeding will be less uniform and even than on the genuine article. There are also electrotype counterfeits that are similar to cast type. They make a somewhat better reproduction of detail, but the seamed edge is more prominent on the electrotypes than in any other type of cast counterfeit.

Die-struck counterfeits are the most difficult to detect because they are struck in the same way as the real coin is. There are two basic ways to spot die-struck counterfeits. One involves showing pictures of the characteristics of real coins and the other involves showing pictures of selected counterfeits. There are thousands of varieties of counterfeits, each with telltale errors that will show up under magnification. It is hard to publish pictures on the subject because the counterfeiters will read the same books and alter their dies to correct errors.

Some of the most widely counterfeited coins are the gold $2.50 and $5.00 "Indians" and $20.00 double eagles, the 1914-D Lincoln cent, and the 1909-S VDB Lincoln cent, the latter being one of the favorites among the counterfeiters.

There are counterfeits that are so well made that one may even slip by an experienced dealer. In this case, the best protection is to have purchased your coins in tamper-proof packaging with photos. A reputable dealer will not hesitate to take back a coin, provided you can show that it is the same coin that you bought.

When buying rare costly dates that are the most likely targets for counterfeiters, it is best to have certification by ANACS. They possess expertise and equipment that is simply not available to the ordinary dealer or investor.

For example, in one phase of their examination, they employ the aid of an AMRAY scanning electron microscope with continuous zoom magnification from 5X to 300,000X. This specially built microscope does things no other microscope can do and can easily produce irrefutable evidence of authenticity.

If you are hesitant to deal with ANACS, even though it is the most recognized certifier in the trade, you might check out the International Numismatic Society Authentication Bureau in Washington, DC, or the National Collectors Laboratories in

New York City. The success rate of these two services, as well
as that of ANACS, is purported to be 100 percent.

Storing Coins

The last major pitfall involves storage. Coins themselves
should be stored in the best containers available. The best
preservation is offered in hard, transparent, Lucite, screw-
together holders. These are very thick and strong and can
withstand almost any common mishap. Avoid cheap containers, especially those made of blue or brown cardboard. Contact with paper will cause coins to become discolored due to
the presence of sulfur in the paper. You want to avoid PVC
plastic since it is reputed that these containers have caused a
strange green slime to appear on coins.

Copper coins are the most susceptible to decay, and you
might avoid investing in the very expensive ones altogether.
The bright red coin with original mint luster will become
downgraded once it becomes chocolate- or dull-colored.
When handling these or any other coins, always hold them by
the edges. A big fat fingerprint, once etched into the surface
by skin acids and oils, will reduce the value of the coin.

Avoid talking, sneezing, or coughing when viewing coins.
Tiny droplets of saliva that come into contact with the surface
will eventually cause black spots to appear on the coin.
Clearly, these spots not only are ugly but also will reduce the
quality of the coin.

Storing your entire collection of coin and bullion is the
other half of the storage problem. The location that comes to
the mind of most people is a safe deposit box at a bank. As this
book has already discussed, these boxes may be safe from
thieves with masks and guns, but how safe are they from
thieves with briefcases and guns (the government type)?
Besides, they are accessible only on weekdays during regular
business hours. What happens when you need your coins on a
Saturday afternoon? You will have to wait until Monday at
9:00 A.M.

An alternative to a bank vault is a private vault which

provides 24-hour, 365-days-a-year accessibility. The best ones have around-the-clock security guards and the strongest vaults money can buy. Still, with all the uncertainties of our world, though it is less likely, there is always a possibility that government men could show up at their doors in a "crisis."

Home storage can be the best and worst place for storage. Improper storage can set you up for thieves, fire, flood, tornadoes, forgetfulness, death, and other acts of God. Probably the best vehicle for home storage is a heavy-duty, best-quality floor safe buried in a cement floor under dense carpet with a heavy piece of furniture covering it.

It is best to be secretive about holdings. When discussing assets, discuss percentages, not dollar amounts. Don't feel secure letting others know you have stored valuables at home simply because you have a secret, impenetrable safe. It is no problem for a thief to hold a gun to your head and threaten you with death unless you reveal the location of your safe and open it. When having your safe delivered, don't let the whole neighborhood see it, and be sure to deal with a highly reputable dealer, or you might be the victim of an "inside" job.

It is also wise, if you are storing wealth at home, not to give the appearance of wealth. Many have been victimized by those who have perceived wealth where there was none. Installing a concealed alarm system and making it look as if someone is always home is the best protection against nomadic thieves who just might stumble into your abode.

In-ground burial is another favorite. Only bury on ground that you own. Sufficient ground must be available to make this effort worthwhile. Your cache must be buried deep enough so that it would call for great exertion to retrieve. This necessitates working at a time when no one can see you, which is not as easy as it sounds. Containers must also be watertight and sturdy.

A danger from in-ground burial could arise from treasure seekers with metal detectors. The best detectors are able to discriminate junk from valuable objects. Very deep burial, which makes it equally difficult for you to retrieve your belongings, must be done to avoid detection. Burying smaller amounts in more spots will also help. One expert recommends buying 10 or 20 tubes of copper-coated BBs to spread around like grass seed after burial is completed. In a week or two these BBs will sink into the ground and become unseen. Anyone coming by with a metal detector will find the detector going haywire.

Don't be so quick to report lots of valuables stored at home to an insurance company. There are lots of unsavory characters that work at these companies who will enter into pacts with burglars who specialize in stealing what you have.

Conflict of Interest

One last investment tip is to take advice from those who have nothing to sell to you. Also, buy from those who are not in the business of disseminating knowledge. You might find advice urging you to buy a certain coin or investment coming from somebody who just happens to be loaded up with that very investment. If you buy from those whose main business is to buy and sell and not to advise, you will avoid a conflict of interest.

Start Your Portfolio *Now*

These strategies and tips have been presented only as general background knowledge. Entire books have been written on each subject, so vast is the knowledge that can be acquired. If you are new to this, let your education begin here, but don't let it end here. Knowledge will be your greatest asset. It is wealth that you carry with you, and it cannot be taken away from you. It is true wealth.

It has been said that, if you think education is expensive, try ignorance. Do everything possible to learn. Seminars and learning from the experts are a good way to pick up knowledge. Ultimately you must become your own expert. Plan, study, learn, and act in the proper way, and you will become invincible.

Finally, there will be many who read this information and,

out of inspiration or fear, make inquiries and plans to get started in building an investment portfolio. Then maybe there is a small drop in the price of some investment vehicle you have interest in and you decide to wait a few days or weeks to catch a lower price. This book gets put on the shelf, and after a week or two you will lose your sense of urgency. You then become a procrastinator. You will fail to act. Because of this you will go down with the ship.

A crude analogy is applicable here. It was said that the *Titanic* was unsinkable. In fact, the crew and passengers had total faith in that statement and acted accordingly. When the ship first hit the iceberg that caused it to sink, reports claim the crew and captain did not react as would normally be expected in such perilous circumstances. When they could no longer deny the obvious, the crew alerted passengers to abandon ship. Many passengers could not be convinced of the *Titanic*'s fallibility and took no heed. There were those asleep in their cabins who could not be persuaded to arise and evacuate because the ship was sinking. They would not believe it. It has even been said that there were those who stayed in the ballroom while the band played, disbelieving any danger would actually befall them. In the meantime, those who did try to escape found there were not enough lifeboats to accommodate a proper salvage operation of passengers. Many latecomers were left behind who wanted to, but could not, escape.

How many will take heed of the sinking of the ship America? Most believe it can't happen as they request, "Strike up the band." The American public is constantly fed a diet of rhetoric that assures us we are the greatest country in the world, we have the best system, we enjoy the most freedoms. If you don't believe it, we are told, try to do this in Russia. The ship America has hit an iceberg and is floundering. The captain and the crew of the ship, the president and the Congress, are not acting properly. The passengers, the American people, have been duped into believing it can't happen here. And those disbelievers who finally take action will find that the salvage operation to secure freedom and wealth, which are the correct investments, is no longer available because the wise have already taken all available seating. The procrastinators and disbelievers will go down with the ship.

No one wants to hear about collapse, and no one wants to believe it. We all do not want it to happen, and that includes the authors of this book. But trends in motion tend to stay in motion, and the overwhelming trend is toward collapse. The future favors the prepared. You cannot do everything today, but you can do something today. Don't gamble with your future, your freedoms. You have been thrown a life preserver. Take advantage, stay motivated, and do something.

11
GOLD—THE FINAL SOLUTION

Our great misfortune is that, because of our irredeemable currency system, we are forced into speculation (which is just another word for *gambling*) as a way of life. Many people cannot understand that our fiat currency is the root cause of all the cheating, lying, and stealing that goes on in order for the common man and his family to maintain a decent standard of living. In 1919, John Maynard Keynes wrote:

> Lenin is said to have declared that the best way to destroy the capitalist system was to debauch the currency. By a continuing process of inflation, governments can confiscate, secretly and unobserved, an important part of the wealth of their citizens. By this method, they not only confiscate, but they confiscate arbitrarily; and, while the process impoverishes many, it actually enriches some. . .
> Lenin was certainly right. There is no subtler, no surer, means of overturning the existing basis of society than to debauch the currency. The process engages all the hidden forces of eco-

nomic law on the side of destruction, and does it in a manner
which not one man in a million is able to diagnose.*

Our present irredeemable currency is a debauched, dishonest currency, no matter in what new shape or style it is
presented to us, and out of necessity it is dependent on a
dishonest standard of behavior. This dishonesty is the precursor of greater evils. Many of our leaders, most of the press,
and a majority of the U.S. Congress support an irredeemable
currency and are extremely reluctant to state accurately the
pertinent facts and principles involved while continuing to
deride a gold standard as archaic, impractical, and a return to
a "barbarous" system of finances. This is compounded by the
fact that most of the population also believes this to be true.
Because this is a problem "not one man in a million is able to
diagnose," the people have unwittingly become part of the
plot to deprive them of their wealth, freedom, and ultimate
happiness.

Not only is there apathy and a great willingness to accept
what we hear from our leaders and the press, but most of our
leaders have themselves become subject to the same ignorance as preached by their predecessors and mentors. Ther is
no major institution of higher learning in this country teach-
ing a full-time course in currency theory. If the leaders are
ignorant, then what can be said of the masses?

Consequently, the general public will advocate the very
expedients that tend to injure them. Their ideas of money go
little beyond the desire for more and more of it. When the
money depreciates, they demand more to compensate for lost
buying power. Many even feel that inflation is prosperity
because they get more money. Talk of redeemability evokes
little sympathy or outright opposition because people fear
they will get less money while they have for so long been
conditioned to a need for more buying power. Somehow,

---

*John Maynard Keynes, *The Economic Consequences of the Peace* as quoted
by Walter E. Spahr, *Our Irredeemable Currency System* (Greenwich: Committee for Monetary Research and Education, Inc., 1976).

embedded in the mores of the people is the belief that gold is the rich man's money, whereas silver and paper money, especially irredeemable paper, are the poor man's money.

Because of this, the public will elect those officials who promise more (through inflation and taxes, of course). This creates a "catch-22" situation as the people and politicians play off each others' greed and ignorance. Our irredeemable currency is unquestionably dishonest. It gives the Treasury, Federal Reserve, and its subordinate cronies the power to create money without the concurrent responsibilities. Monetary reform must be instituted by our leaders, however. We are in dire need of wise leaders who are above reproach and dedicated enough to begin reforms immediately. We need to elect honest statesman who will work for the common good and not mediocre politicians who work for themselves. Maybe this is asking too much, but a nation that lacks such leaders will slowly rot to extinction.

When, in 1933, FDR divested the people of their gold and installed an irredeemable currency, he also stripped them of their power to control directly the government's use of public funds. The New Deal Administration even made the manipulation of the value of the currency an openly proclaimed tool of public policy.

Previously, if individuals disapproved of or distrusted the banks', Fed's, Treasury's, or government's policy, they could register objections directly by presenting their notes and demanding redemption on their promises to pay. This would send a loud, clear signal right to the heart of their nervous system—their gold reserves. With every redemption, the number of warning signals increased, reserves were whittled, and reponses of sounder monetary or fiscal procedures were forced. To the extent of that person's possession of redeemable currency, he or she had the power to voice dissatisfaction through redemption. There was no need for individuals to band together in some organization for the purpose of sending a plea to the Congress, Federal Reserve, or Treasury to beg for a return to prudent, responsible policies. Each person could act alone and send his or her judgment directly.

An irredeemable currency changed all that. The people's power to act individually was destroyed. The only means left to protest damaging or unwanted activities is through organizations, letters to the press, and congressmen, which all result in fruitless efforts because they can be, and will be, ignored. Having cut the line of control over the use of public funds, the government simultaneously freed itself from the concomitant responsibility to serve the people. It now can and generally does ignore their protests, and it now becomes their controller.

With this new liberty of unaccountability, the government resorts to the use of public funds to buy the support necessary to keep itself in office. It then actually seeks the support of special-interest pressure groups that have the ability to deliver large blocks of votes. These pressure groups will deliver their votes to those who promise the most appealing monetary favors, and off they rush to Washington to lobby for the best terms available. One result is that the government becomes inevitably obligated to the special-interest groups, and control of the national treasury is given indirectly to these vote-delivering, favor-seeking groups.

Another effect of an irredeemable currency is to open the door to modern-day socialism, which is an intermediate step toward totalitarianism. Through taxes and inflation, money is taken from helpless groups and transferred to the members of the high-pressure groups. In the name of social justice, redistribution of wealth, and so on, a welfare state is created. The producers are penalized because they have more, and the nonproducers are awarded handouts because they have less.

We are made to believe through government propaganda and machinations of the press and electronic media that middle-class businesspeople and entrepreneurs are greedy capitalists who exploit the underclasses for personal profit and gain. They have achieved their wealth by cheating the poor and therefore must be taxed heavily to relieve the burden of the poor for which they are blamed.

Free competition becomes hampered or destroyed with an endless stream of rules and regulations as the government bestows its favors on the select via wage-price controls, subsidies, grants, tax exemptions, and rent controls. The government also enters into unfair productive competition with private enterprise, unhampered by tax burdens, regulatory and bureaucratic red tape, and interference with which the private sector is forced to deal. Because of this irredeemable currency, the government is able to make special loans at below-market rates, undertake special projects pleasing to the special-interest groups, and use other devices to manipulate and control the marketplace.

Irredeemable currency has allowed profligate spending and a dissipation of the nation's patrimony. All efforts in behalf of economy in government are futile. The leaders are freed from their responsibility to manage properly, and money is made easy for government and its favored groups to obtain. Not only does an irredeemable currency make the road toward totalitarianism easy; it invites it. A gold standard therefore becomes the antithesis to totalitarianism.

It becomes easy to see why the powercrats are so strongly opposed to a gold standard. What better way is there to deal a death blow to their takeover plans? There is probably no single act more debilitating to their dreams of world empire than the reinstatement of a gold standard. The powercrats can ignore the entreaties and objections of the people because of the powers an irredeemable currency bestows. Therefore, the first and most important step in preventing an Orwellian world of *1984* dimensions is the restoration of a gold standard.

The one-worlders would like to see an international currency created. If they are as sincere and humanitarian as they claim, then let them advocate a gold currency that would be readily accepted throughout the entire world. There would be no need to trick or force the people of the earth to accept gold as an international currency, as will be the case with our new paper currency in the coming exchange. If they are really interested in a one-world economy, let them ban irredeemable currency, which only impedes the flow of goods, services, people, and currency itself across international borders. Let them revoke the thousands of government restrictions and controls on private business and put freedom back into the term *free enterprise*. A resurgence of production, trade, and prosperity, both national and international, will not be found in a new, irredeemable currency and more government interference. True internationalism or one-worldism necessitates a gold standard, free exchange of currencies, and the confinement of government solely to policies to ensure free and fair competition and to prevent fraud and national injury.

There are many explanations opponents present against the return to a gold standard. One argument, the scarcity-of-gold argument, claims there is not enough gold (and silver) to go around to act as a currency. This argument fails to realize that scarcity is a requisite of value. The more common an item is, the less value it has. Gold requires sufficient effort to locate, excavate, and refine and is scarce enough to be rare but simultaneously obtainable enough to be widely available. Its scarcity also compels us to practice prudence and frugality in money matters. This built-in feature would automatically curb spendthrift practices in government and the economy.

The cost of goods and services rises because inflation reduces the purchasing power of the dollar. More dollars are needed to buy the same quantity of goods or services. Another way of stating this is the cost of goods and services actually remains the same. It is the value of our currency that diminishes; hence more is needed. The price of gold seems to go up and down in the same manner as that of other goods. The fact is that, generally speaking, the value of gold remains constant; it is the manipulated paper money that is always changing. The following examples will illustrate this.

In America's past, while on the gold standard (1837–1933), an ounce of gold would have purchased a fine-quality man's suit. Today, an ounce of gold will still purchase a fine-quality man's suit. In the past, an ounce of gold would have purchased enough food and groceries to fill the back of a station wagon. Today an ounce of gold will still purchase enough to fill a station wagon.

Another example is that a cup of coffee could be had for one silver dime. Today a cup of coffee can still be purchased with the silver value of that dime. The point is that, if gold and silver coin were again brought back into circulation, their face values in terms of fluctuating paper could be ignored. The value of gold coin would be pegged at its already established level of purchasing power. In other words, if a gold coin the size of a dime had $20 worth of purchasing power, then a gold coin that size could be minted as a $20 piece. Or we could go back to the sizes, weights, and face values of gold and silver coin when such coins circulated as money in our past. A $20 gold eagle was roughly the size of a present-day half-dollar, and a $1 piece was a little smaller than a dime. Instead of having a paper exchange of 100-to-1, we could have such an exchange using gold instead.

Many of us have heard our parents tell of the days when they worked for a week's wages of $20. With that $20, they fed and clothed the family and paid the rent. A return to the days of those weights and values would carry an additional bonus. People would not have to walk around with huge bulges of cash stuffed in their pockets. Wealth could be stored in very concentrated forms. In a 100-for-1 exchange, a copper penny would have the buying power of a dollar, and a $20 gold eagle would equal $2,000. Small coins of great value could easily be concealed and would reduce the chance of theft. Individuals could store their wealth in small secret places and ensure the greatest privacy and safety.

Our dollar is presently equal to $.01 (maybe $.02) of a turn-of-the-century gold dollar. A 100-to-1 exchange would bring prices of goods and services back to levels we had in 1900. According to the U.S. Department of the Treasury, as of June 1983 there was $181,789,283,363 in coin and currency both in circulation and outstanding. A 100-for-1 exchange would reduce that figure to $1,817,892,834, or approximately $1.8179 billion. As of the end of 1982, the U.S. owned 264.03 million troy ounces of gold. If we were to value that gold at $20.67, the price that was set in 1837 and lasted until 1933, our gold would equal $5,457,500,100, or about $5.4575 billion. This equals three times the amount of currency we have in circulation today in equivalents to a 1900s gold dollar. (Without a

100-for-1 recall, the price of gold could be set at $1,000 per ounce. At this price, a money stock of 2.6403 billion could be created.) Or, if necessary, the price could be $2,000 per ounce or whatever would be required if you want to consider things like M_1 (demand accounts plus currency at commercial banks), M_2 (M_1 plus overnight repos [loans], Eurodollars, money market fund shares, savings accounts, and small [under $100,000] time deposits), etc.

So, why must this gold languish in reserve? It could be coined and circulated, and we would have three times the amount of money in circulation if everything was rolled back to 1900 equivalents. Does this sound like there is a shortage of gold? This does not even take into account coins of silver, nickel, and copper. So to say there is not enough gold or silver to go around is not true. Such a statement has no historical or factual basis.

Also to be considered is 800 years of precedent that was set by the Byzantine Empire. As previously stated, the bezant was allowed to circulate freely and roam the world, but never did the empire experience a shortage of gold. Do not forget this situation endured for 800 long years. Good gold and silver coin began to diappear only after the coinage was debauched. A noble government allows the pure noble metals to circulate freely. A corrupt government is reflected in the corrupt alloys that it passes out as coinage.

Once again, we ask why our gold must languish in reserve. Actually, if our money is a fiat currency and is not backed by gold, silver, or even copper, then stockpiles of these metals are not even reserves. We have heard the rhetoric over the last 40 years that gold has no real intrinsic value, is unnecessary, and is solely a reminder of our barbarous past. We have been told our modern economy requires a currency that is able to be expanded when necessary to meet our needs. Economists like Dr. Milton Friedman, and Professor F. A. Von Hayek deprecate a gold standard and tell us any commodity could act as a monetary standard. Professor Von Hayek wants a basket of commodities, while Dr. Friedman facetiously speaks of a pork bellies standard. Others in the past, such as Alfred Kahn, recommended a banana standard, while Jude Wanniski called for a cinder block standard. Through this type of ridicule, our so-called leaders would have us continue to believe that gold is indeed a worthless commodity, undesirable, and impossible to use as money.

But examine these statements a little more closely. If gold is as worthless as has been stated and has no real intrinsic value, then all the more reason to mint coins of gold. It can be no worse than our already truly worthless paper and cupronickel and zinc slugs, which we call "money." If a Susan B. Anthony dollar is equal in size to a quarter but worth four times as much because the government says so, and the government has said that gold has no intrinsic value, then let the government mint coins of this worthless gold and artificially place a value on it. Why should the government stockpile and pay to guard a supply of worthless metal? Copper pennies are no longer made of copper because of the metal's industrial importance and because a copper penny is worth more as scrap than as a penny. If government officials are worried about their M_1, M_2, etc., then let them value gold at whatever they like and keep it there. It will be no different from their constant revaluation of paper.

This becomes a silly argument. The reason gold is held is because it is true wealth and not a useless commodity. It is necessary in the jewelry trade. It can be pounded into extremely thin sheets or stretched to incredible lengths. Next to silver, it is the best conductor of heat and electricity there is. It is impervious to the elements and can be used to coat objects that require protection against not only the elements, but also pollutants, acids, corrosives, etc. But its greatest attribute is its universal acceptance as money. It has an innate appeal to man that transcends all cultures, borders, and time zones. It has been used as money throughout the entire history of the world and has never lost its ability to attract and enamor the minds of men. It has universal appeal that requires no explanation and is readily accepted as valuable by one and all. It would appear that, in the natural order of things, gold was created to be money. It is even mentioned as such in all the scriptures of the world.

So why do the authorities try to convince us that gold is

worthless? Central governments and banks quietly increase their stockpiles of gold while they forbid and condemn hoarders. The IMF, for example, has over 100 million ounces of gold stockpiled but cries out for aid and plays on the guilt of nations for additional handouts. If all these nations, banks, and organizations can circulate worthless paper as currency and give it value because they say so, then it would be no problem to value all their gold at, lets say, $2,000 per ounce because they say so and circulate the gold as money.

Gold in circulation as money at a fixed price would prevent manipulation and cheating by politicians, bureaucrats, bankers, and power brokers in general. Gold currency would facilitate long-term business planning, reduce draining of speculative endeavors, and give people the confidence to save money, which provides capital for industry and business. Obviously, this would also break free the control of the people by the powercrats.

Instead, officials and economists defend their untenable positions with statements about pork bellies, cinder blocks, and banana standards. Pork bellies, bananas, and cinder blocks are all extremely elastic and subject to rapid decay. How could they serve as a currency or monetary standard? What universal appeal do disgusting pork bellies, rotting bananas, or crumbling cinder blocks have as money?

While we are on the subject of decay and elasticity, many have said that in an economic collapse and chaos gold would be worthless. The only thing of value would be food. This argument ignores history. There has always been food, even in the midst of starvation, for those with enough gold to purchase it. Granted, one cannot eat gold, but one cannot eat huge stockpiles of food either. Those who have stockpiles of food greater than needed to ride out a financial collapse face the dangers and difficulties of theft, storage, and decay. What does a farmer do with tons of wheat or corn? He can't eat it all. Storage and decay become difficult, and silos make an easy target for thieves as well as for bugs, explosions, fires, storms, and other acts of God. He could sell everything immediately at harvest time, but if food is the only thing of value, what would he sell it for—different food?

It is obvious that his food would indeed be valuable, but only as sustenance and not as a store of wealth. After stockpiling whatever is necessary to maintain himself and family, it would be foolish to keep his excess wealth deposited in a commodity so subject to the ravishes of time and other calamities.

Historically, gold production has had long-term growth of 2 percent per year. This makes it relatively inelastic. World population growth, long-term, has been 2 percent per year, and long-term economic output of nations has been 2 percent per year. This makes gold a natural as far as the requisites for inelasticity go. As far as decay, gold is practically indestructible. And for the scarcity-of-gold argument, the contention that our gold stock is inadequate or insufficient is false provided gold is properly revalued. And remember, there is also silver, nickel, and copper (even platinum, iron, etc., if you want to stretch the point) that could be used as supplementary coinage.

There is another argument stating that, if gold were used as currency, an inordinate demand for it would develop and hoarding would commence. It was this type of logic that caused many investors to expect a gold rush in the early '70s when it became legal, after a hiatus of 40 years, for the American citizen to own gold coin or bullion. The mad rush to buy gold never materialized, and the speculators never made the money they thought they would. One reason may be that gold had been demonetized and put down for so long that the American people felt unsure and uneasy about the desirability or necessity for using gold as a depository for stored wealth. It was viewed as another commodity in which only the rich could dabble or speculate. Of course this thinking has changed in the last ten years as most of the citizenry have realized the importance of gold, not just as a commodity to speculate in but as a means to preserve assets.

The point is that irredeemable currency is the cause of

hoarding, not vice-versa. This hoarding argument runs diametrically to Gresham's Law. It is historical fact that, when hoarding has taken place, it has been due to the introduction of valueless coin or fiat paper. The way to prevent hoarding, then, is to circulate gold—not withhold it.

There is also apprehension in the minds of many as to how a return to a gold currency could actually take place. In regard to this and the fear-of-runs contention, let us examine what happened in the United States from the years 1860 to 1880.

During this time the government had introduced inconvertible greenbacks to finance the Civil War. From 1860 to 1865, the economy experienced a 116 percent increase in prices. For reasons not necessary to review, the government dragged its feet 14 more years until it returned to full convertibility. A return to gold was finally enacted on January 1, 1879. During the 10 years following the war, from 1865 to 1875, gold and commodities sold for premiums in terms of paper money. In 1875, Congress passed the Specie Resumption Act, which called for a return to full gold convertibility in January 1879. In 1878, a repeal attempt was defeated, which inspired confidence in a doubting public.

Discounts on greenbacks began to fall. By December 17, 1878, premiums on gold disappeared, and the changeover went smoothly and easily. Greenbacks became 100 percent convertible into gold, and in 1879 more gold was turned in for paper money than paper turned in for gold.

The Report of the Secretary of the Treasury for 1879 states:

> The total amount of United States notes presented for redemption, from January 1 to November 1, 1879, was $11,256,678. . . .Meanwhile coin was freely paid into the Treasury and gold bullion was deposited in the assay office and paid for in United States notes. The aggregate gold and silver coin and bullion in the Treasury increased, during that period, from $167,558,734.19 to $225,133,558.72, and the net balance available for resumption increased from $133,508,804.50 to $152,737,155.48.

In the very next year of 1880 (from the Report of the Secretary of the Treasury):

> The amount of notes presented for redemption for one year prior to November 1, 1880 was $706,658. The amount of coin or bullion deposited in the Treasury assay office, and the mints, during the same period was $71,396,535.67.

It would appear that if paper money was made "as good as gold," then many people would hold paper rather than incur the expense of holding gold. Of course, there must also be a bond of trust between the people and government, which must make good on its promise to pay.

This episode in American history demonstrates that, if gold is allowed to circulate alongside a fully redeemable paper currency, there will be less hoarding, not more. It also demonstrates how a return to a gold currency could easily be implemented, provided the authorities act in a trustworthy and confidence-inspiring manner. But even if the people did respond to full convertibility with hoarding, it is their right to do so if they wish. Generally, hoarding is the people's response to an unprincipled government. No government should abuse the people's money or credit in such a way as to provoke hoarding.

Many times in the past it was stated that the general population could not be trusted if a fully redeemable paper currency were reintroduced, that the public might engage in undesirable behavior. They might run to exchange their paper if they became frightened, feared a currency depreciation or inflation, or opposed government spending. This odd contention supposes that the people's money actually is not their own. It is entirely within the right of the people to ask the promisor to make payment on demand without any quibbling or bickering. If there is any fear of hoarding, it is because the governments or banks have created situations whereby the people must react in this manner.

The government and the banks will never be able to command real respect or trust if the populace is denied the ability to hold these entities responsible for the management of their fiscal and monetary affairs. In the days when a fully redeemable currency circulated with gold, promise was made to pay the bearer on demand. There were no contigencies that this right to demand payment would be met only if the bearer were not acting on instinctive or speculative urge; resisting large government expenditures; acting out of a fear of inflation, deflation, recession, or depression; or motivated by fears of unstable international tensions or wars. Of course, our present-day paper money makes no such promises to pay the bearer anything. It used to be that any note was "redeemable in lawful money at the U.S. Treasury or at any Federal Reserve Bank." Now the government and the banks hoard the real money and have magically transformed notes that promised to pay lawful money into money itself.

As previously described, this situation has resulted from the inherent problems found in a fractional reserve system of banking. The bankers wish to reap the benefits of such a system free of obligation to meet promises to pay or other corresponding responsibilities. They are permitted to keep gold reserves, substitute one liability for another in making payments, and use an irredeemable currency to conduct business.

The scarcity-of-gold argument becomes even more foolish in light of the fact that we operate in a fractional reserve banking system. From the years 1915 to 1932, when full convertibility was maintained, the gold supply ratio was between 6.7 percent and 10.9 percent, the average being 8.6 percent. The U.S. fought through World War I without suspension of gold convertibility on ratios ranging from 8.1 percent to 10.9 percent. If the average ratio of 8.6 percent is used, the present gold stock of 264.03 million ounces, if valued at $400 per ounce, would support a paper currency issuance of $1.22805 trillion dollars. The reader is once again reminded that silver reserves are not included, but if used, they would augment the figure greatly.

As can be seen, it is possible to play with these figures endlessly, but no matter what preposterous arguments are advanced, there is certainly enough gold and silver in reserve to be used for currency. Even a 10 percent backing on all paper, though this book calls for a full gold standard, is desirable. The money supply would then be tied to a commodity that cannot be inflated or created from nothing. This would cause some braking action on the runaway deficit spending and inflation that have become our way of life. This could be a starting point even though only a full gold standard would ensure total success.

Another contention has been that the gold standard and fully convertible paper currency did not prevent the crash of 1929 and other wide fluctuations of business cycles and prices. But as we discussed earlier, this great crash of 1929 was actually caused by the greedy policies of bankers and their abuses of credit and the fractional reserve system of banking.

A gold currency cannot prevent price fluctuations due to free market occurrences. For that matter, no currency can. And, if there is an overexpansion of credit or other derelict behavior in financial management that causes economic upheaval, no currency, even gold, but especially a fiat paper currency, will prevent such occurrences. If anything, paper money will augment negative reaction. Gold may not prevent it, but at least gold will not abet this activity.

The function of gold has generally been five-fold:

1. to provide a standard of value
2. to provide a standard of deferred payments
3. to serve as a storehouse of wealth
4. to serve as reserves against promises to pay
5. to serve as a settler of adverse balances of payments

While gold is used to settle balance-of-payments deficits, it is also used for many other purposes, since it is perhaps the most readily marketable commodity in foreign trade. It is used to buy goods and services, to seek a place of safety, to escape currency depreciation, to buy another currency.

Granted that even a gold currency cannot prevent financial

dilemmas brought about by flagrant abuses of a monetary system, it has been demonstrated by thousands of years of history that the most effective way to stabilize currency and prices is through a gold standard.

In a report by Professor Roy Jastram at the University of California, Berkeley, Economics Department, entitled *The Golden Constant*, an in-depth study was made of American gold and commodity prices from the present back to 1880. A painstaking study found that the U.S. wholesale price index, when this country left the gold standard in 1933, was exactly the same as it was in 1880. But as soon as the gold standard was abandoned, the cost of living jumped. According to Professor Jastram, the wholesale commodity index increased 500 percent during the next 43 years after leaving the standard. The professor was also able to trace prices in England all the way back to 1560. During this time, the only long-term periods of price stability occurred when the British were on a gold standard. Other statistics show that, in the 124 years before the creation of the Federal Reserve System, retail prices rose only 16 percent. Since the creation of the Fed, retail prices have increased by a tremendous 900 percent.

Therefore, the return to a gold standard would lay the foundation for economic and fiscal stability. Abolishing the Fed, income tax, and deficit spending and eliminating government interference and the national debt would finish the job. Nineteen-twenty-nine-style crashes, business booms and busts, and price gyrations are usually the result of exploitative interference in the free market. When the government and others in a position to manipulate begin their work is when these economic aberrations occur. To say a gold standard did not prevent these things from happening indirectly indicts the gold standard as a cause of these events when the truth of the matter is that these events occur due to abuses.

To relax the rules through such means as the abandonment of a gold standard presupposes that, if the manipulators are given a freer hand at their art, these reversals could be avoided when, indeed, what is actually required are more stringencies. These stringencies must be of the type that allow free and fair practices to control the marketplace and rebuff the cheaters and manipulators. A gold standard meets this requirement infinitely more so than a fiat currency whose very design is intended to facilitate manipulation.

The gold standard acts as a braking device in economic and fiscal policies. It forces money managers to pursue sound monetary policies. Fiat currency allows bad and damaging money management to take place as well as inviting manipulation. The 1929 crash resulted from a weaker braking power of gold, the greedy expasion of money, and the turning over of the control of money to private individuals, i.e., the bankers of the Federal Reserve.

It is sometimes stated that the gold standard can operate only under favorable conditions or is a fair-weather standard. Once again, this argument ignores the fact that any standard can be abused. When abuses become prominent and drastic action is called for to correct these abuses, then comes the cry that restrictions caused by gold are to blame. There must be greater freedom to act, many will claim, as they incorrectly surmise gold is the culprit rather than abuses themselves.

Based on this fair-weather argument, we hear the time is not proper for a return to gold. We must wait for European or other Western nations to stabilize their economies; a gold standard would devastate Third World economies; we must wait for the rest of the world to adopt a gold standard; we must first balance our budget and eliminate deficit spending; we must reduce federal expenditures; we must wait until we have eliminated our differences with the Soviets and established stable relations lest the Soviets stir up runs on our banks; we have to contend with not just M_1, but M_2, M_3, etc., and increased Federal debt abroad; our gold reserves are presently inadequate; and so on.

These arguments have no validity. The basic reasons for opposition to a stable monetary system are purely political. Monetary stability impedes inflation, which has become the premier political expedient for the shifting of wealth from the productive to the less productive, both at home and internationally. This socialism, both national and international, has become the aim of our age. This internationalism will be the forerunner of totalitarian international big brotherism. Those who have seized control of the creation of money now hold the key to realizing their plans. It can be seen how control of money is the very heart of this vital force, which a return to gold would fatally undermine.

To rebuke these arguments of a fair-weather standard further, consider the following. Our gold stocks are ample if gold is revalued properly, even more so if a fractional reserve system were to remain. A gold standard was maintained from World War I to 1933 on gold reserve ratios of 6.7 percent to 10.9 percent. We maintained a gold standard while currencies abroad were depreciating, being devalued, and collapsing. During the chaos that Europe was experiencing during World War I, the U.S. gold dollar was regarded as as factor of great stability in a world of great instability. Even in the years of 1917, 1918, and 1919, when the federal government ran an unbalanced budget (to the extent of $13.363 billion in 1919), we maintained a redeemable currency.

The continuation of an inconvertible paper money is an extremely perilous position. It is irrevocably based on dishonesty and corrupt morals. The advocates of this system willingly support a governmentally managed economy. These advocates stand on the side of socialists or Communists in rebuking the gold standard and supporting a governmentally managed economy. We also have a government unscrupulous enough to take advantage of the ignorance of the mass of people regarding an irredeemable currency. Compounding the problem are an aggressive number of economists and others in the academic professions rushing to support a governmentally controlled economy and promulgating the deficiencies of a gold-based currency. Unless statesmen who have the good of the people at heart appear and initiate reform, we are doomed to live with a venomous system of currency and its resultant poisonous political and social system, until our day of reckoning teaches once more an old and often repeated lesson.

Under a gold standard, widely fluctuating quotations of the

dollar will disappear, as will inflation. Private enterprise will be revived. Private ingenuity, when given freedom and opportunity, manages to succeed to degrees no government agency can ever hope to equal. Foreign exchange of goods and services will also be stimulated and will benefit. A gold standard will encourage other nations to return to gold and break the barriers restricting free movement of people and their wealth. Unhampered by repressive restrictions, the free flow of goods, services, and ideas should cause a worldwide economic and cultural renaissance to transpire.

A gold currency would instill confidence in government and provide incentive for more saving, more investment, more production, more trade, and overall prosperity. Of course, other reforms and precautions must be taken against future abuses of credit. Foolishness, stupidity, recklessness, or bad management can overcome even a gold standard. The solution is to achieve honest, responsible management under the restraints of gold currency, not to free the money managers from restraints.

A gold standard would return control of public funds to the people, where such power belongs. Use of this power by the people too slowly, too late, or not at all would not negate the threat that at anytime the government or bankers acted irresponsibly their heads might roll. Individuals would have the direct power to voice disapproval of reckless programs, profligate spending, or dissipation of the national patrimony. This single act would invest the people with the power to stop the Socialists, Communists, one-worlders, etc., dead in their tracks. The people could halt the transfer of wealth by withholding their gold, and no degree of manipulation or wrangling could steal its purchasing power. Vote-delivering pressure groups could no longer be purchased via an irredeemable, inflatable currency.

Even though no monetary system can guarantee that there will never be business cycles or price fluctuations, by a return to gold the threat of instability will be canceled and the fluctuations caused by an irredeemable currency will be eliminated. No longer will currency be the controlling factor.

After all, history has shown that the greatest periods of price stability have come under gold standards. Speculation would disappear from common economic exchange, and the dangers inherently present in an irredeemable currency will not enter into people's plans and calculations. An irredeemable currency contains the essence of its own destruction. Ruination comes from within. With gold, danger must come from without.

A resumption of the gold standard would involve a return to principles of honesty and morality in government. Honesty and trust must be found in our leaders, whether they be public or private citizens. Low standards of morality have a demoralizing effect on the people, which diffuses evil influences in many subtle ways throughout the nation. When corruption exists at high levels, then it is permitted, even sanctioned, at lower levels. Strong leaders of impeccable character drive out and expose unscrupulous behavior at subordinate levels. How is it possible to trust someone who is dishonest? Without honesty in government, there can be no trust. And without the trust of the people in their government, how can the government govern effectively?

The leaders of this country must present the facts concerning irredeemable paper and a gold standard immediately, in an accurate, honest fashion. Ignorance may be tolerated and excused, but the population cannot be served well by half-truths, misstatements, and deliberate distortion or neglect of the facts. To argue for an irredeemable currency in favor of gold is to defend a corrupt, infirm monetary system.

Monetary history teaches that a permanent suspension of a gold standard cannot endure. Paper money runs on the promise made by the promisor. These promisors have a notoriously poor track record. On the other hand, the value of gold depends upon the promise of no individual. It ignores human frailties and weakness of character and depends solely on weight and fineness for determination of value. It does not falsify.

The single most important point this book can make, even if everything else that has been written in it is forgotten, is that *there must be a return to a full 100 percent gold currency.* All government gold must be coined and circulated as money. The government should be forbidden from hoarding even one ounce of gold. Gold may be held in the Treasury so that the government can carry out its legitimate functions, but there must be no hoarding whatsoever, particularly for the purpose of backing a paper money issue. As a matter of fact, paper money should be banished from the face of the earth forever.

This book has described many, many problems, and many, many solutions can be put forth to solve these problems. But a return to gold, and the total abolition of paper money, could solve all these problems in a single simple act. Though in the past paper circulated alongside gold when there was full convertibility, even gold-backed currency is dangerous because there is one reason, and one reason only, for its existence, and that is to allow and facilitate manipulation of money.

Gold-backed paper currency leaves intact a system that asks to be abused, especially in a surreptitious manner. It has been said that every endeavor is covered with fault, and gold as a currency may not be perfect, but its drawbacks are minuscule compared to the treacherous deficiencies inherent in paper. Paper money, even if it is backed by gold, can be inflated without public knowledge. The best action is to remove the irresistible temptation by officials to do so. This temptation can be eradicated only through the eradication of paper money. Paper money has been the root cause of so many of the problems described in the previous pages that no solution can be totally effective until all paper is replaced by a full gold standard.

It would appear that the U.S., unless it changes policy, is headed for fiscal, economic, and social disaster. There are many pro-government, pro-Socialists who are determined to continue pursuit of this dangerous endeavor. There are also the one-world powercrats who are the key motivators in this imbroglio. They are resolute in their quest to build their financial and political empires. It may be true that history does not support the possibility that these empires can exist for long. But the term *long* is a relative one. Until a monetary collapse or revolution takes place, the people will experience a slow death, with all the misery and suffering that accompany it. This could take many, many more years to run its course.

The trend can be reversed at any time, though. There must be a grass-roots movement in this land that will recognize and elect responsible leaders or statesmen who will work for the common good. Intelligent, patriotic, moral, religious, and unselfish men and women are needed if we are to succeed in these efforts. The dollar is on a continuous devaluation. The tax burden increases by leaps and bounds. The number of government employees planning and regulating the lives of people down to the minutest detail continues to grow two-three-and four-fold. Larger chunks of the GNP go toward social spending. Inflation, at even so-called modest rates, robs the frugal American, who saves his income, of hundreds of billions of dollars annually. The federal government repudiates its debt by the same amount by progressively reducing the value of the dollar. The sands of time are running out. The people must seek out and entrust leaders of high caliber to take the reigns of government and reestablish integrity. If they do not, agony and despair will plague us as, unfortunately, history once again repeats itself.

INDEX